This is the first general introduction to grammaticalization, the process whereby lexical items and constructions come in certain linguistic contexts to serve grammatical functions, and, once grammaticalized, continue to develop new grammatical functions. Thus nouns and verbs may change over time into grammatical elements such as case markers, sentence connectives, and auxiliaries. The authors synthesize work from several areas of linguistics, including historical linguistics, discourse analysis, and pragmatics. Data is drawn from many languages, including Ewe, Finnish, French, Hindi, Japanese, Malay, and especially English.

This will be a valuable and stimulating textbook for all linguists interested in the development of grammatical forms. Readers in anthropology and psychology will also appreciate the insights it offers into the interaction of language structure and use.

CAMBRIDGE TEXTBOOKS IN LINGUISTICS

General Editors J. BRESNAN, B. COMRIE, W. DRESSLER, R. HUDDLESTON,
R. LASS, D. LIGHTFOOT, J. LYONS, P. H. MATTHEWS, R. POSNER, S. ROMAINE,
N. V. SMITH, N. VINCENT

GRAMMATICALIZATION

GRAMMATICALIZATION

PAUL J. HOPPER
PROFESSOR OF RHETORIC AND LINGUISTICS,
CARNEGIE MELLON UNIVERSITY

ELIZABETH CLOSS TRAUGOTT
PROFESSOR OF LINGUISTICS AND ENGLISH, STANFORD UNIVERSITY

Published by the Press Syndicate of the University of Cambridge
The Pitt Building, Trumpington Street, Cambridge CB2 1RP
40 West 20th Street, New York, NY 10011–4211, USA
10 Stamford Road, Oakleigh, Victoria 3166, Australia

© Cambridge University Press 1993

First published 1993

Printed in Great Britain at the University Press, Cambridge

A catalogue record for this book is available from the British Library

Library of Congress cataloguing in publication data

Hopper, Paul J.
Grammaticalization / Paul J. Hopper, Elizabeth Closs Traugott.
   p. cm. — (Cambridge textbooks in linguistics)
Includes bibliographical references and index.
ISBN 0 521 36655 0 hardback. — ISBN 0 521 36684 4 paperback
1. Grammar, Comparative and general — Grammaticalization.
I. Traugott, Elizabeth Closs. II. Title. III. Series.
P299.G73H66 1993
415 — dc20 92–21612 CIP

ISBN 0 521 36655 0 hardback
ISBN 0 521 36684 4 paperback

TS

In memory of
Dwight Bolinger
1907–1992

CONTENTS

Contents

FIGURES

TABLES

PREFACE AND
ACKNOWLEDGEMENTS

Our aim in writing this book is to present an overview of grammaticalization for the benefit of those students of linguistics to whom this is a new or only vaguely familiar framework for understanding language. We define grammaticalization as the process whereby lexical items and constructions come in certain linguistic contexts to serve grammatical functions, and, once grammaticalized, continue to develop new grammatical functions. It is the process whereby the properties that distinguish sentences from vocabulary come into being diachronically or are organized synchronically. Many terms in linguistics serve two functions, one to describe properties of language (e.g., syntax, morphology, phonology), the other to name the study and theory of that property. The term grammaticalization is no exception. It refers not only to processes observable in language, but also to an approach to language study, one that highlights the interaction of use with structure, and the non-discreteness of many properties of language. In this book we do not advance any particular theory of language, but rather focus on observations that lead to claims about what sorts of concepts an adequate theory must account for. We discuss the kinds of interpretation of data that flow from the approach of grammaticalization, as well as the kinds of data that one would look for in studying some aspect of a language from this perspective. The study of grammaticalization touches on many of the topics that have been central to work in linguistics, whether synchronic or diachronic, most particularly the domains of morphosyntax and morphology. No attempt is made in this book to cover every topic in an encyclopedic way, nor could it be. Some basic knowledge of linguistics is needed. We assume that readers have at least worked through one of the standard introductory textbooks, and have either had a course in historical linguistics or have carefully read a recent textbook in this field.

A word about the choice of the term "grammaticalization." As we note in more detail in Chapter 2, the word seems to have been first used by Meillet (1912). In recent linguistics there is some variation between this word and the newer form "grammaticization." In adhering to the older form of the word, we do not intend any theoretical point other than to maintain a continuity of terminology. We believe that a terminology can and should survive quite radical changes in the ways the terms that comprise it are understood by successive generations of scholars. Some linguists have told us that they avoid the longer word because "grammaticalization" could be understood as "entering the grammar of a language," i.e., becoming "grammatical." "Grammaticization," by contrast, suggests a process whereby a form may become fixed and constrained in distribution without committing the linguist to a view of "grammar" as a fixed, bounded entity. A similar point is sometimes made in a different way: it is said that "grammaticalization" stresses the historical perspective on grammatical forms, while "grammaticization" focuses on the implications of continually changing categories and meanings for a synchronic view of language, thus placing the entire notion of synchrony into question. It is far from obvious to us that any such distinctions in usage exist between the two words, and our own choice does not reflect any particular theoretical position. We note that the titles of several recent major works contain the longer form "grammaticalization" (e.g., C. Lehmann 1985; Heine and Reh 1984; Traugott and Heine 1991; Heine, Claudi, and Hünnemeyer 1991a). While the question has not been settled, an introductory work such as the present one did not seem the right place to change what can still be called the established terminology.

Numerous people have contributed directly or indirectly to this book, among them Joan Bybee, William Croft, Andrew Garrett, Talmy Givón, Joseph Greenberg, Bernd Heine, Paul Kiparsky, Christian Lehmann, John Rickford, Eve Sweetser, Sandra Thompson, and Arnold Zwicky. We would especially like to thank Suzanne Fleischman, who tested an earlier version of the manuscript in classes at The University of California, Berkeley, and Suzanne Kemmer; their careful and insightful comments have been of inestimable worth. Thanks too to the many graduate students who attended our seminar at the Linguistic Society of America's Linguistic Institute at Stanford University in 1987, where many of the ideas for the writing of this book were developed. Portions of the work have been presented at various fora. In addition to the course that we co-taught at the 1987 Institute, we would both like to acknowledge stimulation from colleagues and from students in our own courses at Carnegie Mellon University (Hopper) and Stanford University (Traugott). In particular we appreciate the suggestions made by Nigel Vincent and John McWhorter. Julia Harding and John

McWhorter provided invaluable help with editorial matters. We would also like to thank Penny Carter and Judith Ayling for their help in getting the script to press.

We acknowledge the opportunities provided by Guggenheim Fellowships (Hopper in 1985, Traugott in 1983) for the study of many of the aspects of grammaticalization discussed here. Elizabeth Traugott further acknowledges a Fellowship at the Center for Advanced Study of the Behavioral Sciences at Stanford (1983).

In writing this book we have debated many points with respect for each other's different views. No two authors covering as wide a range of issues currently open to theoretical and methodological debate as are touched on in this book could expect to agree with every concept put forward, and we are no exception. We have welcomed the inspiration that our differing perspectives have provided, and we hope that this book will encourage further debate in the linguistic community.

Additional acknowledgements

The authors and publisher acknowledge permission to reproduce the following:

Rules in (5) and (6) in David Lightfoot, *The Language Lottery: Toward a Biology of Grammars*. The MIT Press, 1982, pp. 159 and 160;

Figure 2. Model of abduction and deduction in the acquisition of language; in Henning Andersen, "Abductive and Deductive Change", *Language* 49 (1973), p. 778;

Table 3, Ratio of CV to total by semantic class of primary, from Peter Edwin Hook, "The Emergence of Perfective Aspect in Indo-Aryan Languages," in Elizabeth Closs Traugott and Bernd Heine, eds., *Approaches to Grammaticalization*, John Benjamins BV, 1991, Vol. 2, p. 69;

Table 3, Occurrence of *that* with *think* vs. *guess* vs. all other verbs, from Sandra A. Thompson and Anthony Mulac, "A Quantitative Perspective on the Grammaticization of Epistemic Parentheticals in English," in Elizabeth Closs Traugott and Bernd Heine, eds., *Approaches to Grammaticalization*, John Benjamins BV, 1991, Vol. 2, p. 320;

Figure in (2) from Charles C. Fries, "On the Development of the Structural Use of Word-order in Modern English," *Language* 16 (1940), p. 201;

Figure 1, Pronouns and person-and-number affixes in Buryat, from Bernard Comrie, "Morphology and Word Order Reconstructions," in Jacek Fisiak, ed., *Historical Morphology*, Trends in Linguistics, Studies and Monographs 17, Mouton Publishers, 1980, p. 88;

Table of Polish clitics in (2), table of agglutination in (5), and table of stress in (7) from Henning Andersen, "From Auxiliary to Desinence," in Martin B. Harris and Paolo Ramat, eds., *Historical Development of Auxiliaries*, Mouton de Gruyter, 1987, pp. 24, 29, and 32, respectively.

ABBREVIATIONS

Linguistic terms

ABL	ablative
ABS	absolutive
ACC	accusative
ADV	adverb
AGR	agreement marker
AGT	agent
AOR	aorist
ASP	aspect
AUX	auxiliary
BEN	benefactive
CAUS	causative
CL	noun classifier
COMP	complementizer
COMPL	completive
CONJ	conjunction
CONTIN	continuative
COP	copula
DAT	dative
DEF	definite marker
DEM	demonstrative
DET	determiner
DUR	durative
EMPH	emphatic
ERG	ergative
FEM	feminine
FUT	future
GEN	genitive
GER	gerundive

ILL	illative
IMP	imperative
IMPF	imperfect
INDEF	indefinite
INF	infinitive
INSTR	instrumental
IOBJ	indirect object
LOC	locative
M	modal
MASC	masculine
NEG	negative
NEUT	neuter
NF	non-final marker
NOM	nominative
NP	noun phrase
OBJ	object
OM	object marker
OV	object–verb word order
PART	participle
PARTIT	partitive
PERF	perfect
PL	plural
PM	predicate marker
POSS	possessive
POST	postposition
PREP	preposition
PRES	present
PRO	pronoun
PROG	progressive
PURP	purposive
RECIP	reciprocal
REFL	reflexive
REL	relative
SG	singular
SUB	subordinator
SUBJ	subject
SUBJUNCT	subjunctive
TNS	tense
TOP	topic
V	verb

VO   verb–object word order
VP   verb phrase
 1   first person
 2   second person
 3   third person

Stages of English

OE   Old English (*c.* 600–1125)
ME   Middle English (*c.* 1125–1500)
ENE   Early New English (*c.* 1500–1750)
PDE   Present Day English (*c.* 1750–)

1
Some preliminaries

1.1 Introduction

(1) Bill is going to go to college after all.

What is the relationship between the two instances of *go* in this sentence? The first *go* is usually analyzed as an auxiliary, the second as a main verb. Are they different morphemes that just happen to look and sound alike, that is, are they homonyms? Are they variants of the same morpheme in different contexts, that is, are they polysemous? Is the auxiliary historically derived from the main verb, and, if so, is this kind of derivation cross-linguistically attested?

What permits the pair in (2) but not the (b) sentence in (3)?

(2) a. Bill is going to college after all.
    b. Bill's gonna go to college after all.
(3) a. Bill's going to college after all.
    b. *Bill's gonna college after all.

These questions and many others are characteristic of the study of grammaticalization. As a first approximation, the answer is that the auxiliary which expresses immediate futurity derives historically from the motion verb *go* in a highly specific context, and that the two coexistent forms are polysemous. Such meaning-form correlations are found in a wide number of languages around the world.

"Grammaticalization" as a term has two meanings. As a term referring to a framework within which to account for language phenomena, it refers to that part of the study of language that focuses on how grammatical forms and constructions arise, how they are used, and how they shape the language. The framework of grammaticalization is concerned with the question of whether boundaries between categories are discrete, and with the interdependence of structure and use, of the fixed and the less fixed in language. It therefore highlights the tension between relatively uncon-

1

strained lexical structure and more constrained syntactic, morphosyntactic, and morphological structure. It provides the conceptual context for a principled account of the relative indeterminacy in language and of the basic non-discreteness of categories. The term "grammaticalization" also refers to the actual phenomena of language that the framework of grammaticalization seeks to address, most especially the processes whereby items become more grammatical through time.

Since Saussure, many linguists have approached language from one of two perspectives: that of its structure at a single point in time ("synchronic") and that of change between two or more points in time (historical or "diachronic"). The synchronic dimension of a language is said to be its system of grammatical units, rules, and lexical items (together with their meanings), that is, its grammar. It is usually conceived as essentially stable and homogeneous. The diachronic dimension, on the other hand, is understood as the set of changes linking a synchronic state of a language to successive states of the same language. The discreteness of categories and rules, and the rigidity of the distinction between the synchronic and diachronic dimensions have been called into question by work on the stuctured variation to be found in various social contexts, and analysis of discourse and language in use. They are also called into question by the study of grammaticalization.

Grammaticalization has been studied from two perspectives. One of these is historical, investigating the sources of grammatical forms and the typical pathways of change that affect them. From this perspective, grammaticalization is usually thought of as that subset of linguistic changes through which a lexical item in certain uses becomes a grammatical item, or through which a grammatical item becomes more grammatical. The other perspective is more synchronic, seeing grammaticalization as primarily a syntactic, discourse pragmatic phenomenon, to be studied from the point of view of fluid patterns of language use. In this book we will combine these two points of view, but with greater emphasis on the historical dimension.

Our example of *be going to/be gonna* illustrates several factors typical of grammaticalization:

(a) The change occurs only in a very local context, that of purposive directional constructions with non-finite complements, such as *I am going to marry Bill* (i.e., *I am leaving/traveling to marry Bill*). It does not occur in the context of directionals in which the locative adverb is present, such as *I am going to London* or even *I am going to London to marry Bill*.

2

(b)   The change is made possible by the fact that there is an inference of futurity from purposives: if I am traveling in order to marry, the marriage will be in the future. In the absence of an overt directional phrase, futurity can become salient.

(c)   The shift from purposive *be going (to* . . .) to auxiliary *be going to* involves reanalysis not only of the *be going to* phrase but of the verb following it. Thus [I am going [to marry Bill]] is rebracketed as [I am going to marry Bill]. It also involves a change of aspect from progressive aspect to "immediate future."[1]

(d)   The reanalysis is discoverable, that is, is manifest, only when the verb following *be going to* is incompatible with a purposive meaning, or at least unlikely in that context, for example, *I am going to like Bill, I am going to go to London*. In other words, the reanalysis is discoverable only because the contexts in which *be going to* can occur have been generalized, or analogized, to contexts that were unavailable before.

(e)   Once the reanalysis has occurred, *be going to* can undergo changes typical of auxiliaries, such as phonological reduction. The reduction of the three morphemes *go-ing to* into one (*gonna*) is possible only because there is no longer a phrasal bracket between *-ing* and *to*.

(f)   The various stages of grammaticalization of *be going (to* . . .) coexist in Modern English, although the change originates in the fifteenth century or perhaps even earlier.

(g)   The original purposive meaning continues to constrain the use of the auxiliary: *be gonna* is the future of intention, plan, or schedule. As an original aspectual, it can occur in constructions where a future formed with *will* cannot:

(4)   a.   If interest rates are going to climb, we'll have to change our plans.
　　　b.   *If interest rates will climb, we'll have to change our plans.

This property of persistence of meaning presumably derives in part from the fact that the older *be going (to* . . .) coexists with the newer use, and hence there is reinforcement of older meanings.

(h)   The main verb *go* is relatively general in meaning, that is, it expresses any kind of motion away from the speaker, including walking, meandering, running, riding, etc.

(i)   In the process of grammaticalization, some of the original relatively concrete meaning of *go* has been lost, specifically motion and directionality. However, some new meanings have also been added; these are more abstract and speaker-based meanings, specifically temporal meanings based in speaker time. The historical development of the construction will be discussed more fully in Chapter 4.

1.2 What is a grammaticalized form?

As is usually the case with words rich in implications, there are a number of different conceptions of grammaticalization. Yet there are central, prototypical instances of grammaticalization which most linguists would recognize, and we start with some of them.

For example, it is usually accepted that some kind of distinction can be made in all languages between "content" words, also called "lexical items," and "function" words, also called "grammatical" words. The words *example, accept,* and *green* (i.e., nouns, verbs, and adjectives) are examples of lexical items. Such words are used to report or describe things, actions, and qualities. The words *of, and, or, it, this,* that is, prepositions, connectives, pronouns, and demonstratives, are function words. They serve to indicate relationships of nominals to each other (prepositions), to link parts of a discourse (connectives), to indicate whether entities and participants in a discourse are already identified or not (pronouns and articles), and to show whether they are close to the speaker or hearer (demonstratives). Frequently it can be shown that function words have their origins in content words. When a content word assumes the grammatical characteristics of a function word, the form is said to be "grammaticalized." Quite often what is grammaticalized is not a single content word but an entire construction that includes that word, as for example Old English *þa hwile þe* 'that time that' > *hwile* 'while' (a temporal connective).

1.2.1 A preliminary classification of grammatical forms

Not all grammatical forms are independent words. Indeed, in some languages they can never be independent words, but must be bound as an affix or other category. Although there is no full agreement on definitions of grammatical forms, in general it is possible to speak of a "continuum" with various "cluster" or "focal areas" of the following nature (cf. Halliday 1961: 249; Bybee 1985; Hammond and Noonan 1988):

(a) Grammatical words with relative phonological and syntactic independence. For example, English prepositions can be found at the end of a clause without a noun phrase, as in *This is where we're at* and *This bed has been slept in.* In this position they have full segmental structure (unreduced vowels and consonants, e.g., [æt] not *[ət]) and full prosodic structure (they can take stress).

(b)   Derivational forms. Content words themselves often contain meaningful parts that are neither inflections nor clitics. Many derivational forms add a meaning component without affecting the category in question. The *-ling* of *duckling* adds to the noun *duck* the new meaning 'young and small,' but does not change the nominal status of the word. Other derivational forms do change the category of the word. For example, in the word *reclusive*, the suffix *-ive* derives an adjective from a noun. In *swimmer*, the suffix *-er* derives a noun from the verb *swim*. Because they not only add meaning but also serve to indicate grammatical categories, such "derivational" morphemes can also be considered to serve a role between contentive and grammatical forms. Derivational morphemes are part of the lexicon: they are added to roots or stems, and the derived stems may be hosts for clitics and inflections.

(c)   Clitics. These are forms that are not affixes, but are constrained to occurring next to an autonomous word, known as the host. Because few of the standard textbooks mention the term "clitic," it will be appropriate for us to discuss it more fully at this point. (For important treatments, see Klavans 1985, Zwicky 1985.) The Greek stem from which the word clitic is derived means 'to lean'; so a clitic is a form that 'leans' against another. The diachronic process whereby a lexical form becomes a clitic is called "cliticization" (the corresponding verb is "cliticize"). The word clitic is actually a cover term for two varieties. A clitic that precedes the host is called a "proclitic," e.g., in colloquial English, *'s* in *'s me* 'it's me.' A clitic that follows its host is an "enclitic." A good example of an enclitic in English is the *'m* in *I'm*. The unstressed form *'m* is said to be a cliticized variant of the full form *am*. The kinds of words that are typically clitics are: special clitic pronouns, which often coexist with autonomous pronouns (e.g., English *'em* versus *them*); copular verbs (e.g., English *I'm*, *you're*, etc.); auxiliary verbs in general (*we'll*, *we've*, etc.); and discourse particles in many languages, e.g., in Latin, *-que* 'and':

(5)   Conticuere omnes, intentique ora   tenebant.
      fell-silent all,   intent-*que* gazes they-held
      'All fell silent and intently held their gaze.'
                              (*c*. 30–19 BC, Virgil, *Aeneid* II,1)[2]

A distinction can be made between "simple" and "special" clitics. Simple clitics occur in a position where their full form would occur, for example, *'s* for *is* and *has* in *Jean's here*, and *Jean's left*. Special clitics occur in a position where an equivalent full form would usually not occur; in many languages this is the second position in the clause. For example, the Latin coordinator *que* 'and' just mentioned must occur to the right of the first lexical item in a coordinated clause, by contrast with *et* 'and', which occurs at the beginning of (or perhaps outside) the clause.

Clitics may be thought of as forms that are half-way between autonomous words and affixes (Jeffers and Zwicky 1980). They may share properties of both, although it is hard to make generalizations about which features will occur in a given instance. For example, clitics may resemble affixes in forming an accentual unit with the host. In Indonesian, where stress tends to occur on the next-to-last syllable of the word, the enclitic pronoun *nya* 'its' in *warná-nya* 'its color' affects the stress in the host stem (contrast *wárna* ·'color'). On the other hand, clitics may behave more like independent words in having no effect on accent, as in Spanish *háblame* 'speak [sg.] to me!,' where the accent of the host *hábla* is unchanged by the extra syllable of the enclitic *me*.

(d) Inflections. These are always dependent and bound; that is to say, inflections by definition are always part of another word. Inflections reflect categories and properties of words such as gender, case, number, tense, aspect, and syntactic relationships. In many languages, inflections are used to show agreement ("concord") in these properties or categories with some other word, e.g., English *this shoe* versus *these shoes*, where the forms of the demonstrative *this/these* reflect the singular/plural contrast in *shoe/shoes*.

1.2.2 Clines

Basic to work on grammaticalization is the concept of a "cline" (see Halliday 1961 for an early use of this term). From the point of view of change, forms do not shift abruptly from one category to another, but go through a series of gradual transitions, transitions that tend to be similar in type across languages. For example, a lexical noun like *back* that expresses a body part comes to stand for a spatial relationship in *in/at the back of*, and is susceptible to becoming an adverb, and perhaps eventually a preposition and even a case affix. Forms comparable to *back of* (*the house*) in English recur all over the world in different languages. The progression from lexical noun, to relational phrase, to adverb and preposition, and perhaps even to a case affix, is an example of what we mean by a cline.

The term "cline" itself has both historical and synchronic implications. From a historical perspective, a cline is a natural pathway along which forms evolve, a kind of linguistic "slippery slope" which guides the development of forms. Synchronically a cline can be thought of as a "continuum": an arrangement of forms along an imaginary line at one end of which is a fuller form of some kind, perhaps "lexical," and at the opposite end a compacted and reduced form, perhaps "grammatical." Both metaphors, "cline" and "continuum," are to be understood as having certain focal points where phenomena may cluster.

The precise cluster points on the cline (i.e., the labels preposition, affix, etc.) are to a certain extent arbitrary. Linguists may not agree on what points to put on a cline, nor on how to define the cline in a given instance. They also may not agree on whether a particular form is to be placed (for example) in the lexical area or the grammatical area of the cline. But the relative positions on a cline are less subject to dispute. For example, most linguists would agree that there is a "cline of grammaticality" of the following type:

content item > grammatical word > clitic > inflectional affix

Another cline, which we will call a "cline of lexicality," would include derivational affixes such as -*ness* in *ugliness*, etc., and presumably also such positions as syntactic phrase, compound, and affix, e.g.:

a basket *full* (of eggs . . .) > a cup*ful* (of water) > hope*ful*

In this book we will be particularly concerned with the cline of grammaticality. It has as its leftmost component a lexical, or content, item and moves through stages of being more syntactic (grammatical word, clitic) and finally morphological (inflectional affix). Each item to the right is more clearly grammatical and less lexical than its partner to the left. Presented with such a cline, linguists would tend to agree that generally the points (labels) on the cline could not be arranged in a different order. A number of such clines have been proposed, based on the many different dimensions of form and meaning that are found in language. It is often difficult to establish firm boundaries between the categories represented on clines, and indeed the study of grammaticalization has emerged in part out of a recognition of the general fluidity of so-called categories. It has also emerged out of recognition that a given form typically moves from a point on the left of the cline to a point further on the right, in other words, that there is a strong tendency toward unidirectionality in the history of individual forms. Heine and his colleagues have suggested that the particular paths along which individual forms or groups of forms develop be called "grammaticalization channels," and the internal structure or relational patterns within these channels be called "grammaticalization chains" (Heine, Claudi, and Hünnemeyer

1991a: 222; Heine, forthcoming). We will discuss unidirectionality and ways
of conceptualizing the cline in some detail in Chapter 5.

1.2.3 Periphrasis versus affixation

As we have seen, the clines discussed in the previous section
demonstrate a cline from freer to more bonded constructions. Often the
same categories can be expressed by forms at different places in the clines.
Thus in English we have phrasal expressions such as:

(6) a. have waited (perfect aspect)
     b. the sound of the engines (possessive)
     c. more interesting (comparative)

These forms can be said to be expressed "periphrastically" (literally "in a
roundabout fashion") or "phrasally." It is also possible to express tense-
aspect, possession, and the comparative through affixes or changes internal
to the stem word, as in:

(7) a. waited (past tense affixed -ed); sang (past tense signaled by
         internal change: contrast *sing*)
     b. the receptionist's smile (possessive affix -s)
     c. longer (comparative -er)

In these forms, the categories of tense-aspect, possession, and comparison
are bound to a host and are said to be expressed synthetically.

The distinction between the morphological and periphrastic expression of
a category is important for the study of grammaticalization because of two
diachronic tendencies. One is for periphrastic constructions to coalesce over
time and become morphological ones. While this and other tendencies are
discussed in more detail later, especially in Chapter 6, a couple of examples
follow:

(a) Definite nouns are marked in many European and other languages
with an article that is separate from the noun, for example, English *the
newspaper*, French *la rue* 'the street,' German *die Stadt* 'the city,' etc. In
such languages definiteness is marked phrasally (cf. English *the five yellow
newspapers*). But in some languages this sign of definiteness is an affix,
which can usually be shown to derive from an earlier definite article or
demonstrative. Thus in Istro-Romanian[3] the Latin demonstrative *ille* 'that'
now appears as a suffix on nouns marking both definiteness and case, as in:

(8) gospodar-i-lor
     boss-PL-DEF:GEN
     'of the bosses'

Here *-i* marks plural and *-lor* is the definite genitive plural suffix deriving from Latin *illorum*, the masculine genitive plural of *ille*. Similarly in Danish, *-en* in *dreng-en* 'the boy' and *-et* in *hus-et* 'the house' are definite singular markers for common gender and neuter nouns respectively, and have their origin in earlier postposed demonstratives (cf. Old Norse *úlfr-inn* 'wolf-the' from **úlfr hinn* 'wolf-that').

(b)   Various tenses and aspects of verbs are formed either with auxiliary verbs (i.e., periphrastic tense–aspect) or with verbal suffixes (i.e., morphological tense–aspect). Thus in Hindi the present tense is formed periphrastically by a verb stem plus the verb *to be*:

(9)   mAI kursii par baiṭhaa hUU.
      I   chair on sit   be:1SG
      'I sit on a chair.'

In Swahili, on the other hand, basic tenses such as the future are formed morphologically, with prefixes on the verb:

(10)   Wa-ta-ni-uliza.
       they-FUT-me-ask
       'They will ask me.'

Morphological tense-aspect formations can often be shown to have developed out of earlier periphrastic ones. The Romance languages supply numerous examples of this, such as the Italian future *canterémo* 'we will sing' from Latin *cantare habemus*, literally 'we have to sing' (> **cantarabémus* > **cantarémus*). We discuss this kind of development in the Romance languages in Section 3.5.1.

The second diachronic tendency that makes the periphrasis/bondedness distinction important is an example of what is known as "renewal" – the tendency for periphrastic forms to replace morphological ones over time. Where a long historical record is available, the process of renewal can be seen to occur repeatedly. The French counterpart of the Italian future just mentioned, for example, is *(nous) chanterons* 'we will sing.' But its Latin source, *cantare habemus*, was a periphrastic future that eventually replaced an older morphological future, *cantabimus*, after competing with it for several centuries. This form in turn evidently contains the verb **bʰumos* 'we are,' inherited from Indo-European, and can be reconstructed as an earlier periphrastic construction **kanta bʰumos*. French *nous chanterons* is itself being replaced by *nous allons chanter*, literally 'we are going to sing.' Something like the following sequence of changes can therefore be established:

(11) **Pre-Latin**   **Latin**   **French**
*?

*kanta bʰumos >   cantabimus
                    cantare habemus > chanterons
                    allons chanter > ?

At each stage two (or more) constructions compete (typically separated from one another by some nuance of meaning such as 'we will' versus 'we are about to'), and eventually the periphrastic one wins out, undergoes coalescence of the two elements that comprise it, and may in turn be replaced by a new periphrastic form (Hodge 1970 provides examples of the renewal by periphrasis from several language families).

The terms "renewal" and "replacement" are somewhat problematic because they may suggest functional identity over time, and even gaps to be filled. In fact, however, it is not only the forms *cantabimus* and *cantare habemus* that differ; their exact semantic functions (and syntactic distributions) differ too, in so far as the overall set of tense options is necessarily different once the two forms coexist (other changes were also occurring elsewhere in the system, further reducing any potential identity). Unfortunately our available linguistic vocabulary or "metalanguage" for expressing the relationship between earlier and later linguistic phenomena is poor. We will not attempt to change it here, but will follow custom and use terms such as "replacement" and "renewal," on the understanding that there is no exact identity over time (and, as will be discussed in 5.4.3., there are no gaps to be filled).

1.3 Some further examples of grammaticalization

We turn now to some relatively detailed examples of grammaticalization to illustrate several of its characteristics, and some of the problems of defining instances of it uniquely.

1.3.1 'Lets'

An initial example will be chosen from contemporary standard English also known as Present Day English (or PDE for short). We begin with this example because it illustrates vividly that grammaticalization is an everyday fact of language. It results in not only the very familiar constructions of language such as *be going to*, but also many of the highly structured, semi-autonomous "formal idioms" of a language that make it unique, but are often regarded as peripheral (Fillmore, Kay, and O'Connor 1988).

In PDE there is a construction involving a second person imperative with the verb *let*:

(12) a. Let us go. (i.e., release us)
      b. Let yourself down on the rope.
      c. Let Bill go. (i.e., release Bill)

The understood subject of *let* is *you*. The objects of *let* in (a), (b), and (c) are all different: *us*, *yourself*, *Bill*, and may be passivized, e.g.:

(12) d. We were let go.

Alongside this ordinary imperative construction with *let* there is a construction sometimes called an "adhortative" (involving urging or encouraging), as in:

(13) Let's go to the circus tonight.

Quirk, Greenbaum, Leech, and Svartvik (1973: Chapter 7, Sections 74 and 76) refer to this construction as a "first-person imperative." Here the subject of *let* is understood as something like 'I suggest that I and you . . . ' *Us* is also the subject of the dependent verb rather than the object of *let*, and can therefore not be passivized: (12d) is the passive of (12a), not of the first part of (13).

    Quirk *et al.* note the spread of *let's* in very colloquial English to the singular of the first person:

(14) Lets give you a hand.

(We will represent the form as *lets* when the subject is other than the first person plural.) Quirk *et al.* describe the *lets* here as "no more than an introductory particle" (1973: 404). In some varieties of English, the first person plural inclusive subject *us* of *lets* has been reinforced by *you and I*, as in:

(15) Let's you and I take 'em on for a set.
               (1929, Faulkner, *Sartoris* III.186; *OED* **let** 14.a)

It has even been extended beyond first person subjects of the dependent verb. The following examples are from Midwestern American speakers:

(16) a. Lets you and him fight.
      b. Lets you go first, then if we have any money left I'll go.

While (16a) was perhaps jocular (a third party egging on two others), the context of (16b) was quite neutral. In other instances there is no second or third person subject pronoun, and *lets* simply conveys the speaker's condescending encouragement, e.g., in addressing a child or a truculent person:

(17) a. Lets wash your hands.

(Cole 1975: 268)

      b. Lets eat our liver now, Betty.

The development of the *lets* construction illustrates a number of characteristics of grammaticalization. Among these are:

(a) (12) shows that a full verb *let* 'allow, permit' has altered its semantic range in some way. We will suggest that grammaticalization in its early stages often, perhaps always, involves a shift in meaning (Chapter 4; see also Traugott 1989). Furthermore, as mentioned in connection with *be going to*, this kind of shift occurs only in a highly specific context, in this case of the imperative *Let us* . . . A first approximation would be to say that the earlier idea of permission or allowing has become extended in one part of its paradigm to include a further one of suggesting or encouraging someone to do something. The sense of *let* has become less specific and more general; at the same time it has become more centered in the speaker's attitude to the situation. This new construction has been available since the beginning of the sixteenth century and probably earlier.

(b) (16) shows that the range of possible subjects of the verb dependent on *lets* is being extended from first person plural to other persons. This was presumably made possible by the fact that *we/us* in English may be interpreted as inclusive of the addressee ('I and you') or exclusive of the addressee ('I and another or others'). So long as the distribution of *let's* is consistent with first person plural subjects in the dependent verb (e.g., 'let's indulge ourselves'), it may still be useful to analyze it as *let* + *us*. But this distribution has now spread to other persons, as suggested by example (14), *Lets give you a hand* (said by one individual to another), where *lets* is singular. As we shall see later on, earlier meanings and functions may persist. Thus (13–17) coexist with (12). Furthermore, the semantic changes proceed by small steps (permission to suggestion, first to second to third person).[4]

(c) A first person plural pronoun *us* became cliticized (*let's*), and from the word-plus-clitic complex a single word was formed, *lets*. As suggested above, so long as the distribution of this form is consistent with the first person plural subjects of the dependent verb, it may still be useful to analyze it as a cliticized form of *us*. But when this distribution spreads to non-first person plural subjects, we are not synchronically justified in continuing to do so. The final *s* of *lets*, then, is losing its status as a separate morpheme, and is in the process of becoming a simple phonemic constituent of a (monomorphemic) word. The historical trajectory:

> (let) us > (let)'s > (let)s

illustrates a more general shift of

> word > affix > phoneme
>
> (cf. Givón 1979: 208–9; Hopper 1990)

(d) Once the monomorphemic stage has been reached, then the form becomes subject to further reduction. Since [ts] is often reduced in rapid speech to the sibilant, it is not surprising that *lets* [lɛts] often becomes *les* [lɛs]. It even goes further and in very colloquial speech is cliticized and attached to the following verb: *sgo*, *sfight*.

(e) Like other emergent constructions, *lets* in some sense fixes, or routinizes, a meaning or discourse function which was formerly freer (see Hopper 1987). It singles out one combination (in this case, *let* + *us*) from what was once a more extensive paradigm of equivalent forms, as in (18), and specializes it in a newly emerging function, the adhortative.

(18) Let him speak now or forever hold his peace.

This new function is provisional and relative rather than permanent and absolute; *lets* may not survive. However, for now a distinctive new grammatical resource has entered the language and is available to speakers for the building of interactive discourse.

A final comment about the development of *lets* is that, although the stages are clearly very local and appear somewhat marginal, nevertheless they are part of a typological change affecting English. This is a shift which has been in progress for over two thousand years from an essentially "object–verb" system (as in *her saw*) with case and verb inflections, in other words, affixal constructions, to an essentially "verb–object" system (as in *saw her*) with prepositions and phrasal verb constructions, in other words, periphrastic constructions. We will discuss word order shifts in more detail in Section 3.5.1. Here it must suffice to mention that in Old English, as in some other older Indo-European languages, the adhortative was expressed by the subjunctive, as shown in (19) (though a phrasal form with *utan* also existed).

(19) Cild binnan ðritegum nihta sie   gefulwad.
      child within thirty   nights be:SUBJUNCT baptized
      'Let a child be baptized within thirty nights.'

                                                  (c. 690, Law Ine 1.1)[5]

The development of *lets*, then, is to be seen as among the class of
innovations that are leading to a phrasal expression of the modalities of the
verb, replacing an earlier inflectional expression. It is part of a very general
change from a morphological way of expressing a function to what is called
"periphrasis" – the use of several words to express a similar function. The
rise of the numerous auxiliary and auxiliary-like verbs and expressions of
Modern Spoken English (such as *may*, *be going to*, *keep V-ing*, and others)
is symptomatic of the same trend, which has been ongoing in English for
many centuries.

1.3.2 A West African complementizer

Our examples so far have for the most part illustrated the
development of verbs into grammatical markers of the kind usually associated with verbs, specifically tense, aspect and mood. We turn now to a
well-known example of a verb being grammaticalized into a connective, in
this case a complementizer that introduces a finite complement clause. A
finite complement clause is equivalent to an English *that*-clause in such
constructions as:

(20) I know that her husband is in jail.

The verb which has the position of *know* in such sentences is called the
"matrix verb," and the clause introduced by the complementizer *that* is the
"complement clause."

Lord presents data from a number of African and Asian languages in
which a locutionary verb meaning 'say' has come to function as a complementizer. Exotic as it may seem, such a construction is by no means
unknown in English, cf.:

(21) *If/Say* the deal falls through, what alternative do you have?

We will cite examples from Lord's work on languages of West Africa, all of
them related members of the Kwa group of Niger-Congo spoken in Togo
and Ghana, especially from Ewe (the examples that follow are from Lord
1976: 179–82).

The process leading to the grammaticalization of a 'say' verb into a
complementizer evidently begins when a general verb meaning 'to say' is

used to reinforce a variety of verbs of saying in the matrix clause. In Ewe, for example, if the matrix verb is the general verb *bé* '*say*,' no further complementizer is needed:

(22) Me-bé me-wɔ-e.
       I-say I-do-it
       'I said, "I did it."/I said that I did it.'

However, if some verb of saying other than *bé* is the matrix verb, *bé* must be used as a complementizer:

(23) Me-gblɔ bé me-wɔ-e.
       I say   say I-do-it
       'I said that I did it.'

(where *gblɔ* is a different verb meaning 'to say').

The next stage is one in which *bé* comes to be used as a complementizer after a whole range of matrix verbs, including, for example:

gblɔ 'say'
ŋlɔ 'write'
lɔ̃ ɖé édzi 'agree' (lit. 'accept reach top')
xɔse 'believe'
nyá 'know'
bu 'think'
vɔ̃ 'fear, be afraid'
kpɔ́ 'see'
ŋlɔ 'forget'
se 'hear, perceive'
ná 'make sure'

The verbs included are verbs of speaking, cognition, and perception. Since these are verbs which in most languages can have objects that are propositions (i.e., clauses), there is an obvious syntactic and semantic relationship between them and 'say.' Even so, the meaning and morphology of the 'say' verb is essentially lost in the process of grammaticalization as a complementizer. For example, in (24) we see that *bé* may no longer take verbal affixes such as person markers (compare *me-dí* 'I-want'), nor may it productively take tense-aspect markers.

(24) Me-dí bé máƥle   awua ɖewó.
       I-want say I-SUBJUNCT-buy dress some
       'I want to buy some dresses.'

15

Furthermore the original meaning of 'say' is in such sentences not easy to recover. Although some of its original context is maintained (it remains a form that introduces a noun clause), it has become available to many more contexts. From being a verb that introduces something said, it has become generalized to introducing other kinds of clauses, such as reports of things seen or thought.

As with English *go* and *lets*, the Ewe example shows not only a semantic shift but also structural adjustment. Not only does the verb 'say' extend and perhaps even lose its original meaning of saying, but a construction originally consisting of two independent clauses is reanalyzed as a matrix verb plus a complement clause introduced by a complementizer. A construction such as (25) is reanalyzed as (26):

> (25) Megblɔ bé [mewɔe].
> I-say   say I-do-it
> 'I said I did it.'

> (26) Megblɔ [bé [mewɔe].
> I-say   [say I-do-it]
> 'I said that I did it.'

We will return later to fuller discussions of reanalysis and analogy in Chapter 3. For the present, it is important to recognize that both are major mechanisms in the process of grammaticalization.

1.3.3 Agreement markers

Our two examples have illustrated grammaticalization as the process whereby lexical items or phrasal constructions can come in certain contexts to serve grammatical functions. We now turn briefly to an example of the way in which already grammatical items can become more grammatical.

A frequently occurring change is the development of personal pronouns into agreement markers. Latin *ille* was a demonstrative pointing to location near third persons, in other words, it was a distal deictic. In French this demonstrative has developed along two lines. The fully stressed form became the pronoun *il*, the unstressed form became the article *le*. As a pronoun, *il* signals number (singular) and gender (non-feminine). It contrasts with *elle*, which is singular but feminine. In standard French *il* and *elle* serve personal pronoun functions only. Thus we find:

> (27) Le garçon est venu hier   soir.   Il est danceur.
> the boy   is come yesterday evening. he is dancer
> 'The boy came yesterday evening. He is a dancer.'

(28) La jeune fille est venue hier   soir.   Elle est danceuse.
     the girl   is come yesterday evening. she is dancer
     'The girl came yesterday evening. She is a dancer.'

But in non-standard French *il* has come to be an agreement marker. It does not fill any NP slot; instead it is bound to the verb and does not signal gender, as in:

(29) Ma   femme il   est venu.
     my:FEM wife   AGR has come

                                        (Lambrecht 1981: 40)

1.4 Grammaticalization and language structure

The examples we have sketched share such characteristics as the following: (a) earlier forms may coexist with later ones (e.g., *go, let, bé*); (b) earlier meanings may constrain later meanings and/or structural characteristics (*bé* in Ewe occurs after verbs of perception, cognition, and saying). Such examples emphasize that language development is an ongoing process, and one that often reveals itself as change that is only incompletely achieved at any given stage of a language.

Ultimately, too, examples such as these suggest more general consequences for linguistic theory and even for our perspective on language itself. Examples such as Ewe *bé* challenge some standard descriptive and theoretical linguistic notions. One is that of categories. Is Ewe *bé* a verb or a complementizer, and what criteria do we apply in determining this? Are sentences such as (22–3) examples of direct speech or of reported speech? Is the clause following *bé* strictly speaking subordinated (embedded) as in PDE, or is it more loosely attached to the preceding clause? Do we need in our analyses to continue to "stop the film" and fix the grammar of a language as we investigate its structure, or do we need to view "grammar" as a provisional way-station in our search for the more general characteristics of language as a process for organizing cognitive and communicative content?

2
The history of grammaticalization

2.1 Introduction

Grammaticalization is the study of grammatical forms, however defined, viewed as entities undergoing processes rather than as static objects. It has had many practitioners, and has occupied at various times both central and marginal positions in linguistics. In this chapter we will survey briefly the thought of some of the major figures in the early study of grammaticalization, and mention some of the contemporary linguists who are interested in the subdiscipline. The most complete histories of grammaticalization are by C. Lehmann (1982) and by Heine, Claudi, and Hünnemeyer (1991a).

2.2 Earlier research on grammaticalization

The term "grammaticalization" itself was apparently coined by the French linguist Antoine Meillet, an Indo-Europeanist who at one time had been a student of Saussure. In a well-known definition, Meillet writes of "the attribution of grammatical character to an erstwhile autonomous word"[1]("l'attribution du caractère grammatical à un mot jadis autonome"; Meillet 1912: 131). Yet Meillet's ideas on the origins of grammatical forms have predecessors in earlier speculations that were often rooted in assumptions about the evolutionary development of human speech.

Perhaps the most sophisticated of these speculations about the origins of grammar was that proposed by the German philosopher and humanist Wilhelm von Humboldt (1767–1835). In a published lecture entitled "On the genesis of grammatical forms and their influence on the evolution of ideas" ("Über das Entstehen der grammatikalischen Formen und ihren Einfluß auf die Ideenentwicklung") given in 1822 he suggested that the grammatical structure of human languages was preceded by an evolutionary stage of language in which only concrete ideas could be expressed. Grammar, he suggested, evolved through distinct stages out of the collocation of concrete ideas (Humboldt 1825).

At the first stage, only things were denoted, concrete objects whose relationships were not made explicit in utterances but had to be inferred by the listener. In modern terms, we might designate this stage as a "pragmatic" stage, using the word pragmatic in Givón's sense (Givón 1979: 223). Eventually certain of the orders in which the objects were presented became habitual, and this fixing of word order introduced a second stage (we might nowadays call it "syntactic"). At this stage, some words began to waver between concrete and formal (i.e. structural or grammatical) meanings, and some of them would become specialized for functioning in more relational ways in utterances. In the third stage, these functional words became loosely affixed to the material words (in modern terminology this might perhaps be called a stage of "cliticization"). In this way "agglutinative" pairs arose, dyads consisting of a material word and a relational word. In the fourth stage these agglutinative pairs became fused into synthetic, single word complexes. There were now stem and (inflectional) affixes that contained simultaneously material and grammatical meanings; we might think of this as a "morphological" stage. At this fourth stage, too, some of the function words would continue their lives as purely formal indicators of grammatical relationships. The functional life of words was reflected in their forms and meanings; during long usage meanings became lost and sounds were worn down.

It is no coincidence that Humboldt's four stages correspond quite closely to a typology of languages that was in the air during the first decades of the nineteenth century. According to this typology, there were three basic types of language: Isolating (Humboldt's stage II), Agglutinative (stage III), and Inflectional or Synthetic (stage IV). Humboldt's proposal can be thought of as an account of these types in evolutionary terms, supplemented by an assumed pre-stage (Humboldt's stage I). He eventually developed this idea into a series of further speculations about language typology and the relationship between language and cultural evolution. (A useful account of Humboldt's later ideas on language can be found in Humboldt 1988[1836], and R. Harris and Taylor 1989: 151–64.)

By the end of the nineteenth century a clear tradition in the study of grammaticalization had been established, lacking only the name itself. A picturesque account of the origins of grammatical forms and their evolution is to be found in the survey of linguistics by the German neogrammarian Georg von der Gabelentz (1891). Gabelentz (1891: 241) invites his readers to visualize linguistic forms as employees of the state, who are hired, promoted, put on half-pay, and finally retired, while outside new applicants queue up for jobs! Forms "fade, or grow pale" ("verblassen"); their colors "bleach" ("verbleichen"), and must be covered over with fresh paint. More grimly, forms may die and become "mummified," lingering on without life as preserved corpses (p. 242).

Gabelentz articulated many of the insights basic to work on grammaticalization. He suggests that grammaticalization is a result of two competing tendencies, one tendency toward ease of articulation, the other toward distinctness. As relaxed pronunciations bring about sound changes that wear down words, distinctions become blurred. So new forms must step in and take over the approximate function of the old ones. For example, the Latin future tense of a verb such as *video* 'I see,' *videbo*, is formed with a suffix *-bo* which was once *$b^hw\bar{o}$*, a first person singular form of the verb 'to be' used as an auxiliary. An old periphrastic construction, that is, a complex of a main verb and an auxiliary verb (*vide* + *$b^hw\bar{o}$*), was collapsed into a single inflectional form. But later this form too "wears down" and is replaced by new periphrastic forms such as *videre habeo* 'I have to see.' Somewhat later, this idea was to be articulated again by Meillet under the rubric of "renewal" ("renouvellement").

A second insight developed by Gabelentz is that this is not a linear process, but rather a cyclical one. Whereas for Humboldt's generation synthetic (inflectional) languages like the classical Indo-European languages represented an evolutionary endpoint, Gabelentz noted that the process of re-creation of grammatical forms is recurrent, and that the conditions for the cycle are always present in languages. Moreover, even the idea of a cycle is an oversimplification. Gabelentz speaks instead of a spiral, in which changes do not exactly replicate themselves but parallel earlier changes in an approximate manner.

Gabelentz's work, unlike Humboldt's, is informed by the awareness of geological timespans, which made it psychologically possible to think of multiple cycles of linguistic change. It also reflects an expanded knowledge of the variety of human languages and of historical texts, especially in the Indo-European languages that the neogrammarians and their predecessors had studied so energetically, now for two or three full generations. Yet Gabelentz's discussion of the origins of grammatical forms and their transformations covers only a couple of pages in his entire book. Although the germs of later work on grammaticalization are contained here, it was Antoine Meillet who first recognized the importance of grammaticalization as a central area of the theory of language change. Meillet was also the first to use the word "grammaticalization," and the first linguist to devote a special work to it.

Meillet's use of the term "grammaticalization" to designate the development of grammatical morphemes out of earlier lexical formatives is clearly descended from Humboldt's and Gabelentz's insights. It was also anchored in a more positivistic view of language, which stressed regularity in linguistic change and systematicity in synchronic description. As Meillet himself noted, the first generation of Indo-Europeanists had speculated intensely about the origins of grammatical forms. But their results had been random and unreliable. Moreover, they had insisted on placing these results in a "glottogonic" context, that is, the context of a supposed evolutionary line that would lead back to the actual origins of language. But this line of investigation had now fallen into disrepute. Meillet showed that what was at issue was not the origins of grammatical forms but their transformations. He was thus able to present the notion of the creation of grammatical forms as a legitimate, indeed a central, object of study for linguistics.

In his article "L'évolution des formes grammaticales" (1912), Meillet describes how new grammatical forms emerge through two processes. One is the well-known fact of analogy, whereby new paradigms come into being through formal resemblance to already established paradigms. (An example of analogy in recent English would be the replacement of the plural *shoen* by *shoes* through analogy to such established plurals as *stones*.) The second way in which new grammatical forms come into being, Meillet suggested, is through grammaticalization, "the passage of an autonomous word to the role of grammatical element" (p. 131).

Meillet illustrates the synchronic result of this process with the French verb *être* 'to be,' which ranges in meaning from a full existential ontological sense, as in *je suis celui qui suis* 'I am the one who is [lit. am],' to a somewhat less full locative sense in *je suis chez moi* 'I am at home,' to an almost redundant sense in *je suis malade* 'I am ill,' *je suis maudit* 'I am cursed,' and to a purely grammatical function as a tense-aspect auxiliary in *je suis parti* 'I left,' *je me suis promené* 'I went for a walk.'

The most significant, and remarkable, part of this fundamental article is Meillet's confident assertion: "These two processes, analogical innovation and the attribution of grammatical character to a previously autonomous word, are the only ones by which new grammatical forms are constituted. The details may be complex in any individual case; but the principles are always the same" (p. 131). Later in the same article, Meillet goes even further. Analogy can only operate when a nucleus of forms has already emerged to which new forms can be assimilated. So analogy is ruled out as a primary source of new grammatical forms. Therefore, " . . . the only process left is the progressive attribution of a grammatical role to autono-

mous words or to ways of grouping words" (p. 132). In every case where
certainty is possible, this is the origin of grammatical forms. Nothing stands
in the way of assuming that when allowance has been made for analogical
extension the same kind of source can ultimately be attributed to forms of
unknown or uncertain origin also.

Considering that during the neogrammarian period all investigations of
grammatical morphology had been essentially investigations of analogy,
Meillet's statement was sweeping and radical. Writing of the transformation
of autonomous words into grammatical roles, he says: "The importance [of
this] is in fact decisive. Whereas analogy may renew forms in detail, usually
leaving the overall plan of the system untouched, the 'grammaticalization'
of certain words creates new forms and introduces categories which had no
linguistic expression. It changes the system as a whole" (p. 133). "Grammaticalization," then, is seen as a process which affects individual words. But it
is evidently also meant to be extended to phrases. Indeed, the combining of
words into set phrases and their eventual amalgamation is presented in the
first part of the article as a defining feature of the event. In the French
future represented by *je vais faire* 'I will do,' literally 'I am going to do,' *vais*
no longer contains any perceptible sense of 'going.' In *je ferai* 'I will do,' the
fusion has gone even further, with no analytic trace remaining of the
original Latin phrase *facere habeo* 'I have to do.' It is a loss, Meillet
suggests, of expressivity. A novel way of putting words together becomes
commonplace ("banal"). In the extreme case, the phrase even ceases to be
analyzable as containing more than one word, but its members are fused
together ("soudé") as one. This phrasal collocation is itself usually a
replacement for an already existent form which has become commonplace.
Consequently, grammaticalization tends to be a process of replacing older
categories with newer ones having the same approximate value: inflected
futures (*ama-bo* 'I shall love') are replaced by periphrastic futures (*amare
habeo* 'I have to love' > 'I shall love'), which in turn are fused (*aimerai* 'I
shall love'), and so on.

At the end of the article he opens up the possibility that the domain of
grammaticalization might be extended to the word order of sentences (pp.
147–8). In Latin, he notes, the role of word order was "expressive," not
grammatical. (By "expressive," Meillet means something like "semantic" or
"pragmatic.") The sentence 'Peter slays Paul' could be rendered *Petrus
Paulum caedit, Paulum Petrus caedit, caedit Paulum Petrus*, and so on. In
modern French and English, which lack case morphemes, word order has
primarily a grammatical value. The change has two of the hallmarks of
grammaticalization: (i) it involves change from "expressive" to grammatical

meaning; (ii) it creates new grammatical tools for the language, rather than merely modifying already existent ones. The grammatical fixing of word order, then, is a phenomenon "of the same order" as the grammaticalization of individual words: "The expressive value of word order which we see in Latin was replaced by a grammatical value. The phenomenon is of the same order as the 'grammaticalization' of this or that word; instead of a single word, used with others in a group and taking on the character of a 'morpheme' by the effect of usage, we have rather a way of grouping words" (p. 148). We see, then, that in this initial study of grammaticalization, Meillet already points to applications of the term that go far beyond the simple change from lexical to grammatical meaning of single words. Indeed, if we pursue his argument to its logical conclusion, it is difficult to see where the boundaries of grammaticalization could convincingly be drawn. If the fixing of word order types is an example of grammaticalization through constant usage, could not all constructions which have been called "grammatical" constructions be said to have their ultimate origins in such habitual collocations? Evidently, how far we shall be prepared to extend the notion of "grammaticalization" will be determined by the limits of our understanding of what it means for a construction to be "grammatical" or have a grammatical function. We will suggest in Section 3.5.1 that, at least at this stage in our understanding of grammaticalization, word order changes are not to be included, although they are deeply interconnected with it.

Meillet also adumbrated other themes in the study of grammaticalization which are still at issue. One of these is the cause of grammaticalization. He attributes the process of grammaticalization to a loss of expressivity in frequently used collocations, whose functions may then be rejuvenated through new collocations filling more or less the same role. Yet often a "loss of expressivity" seems insufficient to capture what happens in grammaticalization. Some of his own illustrations challenge such a motivation. For example (pp. 138–9), the Modern German word *heute* 'today' can be traced back to a presumed Old High German phrase *hiu tagu*, the instrumental of two words meaning 'this day' (compare Gothic *himma daga* and Old High German *hiu jâru* 'this year [instr.]', Modern German *heuer*). It is, first of all, a little startling to find a change of this kind discussed under the rubric of grammaticalization, since it seems more appropriately thought of as illustrating the emergence of a new lexical item rather than of a grammatical formative. It is also questionable whether the change in Old High German from *hiu tagu* to *hiutu* resulted in a less meaningful ("expressive") form. Yet there is surely a difference in Modern German between *heute* and *an diesem Tage* 'on this day' that needs to be characterized in some way.

Evidently some different way of talking about meaning change is needed. We return to this in Chapter 4.

Accompanying this loss of expressivity is a supposed weakening ("affaiblissement") of phonological form and of concrete meaning (p. 139). Meillet's example is the development of the Modern Greek future tense morpheme *tha*, whose origin is in an older construction *thelô ina* 'I wish that'. The change included the following stages (p. 145):

thelô ina > thelô na > thena > tha

and the semantic development is from 'wish, desire' to 'future tense.' It is not difficult to see "weakening" in the phonological process, since there is undeniably a shortening and hence a loss of phonological substance. But it is not so obvious that the concomitant semantic change should also be seen in the same way. Like all the writing on grammaticalization at his time, and much since then, Meillet's account of grammaticalization in general is couched in terms which stress deficits of various kinds: loss, weakening, attrition. Such metaphors suggest that for all his linguistic sophistication there is still a slight residue of the "classical" attitude toward language in Meillet's thought, the attitude that equates change with deterioration.

Still, this first full-length paper on grammaticalization, in which the term itself is proposed, is astonishingly rich in its insights and the range of phenomena which are analyzed. Subsequent work on grammaticalization has modified, sometimes quite radically, Meillet's views, and many more substantive examples have been described, but time and again the germs of modern ideas on grammaticalization are to be found, implicitly and often explicitly, in this initial paper.

2.3   More recent research on grammaticalization

After the work of Meillet in the first two decades of the century, the topic of grammaticalization was taken up mainly by Indo-Europeanists. However, many other scholars who saw themselves as historical linguists, but not necessarily Indo-Europeanists, did not concern themselves with grammaticalization as a subdiscipline or even as a topic in its own right. The term is consistently overlooked in the textbooks of synchronic and historical linguistics of the period. Indeed the tradition of what C. Lehmann has called "amnesia" about grammaticalization extends up to the present, for the word does not appear in the index of Hock's *Principles of Historical Linguistics* (1991 [1986]), even though some of its principles do, nor does it figure in recent textbooks of linguistics such as Finegan and Besnier (1989).

"Mainstream" linguistics was strongly synchronic in its approaches and assumptions, which meant that historical factors, including grammaticalization, were of secondary interest. Language change came to be seen as sets of rule adjustments, beginning with one stage and ending with another but with little interest in the gradual process that must have been involved in between: "the treatment of change as the change in rules between synchronic stages isolates the description of change from the change itself" (Ebert 1976: viii–ix). The only significant studies of grammaticalization during this period were done by Indo-Europeanists such as Kuryłowicz (especially 1964, 1965) and Calvert Watkins (1964) who worked outside the dominant theoretical paradigm. But their work, unfortunately, was read almost exclusively by other Indo-Europeanists. Significantly, Meillet's student Émile Benveniste, in an article "Mutations of linguistic categories" written in 1968, found it necessary to repeat much of what Meillet had said in 1912 concerning the grammaticalization of auxiliary verbs out of lexical verbs such as 'have, hold'. Benveniste coined a new word, "auxiliation," to refer to this process. Even though he used several of the very same examples which had been proposed by Meillet (e.g., the Modern Greek *tha* future from an earlier *thelô ina*), at no point in the paper did he explicitly refer to Meillet's work or use the term "grammatic(al)ization" or its equivalent.

That such an influential linguist as Benveniste could appear to be starting afresh in the study of the origins of grammatical categories indicates the extent to which Meillet's insights had become submerged by twentieth century structuralism. We have seen that grammaticalization presents a challenge to approaches to language which assume discrete categories embedded in fixed, stable systems. It is therefore not surprising that grammaticalization again appears as a major theme of general (as opposed to specifically Indo-European) linguistics in the context of the questioning of autonomous syntactic theory which occurred in the 1970s. During this decade the growing interest in pragmatics and typology focused attention on the predictable changes in language types. Linguists thereby (largely unconsciously) revived the same line of investigation that had been dropped earlier in the century, a line which went back at least to Humboldt. An early paper by Givón perhaps began this revival. Entitled "Historical syntax and synchronic morphology; an archeologist's field trip," it announced the slogan "Today's morphology is yesterday's syntax" (Givón 1971: 413), and showed with evidence from a number of African languages how verb forms that are now stems with affixes could be traced back to earlier collocations of pronouns and independent verbs.

If one of the main tenets of twentieth century structuralism, especially as developed in the United States, was homogeneity, another was the arbitrariness of language, that is, its alleged independence from external factors such as the nature of things in the word (the referents of language). Saussure had drawn attention to the arbitrariness of the sign, for example, to the total independence of a word such as *dog* of the animal it names. But he also stressed the fact that arbitrariness is limited by associations and "relative motivations." These include word compounding as in *twenty-five*, derivational affixation as in French *pommier* 'apple-tree' (*pomme* 'apple' + *-ier*), *cérisier* 'cherry-tree' (*cérise* 'cherry' + *-ier*), and inflectional paradigms such as Latin *dominus, domini, domino* 'master-NOM, master-GEN, master-DAT.' Indeed, he regarded grammar, the set of structural rules, as setting limits on the arbitrariness and the chaotic nature of language (1986 [1922]: 130).

One name given to the principle that ensures non-arbitrariness is "iconicity." Iconicity is the property of similarity between one item and another. The philosopher Peirce made a useful distinction between imagic and diagrammatic iconicity.[2] Imagic iconicity is a systematic resemblance between an item and its referent with respect to some characteristic (a photograph or a sculpture of a person are imagic icons). Diagrammatic icons are systematic arrangements of signs. None of the signs necessarily resembles its referent in any way, but, crucially, the relationship among the signs mirrors the relationship among the icon's referents: "those [icons] which represent the relations . . . of the parts of one thing by analogous relations to their own parts are diagrams" (1931: Vol. 2, Par. 277). For example, the model of language change in Chapter 3 is an iconic diagram of the relationship between grammars of different generations. It is diagrammatic iconicity which is of chief importance in linguistics, and which has suggested significant insights into the organization of language and into grammaticalization in particular. A very well-known example of diagrammatic iconicity in language is the tendency for narrative order to match the order of events described; if the order is not matched, then some special marker or "diacritic" (usually a grammatical form) must be used. Thus Caesar's famous *Veni, vidi, vici* 'I came, I saw, I conquered' is a much-cited example of the way in which order of mention mirrors order of action described; any other order would require complex structures such as 'Before I conquered, I came and I saw.' Another famous example of diagrammatic iconicity in language is the way in which politeness (social distance) is typically reflected in language by complex morphology and formal vocabulary (often itself complex in structure), as exemplified by

Good morning (versus *Hi!*), *Would you please pass the butter* (versus *Can I have the butter?/Pass the butter!*).

Although iconicity was a major topic in much European linguistics, especially in the approach known as "semiotics" or "semiology," it was largely ignored as a principle in American linguistics in the first three quarters of this century, when interest was focused on the arbitrariness of language. Attention to iconicity was, however, renewed by several linguists working with issues germane to grammaticalization, most notably Jakobson (1966), Haiman (1980, 1983, 1985a), and Givón (1985), who laid the foundations for much recent thinking on the subject. The value of the principle of iconicity is most apparent in the context of cross-linguist work, and it is not coincidental that the period when iconicity came to be recognized again was also a period of interest in typology of languages.

This was a period, too, of intense interest in language universals, and some linguists began applying the idea of grammaticalization to general problems of synchronic description that had arisen in the course of the search for these universals. The work of Li and Thompson was especially influential among those working on historical issues. In their studies of serial verb constructions in Chinese and other languages they showed that verbs could be reanalyzed as prepositions and case markers, and thus revived interest in the question of how categories come into being. For example, in seventh to ninth century Chinese a "verb" *ba* occupied an ambiguous status between verb and prepositional case marker. In the example that follows, these two possibilities are suggested by two different translations of the same sentence:

(1) Zuì   bǎ zhū-gēn-zǐ   xì   kàn.
    drunk *ba* dogwood-tree careful look
    'While drunk,
    (i) I took the dogwood tree and carefully looked at it.'
        (*ba* = 'take')
    (ii) I carefully looked at the dogwood tree.' (*ba* = accusative
        case)

　　　　　(8th c. AD, Dù-fǔ poem, Li and Thompson 1976a: 485)

Such contexts provide the staging for a reanalysis of the former "verb" *ba* 'take' as a marker of the direct object of the verb and the collapsing of what had once been a sequence of two clauses (interpretation (i)) into a single clause (interpretation (ii)).

Li and Thompson's work on word order and especially on topicalization showed, as Meillet's had done, that syntactic development was also governed by processes analogous to or even identical to grammaticalization. Consider, for example, the distinction between a "topic" such as the initial noun phrase in (2), as opposed to the initial noun phrase in (3):

(2) That new yacht of his, he has spent a fortune on it.

(3) That new yacht of his has cost him a fortune.

In the first sentence, *that new yacht of his* is said to be a "topic," while in the second sentence the same noun phrase is a "subject." At this time there was considerable interest among linguists in arriving at a definition of the notion of "subject" that would be cross-linguistically valid. One of the chief obstacles was that in many languages the "subject" of a sentence was little more than a noun phrase in a very loose relationship to the verb (for instance, in some languages the sentence 'fire engines last night not have sleep' would be the normal way of saying 'I couldn't sleep last night because of the fire engines').

A number of properties, depending on the language involved, might set topics off against subjects. For example, there might be verb agreement between subject and verb but not between topic and verb; sometimes subjects but not topics could be referred to by a reflexive pronoun in the same clause. Moreover, in some languages there appeared to be no or very few topics, but a strongly developed notion of subject, while in other languages the topic appeared to be the usual role of a primary noun phrase. These facts had often been noted, but Li and Thompson's work, by placing them in the context of grammaticalization, revealed the diachronic relationship between the two categories. Evidently the difference between a "topic" and a "subject" was one of degree of grammaticalization only: "Subjects are essentially grammaticalized topics . . . " (Li and Thompson 1976b: 484). This work suggested to many linguists at the time that a diachronic perspective might offer more than merely an interesting historical comment on synchronic facts; the synchronic "facts" were indistinguishable from the diachronic and discourse pragmatic process they were caught up in (see, for example, Bolinger 1975).

Greenberg's empirical cross-linguistic study of word order (Greenberg 1966a) was foundational for the language universals movement. In this work a number of absolute and dependent ("implicational") generalizations about syntax were claimed, such as a statistical relationship binding languages that had verb-final word order, postpositions, and genitive preceding possessed noun in the possessive construction. Clearly, a diachronic perspective on these universals was possible; not only could changes in

word order be understood typologically, but synchronic syntax and morphology could be seen as the temporary – and not necessarily stable – reflexes
of ongoing shifts. Other cross-linguistic work by Greenberg that was
seminal for work in grammaticalization included his study of the development of demonstratives into articles and ultimately gender markers (noun
classifiers) via agreement markers (Greenberg 1978a), and of numeral
systems and their structure in terms of the order of elements in the numeral
phrases, and their syntactic relation to the noun head (Greenberg 1978b).
The first of these was primarily historical in focus, the second primarily
synchronic, but both highlighted the importance of a dynamic approach to
language structure.

Cross-linguistic projects that developed large computerized data banks
and often series of working papers owe much to the original inspiration of
the Stanford Project on Language Universals, headed by Charles Ferguson
and Joseph Greenberg, which culminated in Greenberg, Ferguson, and
Moravcsik's *Universals of Human Language* (1978), a four volume set of
papers, many of them on topics central to grammaticalization. Other such
projects include the Cologne Project on Language Universals and Typology,
headed by Hansjakob Seiler and disseminated through the publication
Arbeiten des Kölner Universalien-Projekts (*AKUP* for short). Especially
influential has been a survey of the morphology associated with the verb in
fifty languages headed by Joan Bybee at the University of New Mexico, and
exemplified by her book *Morphology: A Study of the Relation between
Meaning and Form* (1985). The most recent project at the time of writing is
a typological study of the European languages headed by Ekkehard König
of the Freie Universität Berlin, the publications of which are the working
paper series *Eurotyp*.

To return to our brief history of work in grammaticalization, Givón's
book *On Understanding Grammar* (1979) was a highly influential, if slightly
idiosyncratic, summing up of the decade's thought on these matters. It
firmly placed all linguistic phenomena in the framework of "syntacticiza-
tion" and "morphologization" (terms which Givón preferred to "grammaticalization"), and emphasized the essential function dependency of linguistic
rules and categories. The forms of speech, Givón proposed, were to be
viewed as being located on clines and as shifting between such poles as
child/adult, creole/standard, unplanned/planned, pragmatic/syntactic. In
each pair of these, the first is labile or "loose," the second fixed or "tight,"
and movement – i.e., change – is generally in the direction of the "tighter"
pole. This work distilled for the growing community of workers in grammaticalization some of the highly relevant research on morphologization in

pidgins and creoles such as is represented by Bickerton (1975), Sankoff (1980), and, in child language acquisition, by Slobin (1977). Unfortunately, a fuller integration of sociolinguistic and developmental research with research on grammaticalization still remains to be worked out.

2.4 Current trends in research on grammaticalization

The 1980s saw grammaticalization (or "grammaticization") assuming a significant place as a topic in its own right in the research of a number of linguists. As mentioned above, Bybee's large scale project on morphology, primarily verbal (e.g., Bybee 1985), has been a prominent and highly influential source of ideas and data. Some of this work will be discussed later. Here we will mention two important monographs, from the earlier part of the decade. C. Lehmann's *Thoughts on Grammaticalization: A Programmatic Sketch* (1982) was the first modern work to emphasize the continuity of research from the earliest period (roughly, Humboldt) to the present, and to provide a survey of the significant work in grammaticalization up to that time, with emphasis on work in historical linguistics. This book, which unfortunately was circulated only as a working paper of the Cologne Universals Project, provided by its comprehensiveness and its historical perspective a useful antidote to the "amnesia" that beset linguists of the previous decade, many of whom seemed to believe that the field had been newly invented. The second book that should be mentioned is that of Heine and Reh, *Grammaticalization and Reanalysis in African Languages* (1984). This book was perhaps the first to address an entire linguistic area (Africa) synchronically from the point of view of grammaticalization. It provided not only a classification of the phenomena to be addressed, with copious examples, but also an exhaustive index of the typical pathways of grammaticalization discovered by the authors, particularly with respect to morphosyntax and morphophonology. It goes without saying that most of these phenomena are not restricted to Africa, but have counterparts elsewhere in the world. Heine and Reh's book was a convincing demonstration of the power of grammaticalization theory as a tool of descriptive linguistics and especially of the wide range of linguistic facts that grammaticalization could characterize. These two books have been indispensable foundations for the (re-)establishment of grammaticalization as an important direction of modern linguistic research.

At the time of writing, Heine, Claudi, and Hünnemeyer published another major work, *Grammaticalization: A Conceptual Framework* (1991a). As in Heine and Reh, the data is mainly African and synchronic, but the focus is on pragmatic and cognitive factors that motivate grammaticalization, and the meaning changes that forms may undergo as they grammaticalize.

A two volume collection of papers arising out of a 1988 conference organized by Givón, and edited by Traugott and Heine under the title *Approaches to Grammaticalization* (1991), addresses many of the themes of current concern to a wide range of linguists working from the perspective of grammaticalization, many of which will be elaborated in the following chapters, for example:

(a) Can diachronic and synchronic approaches to grammaticalization be reconciled, or is a new approach required?

(b) Is grammaticalization a continuous or discontinuous process?

(c) To what extent is grammaticalization the result of discourse pragmatic forces?

(d) What constraints are there on the choice of concepts and forms serving as the input to grammaticalization?

(e) When can incipient grammaticalization be recognized?

(f) Is grammaticalization a unidirectional phenomenon?

(g) What phenomena in language are not examples of grammaticalization?

Our aim in the remainder of this book is to develop a synthesis of current thinking on grammaticalization that will provide the basis on which further work can be built. It is to this task that we now turn.

3
Mechanisms: reanalysis and analogy

3.1 Introduction

We turn now to some central concerns in any discussion of language change, with focus on those that are particularly important for an understanding of grammaticalization. In particular, we attempt to answer the questions: what motivates grammaticalization in the first place, what mechanisms lead to it, what are its probable paths of progression through time, and what are its end results? Particular changes do not have to occur, nor do they have to go through to completion, though some degree of change is inevitable. As elsewhere in this book, therefore, we will be referring to phenomena that make change possible or facilitate it, sometimes singly, sometimes together, not to factors that are absolute or obligatory. In this chapter we consider the mechanisms by which grammaticalization takes place: reanalysis primarily, and analogy secondarily. In Chapter 4 we will discuss speaker/hearer asymmetries and processes of inferencing as among the possible motivations for the operation of these mechanisms. Further possible motivations, acquisition and transmission, will be touched on in Chapter 8. The unidirectionality of paths of change will be the subject of Chapters 5, 6, and 7.

Reanalysis and analogy have been widely recognized as significant for change in general, most especially morphosyntactic change. Reanalysis modifies underlying representations, whether semantic, syntactic, or morphological, and brings about rule change. Analogy, strictly speaking, modifies surface manifestations and in itself does not effect rule change, although it does effect rule spread either within the linguistic system itself or within the community. Unquestionably, reanalysis is the most important mechanism for grammaticalization, as for all change.

A discussion of mechanisms from the point of view of grammaticalization tends to focus on their local operation, and their gradience (see also papers in Li 1977 under the name of "syntactic change") rather than on global characteristics or formalisms, though these are of course relevant too, and some will be discussed briefly in connection with recent hypotheses regarding the relationship between change and acquisition.

3.2 Some background assumptions about change

This is the not appropriate context for discussing principles of language change in detail. For fuller accounts of these principles, see Hock (1991 [1986]), Anttila (1989 [1972]), and more specifically on syntactic, morphological, and phonological change respectively, Lightfoot (1979, 1988, 1991), S. Anderson (1988), and Kiparsky (1988). However, before we proceed, some initial comments on language change will be helpful in clarifying certain assumptions behind the material to follow.

First, when we speak of change, what is thought to be changing? We speak loosely of "language change." But this phrase is misleading. Language does not exist separate from its speakers. It is not an organism with a life of its own; rather, each speaker of a language has to learn that language anew. Change is replacement (Hoenigswald 1966), on the understanding that "replacement" does not entail strict identity of an earlier function or category with a later one (see discussion at the end of 1.2.3). However, in so far as language is characterized by an abstract set of rules independent of languge users, the **rules** (or set of rules) can be said to change.

Different models of rule change have been suggested. The one most influential in the last three decades has been the generative model. This conceptualizes rule change in terms of high level global organization and of the whole set of rules (the "grammar") rather than in terms of individual rule changes. Furthermore, it assumes that in general, or as an idealization, major changes (called "restructurings") can occur only in the discontinuity of transmission from one generation to another, in particular during the process of child language acquisition in a homogeneous speech community. The factors that enable this transmission are twofold: universal capacities for language and universal reasoning processes that language users bring to the output of the earlier grammar. Andersen (1973: 778) characterized the sequence of change as shown in Figure 3.1.

In this model, Grammar1 is the internalized set of rules in an earlier generation. This speaker's verbal output (Output1) is determined by Grammar1. The language learner, endowed with certain universal capacities for language, hears Output1. Using the universal capacities (here called "Laws"), and universal reasoning processes (modeled by the curved arrow), the learner infers an internalized grammar which may be different from that of the earlier speaker, in which case it is termed Grammar2. This interna-

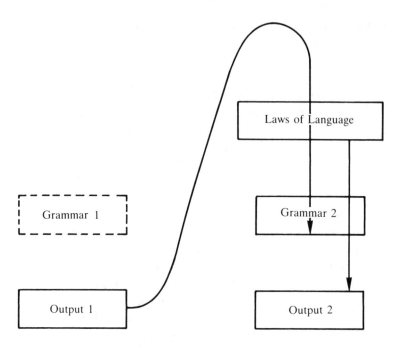

Figure 3.1 A model of language change

lized grammar is verbalized by output which is different from Output1 because it is the verbalization of a different grammar.

The model is a useful one for conceptualizing change, and will serve our purposes in this book provided it is understood in the light of assumptions about grammaticalization rather than the more rigid generative ones to which it has largely been adapted. However, attention should be drawn to some of the original assumptions and how they need to be modified, and it is to this task that we now turn.

Although the model itself does not force the issue, it was designed to characterize a grammar of relatively fixed structure at any one period, and uniformity of input. Such assumptions, as we have seen, are challenged by the study of grammaticalization (and of sociolinguistics). The model does crucially claim that there are universal laws of some kind, but, as a model, does not specify what kinds of laws they are. Andersen speaks of them as: "the properties of [the learner's] constitution that completely determine the nature of linguistic structure, and hence the relation between a grammar and its output" (Andersen 1973: 776). The key phrase here is "completely determine." The hypothesis is that human beings are born with a set of constraints on what possible language structures can be, and ways in which they can vary. A characterization of this hypothesis has been the major focus of much recent generative theory. Specifically, it has been proposed that all human beings are genetically endowed with Universal Grammar (UG). This UG is conceived as consisting of two components: unchanging "principles" that characterize the fundamental structure of language and restrict the class of attainable grammars, and "parameters" that define the space of possible variation and are fixed by experience. Differences between languages across geographic and social space or across time are conceived as being the result of different settings of the parameters in the process of language acquisition (Chomsky 1981). Recently Lightfoot has elaborated on the idea of principles and parameters for change, and has argued that changes from one generation to another are the result of the fact that different learners select different possibilities from among a restricted set of structures that are genetically encoded. Specifically, Lightfoot hypothesizes that children contribute to language learning and hence to change at least a "disposition to learn". This disposition is conceived as a selective one: "an organism experiences the surrounding environment and selects relevant stimuli according to criteria that are already present internally" (Lightfoot 1989: 321; 1991: 2). Such a selective disposition is contrasted to an "instructive" one, which is essentially flexible and modifiable by outside stimuli. The claim that the disposition is selective means that, according to Lightfoot, only certain data are attended to by the child: precisely those data that can be matched to the child's extant internalized grammar.

An alternative approach, more akin to the objectives of researchers in grammaticalization, is to regard the universal component as one which does not "completely determine the nature of linguistic structure," but rather as one which characterizes broader properties of the human constitution and can be modified by outside stimuli (Jackendoff 1983) and by the functional purposes to which language is put (Givón 1989). We will adopt this more flexible view of universals.

One of the consequences of the assumption that Grammar1 and Grammar2 are relatively fixed is that the model can be (and has been) taken to suggest that rule or form A is replaced directly by a different rule or form B. Consider Ewe *bé*. From the model it might appear that a later generation abruptly replaces the earlier generation's lexical V meaning 'say' with a particle meaning 'that' (along with accompanying changes in syntactic structure) and that, for the language learner, the earlier meaning and structure have disappeared altogether. But, as we have seen, older and newer forms coexist for individual speakers as well as for communities over time. Indeed, A probably never "becomes" B without an intermediary stage in which A and B coexist:[1]

$$
(1) \quad A > \left\{ \begin{matrix} B \\ A \end{matrix} \right\} > B
$$

Such coexistence may last several hundred or more years, as in the case of Ewe *bé* or English *be going to*. Alternatively, it may be quite short, as in the case of the brief development and demise during Middle English of "egressive" aspectual verbs *stint* and *fin* (meaning approximately 'leave off V-ing,' 'stop V-ing') (Brinton 1988: 151). We will discuss the phenomenon in greater detail in Section 5.5.1.

When accounting for Figure 3.1 in the light of the claim that it is rules that change, not languages, a distinction needs to be made between change and spread of the change (for discussion from the point of view of grammaticalization, see Lichtenberk 1991a). When B enters the grammar alongside of A, it does so abruptly: an Ewe language user either does or does not use *bé* as a complementizer.[2] However, the spread of the complementizer analysis across verbs of locution and cognition (see 1.3.2) is gradual; this kind of spread through the linguistic system is called "generalization" and will be discussed in fuller detail in Chapter 5. Spread across linguistic contexts is to be further distinguished from spread across genres and social groups. For example, each individual reanalysis of a verb of locution or cognition could potentially have its own trajectory through social space, though often there will be cumulative effects from one change to another.

As indicated above, Andersen's model has been understood as designed to reflect changes in the abstract grammars of individual speaker-hearers of different generations. The problem is that "one swallow doth not a summer make," and one change in the grammar of an individual does not constitute what we think of as a change in "a language." From the viewpoint of generative grammar, there is no such thing as "a grammar of OE," or "a grammar of PDE," only grammars of individuals; therefore, when we use such expressions as "change in the grammar of X" we are essentially using "a convenient fiction permitting the statement of certain generalizations and ignoring certain types of variation" (Lightfoot 1991: 162). But this leaves the question of how to think about the sometimes significant differences that can be observed over time. The answer from the generative perspective is that, however abrupt a change may appear to be in models such as that in

Figure 3.1, once the change has occurred, it is the aggregations of gradual changes across time that give the impression of "changes in the language." In an effort to refocus attention on breaking down diachronic development into its "smallest appreciable constituent steps," an effort highly consonant with grammaticalization, Andersen points out that:

> each and every step in such a development is an innovation, not only the initial act, through which a new linguistic entity comes into being. It is through innumerable individual acts of innovation – of acceptance, adoption, and acquisition – that any new entity gains currency and enters into competition with traditional entities in the usage of a linguistic community.
>
> (Andersen 1989: 14)

Another way to think of what constitutes a change is to think of grammars not of the individual but of the speech community: "The grammars in which linguistic change occurs are grammars of the speech community" (Weinreich, Labov, and Herzog 1968: 188). But this approach too ultimately leaves us with unresolved questions: what is the status of "grammar of the speech community," and, again, when can we say that a change has occurred?

Although evidence for either approach could presumably be empirically tested in contemporary language development, the exigencies of most historical records make both difficult to apply. Although caution must always be exercised, in practice many linguists tend to see a single example of a change that later spreads to other texts and other constructions as a "first example of change X." This approach naturally follows from thinking of change in terms of differences in the grammars of individual language users. As will be discussed in more detail later, the ancestor of PDE *will*, as in *She will run for Governor*, was a main verb meaning 'intend,' cf. *She willed herself to succeed*. The following example is a rare instance in ninth century Old English of the past tense of *willan* 'want' in a context that suggests it can only have been meant as a marker of later time (equivalent of PDE *would* for *will* in reported speech):

(2) Þa   Darius geseah þæt he overwunnen beon wolde, þa
     when Darius saw   that he overcome   be   would, then
     wolde he hiene selfne on ðæm gefeohte forspillan.
     wanted he him self   in that battle   kill-INF
     'When Darius saw that he would be overcome, he wanted to commit suicide in that battle.'

(*c.* 880, Orosius 3 9.128.5)

Does this citation exemplify a change at least in the grammar of the language user who wrote this passage, if not in the "convenient fiction of the grammar of Old English"? The rate of use of *wolde* in the sense of 'would' increased in Middle English. Therefore (2) appears to be a legitimate early example of a structure that signals a rule change at a minimum in the individual even though it appears only rarely elsewhere. By contrast, a novel construction that does not reappear or spread is taken to be a "scribal error," or a "nonce-formation," and not an example of change or even of a precursor to change.

Methodologically it is certainly preferable to recognize change only when it has spread from the individual to a group, and only when the constraints of the former linguistic environment are no longer obligatory. Thus we know that *let's* has begun to be grammaticalized when the constraint to the permission context no longer holds. When this happened, the paradigmatic relationship of the first person plural pronoun to other pronouns and nouns no longer held, and the stress on *let* could be reduced.

Another assumption behind the model worth mentioning is that the focus on universals privileges the uniformity of rule types and reasoning types across languages and times. Indeed, what has come to be called the "uniformitarian principle" (Labov 1974, Romaine 1982) is an essential ingredient of most work in historical linguistics. According to this principle, the linguistic forces that are evidenced today are in principle the same as those that operated in the past. Operationally, this means that no earlier grammar or rule may be reconstructed for a dead language that is not attested in a living one. There is no reason to believe that grammaticalization did not occur in languages spoken ten thousand years ago in much the same way as it does now.

So far we have only mentioned the reasoning process modeled in Figure 3.1 by the curved arrow leading from Output 1 to Grammar 2, and have said that these processes are important in grammaticalization. Here we pause to consider some basic logical principles of reasoning, known as induction, deduction, and, most importantly for change, abduction.

3.3 Induction, deduction, abduction

An idealized artificial language, for example, a computer language, can be thought of as a coding device in which ready made ideas are converted into symbols that serve one and only one function. Here a principle of "one form – one meaning" operates, and every "utterance" conveys an unambiguous message. Such transparency is not found in human language. This is partly because in real world languages a small set of units and constructions must serve a much larger set of functions. Moreover, language is a social institution, and one of its important functions is to maintain social networks and sustain interest in a verbal interaction. Therefore indirectness (such as is found in politeness phenomena), metaphor, and other non-literal meanings are an essential part of language. "One form – one meaning" would in these circumstances be dysfunctional. For example, *Do you mind not smoking in here?* can serve as a request for information, or a command to stop smoking in the guise of an inquiry. After extensive use as the latter it can be felt as too "routine," hence too close to *Please stop smoking*, and therefore can be substituted in some circumstances by a lengthier paraphrase such as *Would you mind awfully if I were to ask you not to smoke in here?* Part of the human ability to understand and use language is the ability to reason from the form of what is said to the intent of what is said, as well as from the string of sounds that occurs as input to the structure behind that input.

Logicians have focused until recently on two types of reasoning: induction and deduction. If human language were an artificial language then these logics might suffice. However, neither of these logics accounts adequately for indirectness, expressiveness, or change. For this a third type of reasoning, abduction, first identified by C.S. Peirce (1931), needs to be considered. The importance of abduction for language change has been stated particularly clearly by Andersen (1973). The following is based on Andersen's main points (especially 774–86; see also Lightfoot 1979: 343–73; Anttila 1989 [1972]: 196–8).

Types of reasoning are exemplified by three propositions that consititute a syllogism:

> The Law (e.g., All men are mortal)
> The Case (e.g., Socrates is a man)
> The Result (e.g., Socrates is mortal)

Deductive reasoning applies a law to a case and predicts a result (e.g., *All men are mortal, Socrates is a man, therefore Socrates is mortal*). Strictly speaking, the conclusion asserts nothing that is not given in the premises; furthermore, if the premises are true, then the conclusion is also. Inductive reasoning proceeds from observed cases and results to establish a law (e.g., *Socrates is a man, Socrates is mortal, therefore all men are mortal*).

Abductive reasoning is different, although it is often confused with inductive reasoning: "Abduction proceeds from an observed result, invokes a law, and infers that something may be the case. E.g. given the fact that Socrates is dead, we may relate this fact to the general law that all men are mortal, and guess that Socrates was a man" (Andersen 1973: 775). Even if the premises are true, the conclusion need not be so: one may match the wrong result with the law. Perhaps Socrates is not a man but a lizard, a wrong conclusion but nevertheless one that is compatible with the other two premises. The law may be an established truth, or it may be a tentative generalization. Peirce was interested in abduction because, although he saw it as a weak form of reasoning, he also saw it as the basis of human perception and as the only kind of reasoning by which new ideas could originate.

Andersen, and many linguists after him, have regarded abduction as essential to development of cultural patterns, including language. Of the process itself, Andersen says: "In acquiring his [sic] language, a learner observes the verbal activity of his elders, construes it as a 'result' – as the output of a grammar – and guesses at what that grammar might be" (1973: 776). The guesses are processes of reasoning based on universal principles, the basic goal being the construction of a grammar (the case) that in some way conforms to the observed data (the result). As will be discussed below, abduction is the mode of reasoning that leads to reanalysis. It is constantly tested out by the process of induction (the matching of a hypothesis to the data) and by deduction (the production of new utterances based on the hypothesis). As indicated above, the curved arrow from Output1 through Laws of Language in Figure 3.1 as developed by Andersen models abduction. The straight arrow from Laws of Language through Grammar 2 to Output 2 models deduction.

Whatever our model for change, we need to consider the ways or "mechanisms" by which change takes place and the factors that enable them to occur. In the remainder of this chapter we focus on the principal ways in which grammaticalization may occur.

3.4 Reanalysis

In a major paper on syntactic change, Langacker defined reanalysis as: "change in the structure of an expression or class of expressions that does not involve any immediate or intrinsic modification of its surface manifestation" (1977: 58). Subsequently, reanalysis has been thought of in terms of shift from one parametric setting to another, as will be briefly discussed in Chapter 8. For purposes of our initial discussion here, we will focus on Langacker's approach.

One of the simplest types of reanalysis, and one very frequently found in grammaticalization, is fusion: the merger of two or more forms across word or morphological boundaries. A typical example is compounding: the combining of two or more words into one, usually with consequences for semantics, morphology, and phonology (and sometimes also syntax) from the perspective of the new whole word and the former individual parts. An example of compounding is the development of many highly productive derivational affixes in English. Present Day English *-hood, -dom, -ly* originated in full nouns meaning 'condition,' 'state, realm,' and 'body, likeness' respectively that were compounded with other nouns, as in:

(3) cild-had 'condition of a child' > childhood
     freo-dom 'realm of freedom' > freedom
     man-lic 'body of a man, likeness of a man' > manly

Such affixes usually have their origin in lexical items of a relatively general or abstract sort, and the same items tend to recur in language after language. Heine and Reh (1984: 269–81) have catalogued many of them for African languages. Words for body parts in particular often begin to function as emphasizers, as in *talk one's head off, work one's tail off*. They frequently come to emphasize pronouns and later may become reflexive pronouns. Heine and Reh list "body, head, belly, soul, breath, person" as among the nouns which typically develop as reflexives (1984: 272).

Fusion involves changes in the assignment of boundaries (i.e., rebracketing). But rebracketing does not always lead to fusion. The examples of grammaticalization in Chapter 1 are all examples of reanalysis that involves rebracketing of elements in certain constructions, and reassignment of morphemes to different semantic-syntactic categories: *be going to* from main verb + progressive aspect + purposive preposition to tense marker; *let us* from main verb + object to modal particle + subject; and Ewe *bé* from main verb to complementizer.[3] In each case we can posit ambiguity in some contexts (also called "opacity") that allowed for the structure to continue to be analyzed as before, and for a new analysis to coexist with it.

Reanalysis is the result of abduction. For example, given the reanalysis of a construction consisting of a head noun and a dependent noun (4a) as a (complex) preposition and head noun (4b):

(4) a. [[back] of the barn] >
     b. [back of [the barn]]

the abduction account of what has happened here is as follows. A hearer has heard the "output" (4a) (the "result"), but assigns to it a different structure (4b) (the "case") after matching it with possible nominal structures (specified by the "laws"). The conclusion is not identical with the original

structure of which (4a) is a manifestation, b|
with (4a) in that the surface string is the same

Below we give more examples of reanalys|
of reassignments that occur. All three involv|
although the first and second pertain primarily t|
ment of the Romance future, and of the thi|
Uto-Aztecan language, Tarahumara), and the t|
ment of English modal auxiliaries).

3.4.1 The French inflectional future

The history of the Romance future has |
fuller accounts, see especially Fleischman 1982, P|
reviewing specifically the development from Latir|
French such as *je chanterai* 'I will sing.'

As mentioned in Chapter 2 in connection with |
order as a kind of grammaticalization, Latin was a|
object–verb word order structure, but allowed a|
convey different rhetorical strategies (e.g., the three|
of *Petrus Paulum caedit*). It had verbal inflections|
future, as well as other temporal relations. As mentioned|
future was an inflection that combined person, number, a|

(5) cantabo
     sing-1SG:FUT
     'I will sing'

The question is how phrasal constructions such as (6), consisting of an
infinitive and a form of the verb *habere* 'to have,' came to compete with and
eventually replace constructions such as (5):

(6) Haec habeo   cantare.
     these have-1SG:PRES sing-INF
     'I have these things to sing.'

It was constructions such as the one in (6) which were reduced, in various
ways in the various Romance languages, to form the new inflectional future
illustrated by *je chanterai*.

One of the verbs in Latin was a verb of possession and belonging, *habere*
'to have,' cognate with English *have*. As a possessive, it was a transitive verb
and could originally introduce only a nominal object. In many contexts it did
not have the strict meaning of possession, but rather had a more general
locative meaning of 'belonging, being in presence of,' etc. (for the cross-

linguistic interrelationship of locative-possessive-existential, see Lyons 1968, Clark 1978). In some contexts, especially those in which the object was predicated by a gerundive, for example (7), this verb acquired a sense of obligation, or at least future orientation, presumably transferred from the gerundive, which itself once expressed obligation.

(7) Aedem habuit tuendam.
    house   had   look:after-GER
    'He had a house to look after.'
            (*c.* 40 BC, Cicero, *Ver.* II.1,130; cited in Pinkster 1987: 208)

Thus if I have a house to look after, I may have obligations to look after it, and I may have future purposes, such as living in it, passing it on to my descendants, etc. Pinkster (1987) suggests that *habere* + infinitive originated as an alternative to *habere* + gerundive, most particularly in contexts of verbs of speaking:

(8) a. Quid habes   dicendum?
      what have-2SG say-GER
      'What do you have to say?'
   b. Quid habes   dicere?
      what have-2SG say-INF
      'What do you have to say?'

The first instance, according to Pinkster, of *habere* with an infinitive is in the context of a verb of speaking that introduces a sentential complement:

(9) Multos ferro,   multos veneno   (occidit); habeo
    many   dagger-INST, many   poison-INST (killed); have-1SG
    enim dicere   quem . . .   de   ponte in Tiberim deicerit.
    even tell-INF someone . . . from bridge in Tiber   threw
    'Many he killed by the dagger, many by poison; I can even give you an example of one man whom . . . he threw from the bridge into the Tiber.'
            (*c.* 40 BC, Cicero, *S. Rosc.* 100; quoted in Pinkster 1987: 206)

Several examples such as (6) occur in texts with the 'have'-verb separated from the infinitive, as in (9), or preceding it, as in (10):

(10) De   re   publica nihil   habeo   ad te
     about matter public   nothing have-1SG:PRES to you
     scribere   nisi . . .
     write-INF except . . .

'I have nothing to write to you about the commonwealth[4] except . . . '

(*c.* 40 BC, Cicero; cited in Fleischman 1982: 121)

But a different order is also attested, notably:

(11)   Haec cantare habeo.

Examples include:

(12)   Et   si interrogatus fueris,   quomodo
       and if asked   be-2SG:PERF:SUBJUNCT, how
       dicere   habes?   Veritatem dicere
       say-INF have-2SG:PRES:SUBJUNCT truth   say-INF
       habeo.
       have-1SG:PRES
       'And you, if you are asked, what do you have to/will you say?
       I will have the truth to say/I will speak the truth.'

(Later Latin; cited in Fleischman 1982: 59)

From the perspective of reanalysis, the important fact is that constructions such as (12) contain a main verb *hab-* and an infinitive complement, in a structure of the type: [[cantare] habeo], and in contexts that can be understood to be obligative or at least future oriented. If one is asked what one can say, the inference can be that one ought to say it. In such contexts, processes of abduction could lead a language user to interpret the input string not as representing two underlying clauses, but rather as bracketed together in a structure of the type [cantare habeo], provided of course that the forms are adjacent.

Once this reanalysis had occurred, further changes were possible. These include fusion across morpheme boundaries and phonological attrition, and also semantic reanalysis to a future tense marker. We may posit a development of the kind sketched in Section 1.2.3:

(13)   Classical Latin [[cantare] habeo] >
       Late Latin [cantare habeo] >
       French [chant-e-r-ai]

3.4.2   *The Tarahumara third person pronoun*

Another example of successive stages of reanalysis is provided by the development of the third person singular pronoun *binoy* in Tarahumara (Uto-Aztecan) (Langacker 1977). Langacker reconstructs this pronoun as deriving from a clause consisting of a Proto-Uto-Aztecan third

44

person singular animate pronoun $*p\dot{t}$-, the reciprocal $*na$, a general locative postposition $*k^wa$ (POST), and the verb $y\dot{t}$- 'be', and meaning 'He is by himself.'

(14) PRON-REFL-POST-BE
      p $\dot{t}$-na-k^{w}a-y $\dot{t}$
      he-himself-by-is
      'he is by himself'

(Langacker 1977: 89)

When appended to another clause with coreferential subject, the reciprocal *na was presumably understood (i.e., reinterpreted) as an emphatic locative reflexive, and constructions of the type 'The man is working (and) he is by himself' can be reconstructed (p. 88).

In order for the clause in (14) to be reanalyzed as a phrase, the segments signaling clausal status (the third person pronoun *p$\dot{t}$* and the verb *y$\dot{t}$*) must have been reinterpreted as having different functions from those they had before. Langacker hypothesizes that *p$\dot{t}$* was reinterpreted as having the function "reflexive," and the remainder as a locative postposition. In other words, the original four segments were reanalyzed as two, the second of which resulted from boundary loss. Thus from (14) above, the following Proto-Uto-Aztecan locative emphatic reflexive was derived (presumably by other smaller intermediate steps):

(15) REFL-POST
      p$\dot{t}$-nak^{w}ay$\dot{t}$
      'himself by'

(ibid.)

Further semantic reanalysis and further boundary loss, as well as regular phonological changes, gave rise to the third person Tarahumara monomorphemic pronoun *binoy*.

3.4.3 The English modal auxiliaries

We turn now to an example of reanalysis with far wider reaching ramifications than the development either of the French inflectional future or of the Tarahumara third person pronoun. The development of the English auxiliaries was one of the first topics to draw the attention of generative linguists working on syntactic change (see Traugott [Closs] 1965, Lightfoot 1979). Originally conceived as a prime example of syntactic change, it is clearly also an instance of the larger process of grammaticaliza-

45

tion. It concerns change in the status of lexical verbs such as *may, can, must, do* such that they become auxiliaries.

In Middle English around 1380 (as represented by texts by Chaucer and Wycliffe) and in the fifteenth century (as represented by the Paston Letters and other texts) the following kinds of constructions were available:

    (i)   Question inversion and negation without *do*:

(16) a. 'Felistow', quod sche, 'thise thynges, and entren thei aughte in thy corage?'
          'Do you feel', she said, 'these things, and do they enter at all into your feelings?'

(c. 1380, Chaucer, Boethius, I.iv.1)

      b. it aperteneth nat to a wys man to . . .
          'it does not suit a wise man to . . . '

(c. 1380, Chaucer, CT, Melibee 2170)

    (ii)   Transitive clauses consisting of verbs such as *can* or *may* followed by an object NP, as in (17), or a *to*-infinitive complement as in (18):

(17)   She koude muchel of wandrying by the weye.
       'She knew a lot about travel.'

(c. 1390, Chaucer, CT, Prol. A. 467)

(18)   any man þe whiche hadde mowȝt to scapen þe deth
       'any man who had been able to escape death'

(c. 1382, W. bible 2 Par. 20.24 [MED mouen 11b])

    (iii) Modal verbs in past participle form, like *mowȝt* in (18).
    (iv) Sequences of modal verbs:

(19)   No-þing to hafe is sum-tyme of need, bot noȝt to may will haue is of grete vertew.
       'To have nothing is sometimes a necessity, but to desire [lit. to be able to will to have] nothing is a great virtue.'

(1434, Misyn ML 128/8 [MED mouen 10a])

By Early Modern English of the early sixteenth century constructions such as those in (17–19) had become almost non-existent, and *do*-constructions were rapidly replacing those in (16). For detailed studies of this replacement and how to model it, see Kroch (1989a, 1989b).

Work by Lightfoot has provided one perspective on the changes in the auxiliary verb constructions from Old and Middle English to Early Modern English. He suggests that "in Old English *can, could, may, might, must,*

shall, should, will, would, do, did behaved exactly like normal verbs"
(Lightfoot 1982: 159) and this fact can be captured by a partial grammar of
Old and Middle English of the type shown in (20):[5]

(20) S → N″ AUX V‴
      AUX → Tense
      V‴ → Specifier V′
      V′ → V . . .
      Specifier → Perfective Progressive
      V → cunn-, will-, mot-, mæg-, scul-, do-, see-, scape-, lufe-,
      write- . . .

Negation and inversion operated on AUX + the first verb of the clause
(whether specifier or main verb) as in (16). During the early sixteenth
century a change occurred such that constructions of the type (16–19) are no
longer found, or are found only in highly restricted contexts. A subset of the
main verbs, notably *may, can, shall, do*, etc., has been reanalyzed as a
separate category: Modal. Inversion and negation now make reference to
this category. The new Early Modern English grammar, according to
Lightfoot, was as shown in (21) (1982: 160, with slight modifications):

(21) S → N″ AUX V‴
      AUX → Tense Modal
      V‴ → Specifier V′
      V′ → V . . .
      Specifier → Perfective Progressive
      Modal → can, could, will, would, must, shall, should, may,
      might, do
      V → see, escape, love, write, will . . .

Note that the AUX rule has changed, by addition of Modal. The V rule has
also changed, by loss of some former members; the remaining *will* verb
means 'to will something (to someone).' As presented here, the reanalysis
consists of the development of a new grammatical category, as the result of
the restriction of a small subset of former main verbs into a closed class. An
alternative view, which is also more responsive to the data, focuses not so
much on the establishment of the new category Modal, but on the
development of *do* as most Vs lose the capacity to be moved in questions
and to occur before the negative, as in (16) (Kroch 1989b). Lightfoot
incorporates the two views in his (1991) analysis, and argues for two
successive changes, the first involving identification of *will*, etc. as auxiliaries, followed later by the failure of non-auxiliaries to be inverted in

questions and to precede the negative. The changes, most especially the latter, had consequences for the texture of English that make it very different not only from earlier stages but also from several other European languages, including French and German.

An important aspect of Lightfoot's analyses is that he shows that there was a cluster of factors that set the scene for the reanalysis. Together, he suggests, they made *may, can, shall, do*, etc. appear to the language learner as a rather special subset of main verbs – by the early sixteenth century most had ceased to take a direct object or a *to*-infinitive, and, being preterit presents, most had special morphologies. As study of grammaticalization in context continues, it is likely that many, if not most, instances of reanalysis will also be shown to arise out of a cluster of factors rather than out of a single one.

The characterizations Lightfoot proposes are at a level so general that they obscure many of the more fine-grained properties that a perspective from grammaticalization would focus on. For example, (20) and (21) suggest that all the relevant verbs changed at the same time. Indeed, in earlier work, Lightfoot wrote of "a sudden, cataclysmic, wholesale restruc-turing" (i.e. reanalysis) (Lightfoot 1979: 122). However, the changes occurred in different verbs at different times (a point accepted in Lightfoot 1991: 161). Some go back to Old English times (for discussion see Warner 1983, 1990; Plank 1984; Fischer and van der Leek 1987; Bybee 1990; Denison 1990). Furthermore, some of the changes are still ongoing. Consider, for example, the set of verbs known as "quasi-modals": *be to, dare to, need to* and *ought to*, some of which do and some of which do not require *do* in negatives and questions (e.g., *You needn't go, Do you need to go, *Need you go, *You don't ought to leave, ?You oughtn't to leave, Ought you to leave?*). We will discuss further ways in which the perspective of grammaticalization differs from that proposed by Lightfoot in Section 8.2. Here the focus has been on demonstrating the interrelationship of gramma-ticalization and reanalysis.

3.5 The independence of reanalysis and grammaticalization

As indicated above, reanalysis is a major factor in change. Meillet appears to have identified reanalysis with grammaticalization. However, although many cases of reanalysis are cases of grammaticalization (including those discussed in 3.4.1–3), not all are the result of reduction of a lexical item or phrase into one that is more grammatical, less lexically categorical, etc.

In 3.4 we mentioned compounding, a process resulting from reanalysis in which the boundary between words or morphemes is weakened, if not entirely lost. When new grammatical affixes arise out of the process, then we can say that reanalysis has led to grammaticalization. But new affixes do not always arise out of the process, and then the effect seems to be primarily on the lexicon, not the grammar. Examples of non-affixes include *bo'sun* from *boat* + *swain* 'man,' *hussy* from *house* + *wife* 'woman,' *fishwife* from *fish* + *wife* 'woman,' *sweetmeat* from *sweet* + *meat* 'food' (Anttila 1989 [1972]: 151). *Swain, wife, meat* have not been reanalyzed as grammatical morphemes, nor do they seem destined to be. Here then, we have a case of reanalysis without necessary grammaticalization.

Sometimes reanalysis results in a change that has grammatical effects, but nevertheless involves a shift from grammatical to lexical structure, rather than from lexical to grammatical structure (the norm for grammaticalization). Examples are the use of *up, down, ante*, etc. as verbs or nouns, cf. *to up the ante, to ante up, what a downer*. The process whereby a non-lexical form such as *up* becomes a fully referential lexical item is called "lexicalization." It is relatively uncommon, but instances can be found in most languages. A rather different instance is the development in English of *bus*, a borrowed Latin ablative plural that has been detached from the adjective stem *omni-* (*omnibus* 'for all') and promoted to nominal status. Since the form derives from a borrowing, and the Latin paradigm of case inflections is virtually inaccessible to most English speakers, the development of an inflection into a noun illustrated by *bus* has status only as a unique innovation, not as a regular type of change.

Another case of reanalysis leading to the autonomy of an earlier affix, this time one that resulted from sound change, is that of the emphatic particle *ep* in Estonian (Campbell 1991: 291). At an earlier stage the particle was a bound clitic, cf. Finnish *-pa, -pä*. By regular phonological change, the final vowel disappeared, leaving *-p*, cf. *päällä* 'on (top of)' > *pääll*, and *päällä-pä* 'right on (top of)' > *päällä-p*. The vowel of the clitic had originally required vowel harmony; with the loss of the vowel of the clitic, the vowel harmony rule no longer applied, and the emphatic form became *peallep*. The emphatic *peallep* no longer had any transparent relationship to the non-emphatic *päällä*. *Pealle-p* was reanalyzed as *peal-ep*. Later *-ep* was reinterpreted as an autonomous particle, and came to precede the word it emphasized. Reanalysis here led to the development of new independent particles, which themselves then could become subject to grammaticalization.

More widely attested cases of reanalysis that call into question the identification of reanalysis with grammaticalization include word order changes, which we discuss immediately below. These can have major effects on the morphosyntactic organization of a language, but do not exemplify the unidirectionality typical of grammaticalization. It is best, then, to regard grammaticalization as a subset of changes involved in reanalysis, rather than to identify the two (Heine and Reh 1984: 97; Heine, Claudi, and Hünnemeyer 1991a: 215–20).

3.5.1 *Word order change*

Langacker's major paper on reanalysis (1977) focuses on boundary creation, shift, and loss, but does not include discussion of word order changes. However, the latter involve changes in constituent order. As we will see below, word order changes can have far-reaching effects on grammatical rules as well as on the texture of a language. The question is whether word order changes are a type of grammaticalization.

As mentioned in 2.2, Meillet, at the end of his path-breaking article (1912), suggests that words are not the only sources of grammatical expression: word order changes may be too. He compares word orders that signal nuances of meaning (what we would call pragmatic meanings), such as alternative word orders in Latin, with grammatical word orders that signal the syntactic cases subject and object, as exemplified by Present Day English. Meillet therefore included word order changes among instances of reanalysis. Lightfoot has done likewise. The question for us is whether word order changes, which exemplify a kind of reanalysis, also exemplify grammaticalization, as Meillet suggests, or whether they are to be considered as types of reanalysis that do not necessarily involve grammaticalization. To anticipate, word order changes may be the outcome of, as well as the enabling factors for, grammaticalization in the narrower, prototypical sense used in this book of the process by which lexical items used in certain contexts come to mark grammatical relations. These changes are not unidirectional. Therefore, they should not be identified with grammaticalization in the narrower sense. However, given a broader definition of grammaticalization as the organization of grammatical, especially morphosyntactic material, they cannot be excluded from consideration.

For our purposes it is important to stress that word order changes can have a profound effect on the grammatical structure and the morphological texture of the language, because different constituent orders are typically associated with "verb-initial" and "verb-final" languages. Verb-initial languages include those with the order VSO (verb–subject–order), e.g.,

Hebrew, Masai, and Welsh, and SVO, e.g., English, Finnish, Malay, and Swahili. Verb-final languages include those with the order SOV, e.g., Basque, Hindi, Japanese and Quechua (for more combinations and discussion of word order typologies, see Greenberg 1966a, Vennemann 1975, W. Lehmann 1978a, Hawkins 1983, Dryer 1991; for a collection of papers on word order and word order change, see Li 1975). According to some analyses, the differences between OV and VO order represent the more global relationship Dependent–Head (OV) or Head–Dependent (VO) (see especially Vennemann 1975). More recently a number of different views regarding the status of "heads" have been developed (see Nichols 1986, Zwicky, forthcoming; and Vincent forthcoming a for an overview), but the following generalizations regarding word order still hold for many languages. Verb-initial languages tend to be prepositional, the adjective follows the noun, the relative clause follows the noun, the possessive follows the noun, the auxiliary precedes the verb, and the question particle marking yes–no question occurs in initial position in the clause. By constrast, although verb-final languages tend to show the order in reverse, they also tend to be more inconsistent with respect to the characteristics. Some sample constructions are shown in (22):

(22) **OV**   **VO**
     him saw   saw him
     house in   in house
     that old man   man old that
     man's hat   hat of man
     killed been has   has been killed
     he left whether?   whether he left?

There is no "ideal" OV or VO order language. Instead, there are languages which may have predominant OV or VO order, or which may exhibit properties of both. This is because coding is constantly in flux, and because there are competing motivations in creating discourse (see Section 4.1). For example, topicalization typically moves material to the beginning of a clause, bringing information to attention and deroutinizing it. On the other hand, routine orders serve as "normative structures" in the everyday flow of communication (useful sources are Vincent 1979, on "iconic" versus "symbolic" orders; and Haiman 1985a, Chapter 6, on three conflicting principles: (i) what is old information comes first, what is new information comes later in an utterance; (ii) ideas that are closely connected tend to be placed together; (iii) what is at the moment uppermost in the speaker's mind tends to be the first expressed).

In some languages, OV order favors the development of inflections, though by no means all languages with OV order are inflectional (Li and Thompson 1974). When they arise, inflections tend to be derived from prior lexical items. An example is provided by the development of the French future, illustrated in 3.4.1 above. When VO order arises from OV order, the change will often be accompanied by the innovation of new phrasal ("periphrastic") ways of coding what at an earlier stage was coded inflectionally. The history of English modals illustrates among many other things the replacement of certain subjunctive inflections by periphrastic expressions. We suggested in 1.3.1 that the development of *lets* may also be an instance of the larger change of English from OV to VO.

If inflections develop in OV languages, they typically do so via reanalysis of enclitics or bound forms through boundary loss, fusion, and phonological attrition of already bound forms. By contrast, when new periphrastic constructions arise in the shift from OV to VO, they typically develop through reanalysis of lexical items as grammatical ones. They are examples of what Meillet called "renouvellement" – renewals of old functions, possibly originally more expressive ways of saying the same thing. These periphrastic constructions may themselves in turn become inflections (prefixes rather than postfixes). Because they derive in different ways, and at different times, the resources used in the development of OV and VO orders may look very different from a relatively synchronic point of view. For example, there is no form–meaning, i.e., "cognate," relationship between the inflectional or clitic genitive -s in English and the preposition *of* that partly replaced it. Nor is there any cognate relationship between the OE inflectional subjunctive (typically -*e(n)*) and *might, should*, etc.

Cross-linguistic studies suggest that there are no constraints depending solely on word order that delimit the lexical resources that can be used in the development of grammatical items. Rather, the relevant factors for selection are semantic suitability, inferences (both "logical" and "conversational") from context, and potential constructional ambiguities arising from such inferences. Such factors will be discussed in the next chapter.

We give here an example of the same lexical item giving rise to both inflection and to periphrasis (but in local constructions with different word orders). We turn again to Romance. As we have seen, the Late Latin verb *habere* 'to have' was reanalyzed in post-verbal (OV) position as a future inflectional marker. As Romance developed, a new periphrastic complex perfect construction developed alongside of the future inflection, replacing the earlier perfect inflection -*v*-; e.g., *probavi* 'I have tried' was replaced by *habeo probatum*. This complex perfect, like the future, arose out of a *habere* construction, but in this case it originated in a construction consisting of an inflected form of *habere* 'to have' and a past participle that agreed with the object of *habere* (see, with somewhat different interpretations, Benveniste 1968, M. Harris 1978, Fleischman 1982, Vincent 1982, Pinkster 1987).

In Late Latin both the future and the perfect occur in both OV and VO orders. Thus we find:

(23) a. cantare habeo ~ habeo cantare (OV ~ VO)
     b. probatum habeo ~ habeo probatum (OV ~ VO)

The type *cantare habeo* has been illustrated in (12), the type *habeo cantare* in (8b) (and with intervening material in (9) and (10)). The type *probatum habeo* may be illustrated by (24 a,b) and *habeo probatum* by (25):

(24) a. Promissum   habeo . . .   nihil
         promised-NEUT/SG(?) have-1SG . . . nothing:NEUT/SG
         sine   eius consilio agere.
         without his advice do-INF
         'I have promised to do nothing without his advice.'
             (sixth century, Gregory of Tours: cited in Fleischman 1982: 120)

     b. Quae cum ita sint,   de   Caesare satis hoc
         which since thus be-SUBJUNCT, about Caesar enough this
         tempore dictum habeo.
         time   said   have-1SG
         'Under the circumstances, I shall regard what I have said of
         Caesar as sufficient at present.'
             (*c.* 40 BC, Cicero, *Phil.* 5,52; cit. Pinkster 1987: 204)

(25) Metuo   enim ne ibi   vos habebam fatigatos.
      Fear:1SG For   lest there you have-1SG tired
      'For I fear that I have tired you.'
        (early fifth century, Augustine; cited in Fleischman 1982: 120)

Both the future and the perfect eventually became fixed units and involved reanalysis of an inflected form of the independent verb *hab-* as dependent on the non-finite verb with which they occurred. They differ in that the path from *habere* to the future was via an obligative or future-oriented sense of the verb, whereas the path from *habere* to the perfect was via the locative-posssessive-existential in transitive contexts of cognitive and sensory states.[6] Furthermore, the first became an inflection and the second remained as a periphrasis. Fleischman (1982: 121) hypothesizes that the future was grammaticalized while OV was still the chief word order, and that the perfect was grammaticalized later when the shift to VO had already taken place. However, this hypothesis is not necessary, since earlier orders do continue or reappear in languages and indeed can become quite productive. An example is the retention of the clitic genitive *-s* despite the existence of the periphrastic preposition, as in *the neighbor-across-the street's peaches are ripe* versus *the peaches of/belonging to the neighbor across the street are ripe*. An example of reappearance of an older order is the process by which "noun incorporation" can take place (cf. *baby-sit, mountain-climb*) and word formations such as *sky-scraper*.

So far, we have discussed only shifts from OV to VO, both at the general level of verb phrase constituent structure and at the more local level of individual morphosyntactic changes. Before leaving the subject of word order, it is important to point out that a shift from OV to VO or vice versa rarely, perhaps never, occurs independently of other word order factors. To oversimplify the complex factors that led to the reanalysis of Old English OV order as Middle English VO, a contributor to the change was the existence in Old English, and most Germanic languages, of two rules that operated in main clauses. One is known as "heavy NP shift," a rule whereby lexical (as opposed to pronominal) NPs and PPs were moved to the right of the clause, typically after the verb. The other is known as "verb second" or "V2," although it was actually a verb-fronting rule, which moved the verb to the left of the clause. The reason it is known as "verb second" is that the fronted verb typically follows an adverb such as *þa* 'then,' *her* 'here, in this year,' *ne* 'not,' or a topicalized NP, which can be subject, object, or some other NP (Kemenade 1987). Relics of both these rules still linger on in PDE. For example, we say *I have several books crumbling with age*, rather than *I have several crumbling with age books*; here (the "heavy" adjectival phrase is to the right of the noun it modifies). Furthermore, we are more likely to say *I gave her the pictures that had been damaged in the flood* than *I gave the pictures that had been damaged in the flood to her* because *to her* is "light." Examples of relics of V2 in PDE include *Hardly had he left, when . . .* , *Never had I seen such a mess*. But neither construction is in wide use, whereas in OE they occurred so frequently that they finally led to the reanalysis of the basic word order.

As a generalization, OV order is found in OE chiefly in subordinate clauses and in some coordinate clauses.[7] Typical examples are shown in (26–7):

> (26) nimþe se   cyng alyfan wille, þæt man wergylde alysan mote
>   unless the king allow will   that one ransom   pay   may

'unless the king will allow one to pay ransom'

(c. 1050, Law Grið 15)

(27) and Eraclyus sona   his swurd ateah and hine
      and Eraclyus immediately his sword drew and him
      beheafdode
      beheaded
      'and E immediately drew his sword and beheaded him'

(c. 1000, ÆLS (Exalt of Cross) 74)

In (26) the infinitives (*alyfan, alysan*) are followed by the pre-modals (*wille, mote*); these infinitives are the objects of the pre-modals. In the second clause the nominal object (*wergylde*) precedes the verb object. In (27) the order is coordinator–subject–temporal–object–verb. By contrast in main clauses we find:

(28) Hi   habbað mid him   awyriedne engel, mancynnes feond.
      they have   with them corrupt   angel, mankind's enemy

(c. 1000, ÆCHom II,38 283.113)

Here the order is subject–verb–prepPhrase–object. The PP contains a pronoun, in other words, is "light," and the object is not only lexical but also has an attributive phrase attached to it, in other words, it is heavy. Sometimes (but by no means always), subordinate and main clauses show mirror image word orders, because of the effect of heavy NP shift and V2, e.g.:

(29) Ða   he þiderweard seglode fram Sciringes heale, þa   wæs
      when he thither   sailed from Skiringssalr,   then was
      him   on þæt bæcbord Denamearc.
      to-him on that larboard Denmark
      'When he sailed there from Skiringssalr, Denmark was on his larboard side.'

(c. 880, Orosius 1 1.19.24)

The order here is subordinator–subject–directional–verb–directional, followed by adverb–verb–indObject–locative–subject.

The kind of word order illustrated by (28) and the main clause in (29) was used so extensively that eventually reanalysis occurred, probably in two stages. The first, occurring *c*. AD 1200, was OV > VO as a result of loss of case morphology, and of heavy NP shift. The second, occurring *c*. AD 1400, was the loss of V2 (Kemenade 1987).[8]

This short outline has hardly touched on the complexities of the history of English word order. Nevertheless, it gives a glimpse into the interaction of clause level strategies (e.g., heavy NP shift) with more local ones, e.g., the development of periphrasis as VO became the rule. As indicated at the beginning of this section, it does not illustrate grammaticalization in the prototypical sense of a unidirectional process discussed in this book, but it highlights its interconnection with strategies for organizing linguistic material.

3.6 Analogy/rule generalization

As we have seen, Meillet made a distinction between the development of new grammatical forms and arrangements on the one hand, and analogy on the other. The first, which he called grammaticalization, is the result of what we now call reanalysis. As we have defined it, reanalysis refers to the development of new out of old structures. It is covert. Analogy, by contrast, refers to the attraction of extant forms to already existing constructions, for example, the attraction of Ewe verbs of locution and cognition to the complementizer construction, modeled after *bé*. It is overt. In essence reanalysis and analogy involve innovation along different axes. Reanalysis operates along the "syntagmatic" axis of linear constituent structure. Analogy, by contrast, operates along the "paradigmatic" axis of options at any one constituent node (Jakobson and Halle 1956).

When Meillet was writing, there was a rather narrow, local interpretation of analogy, which was defined as a process whereby irregularities in grammar, particularly at the morphological level, were regularized. The mechanism was seen as one of "proportion" or equation. Thus, given the singular–plural alternation *cat–cats*, one can conceive of analogizing *child–children* as *child–childs* (as indeed occurs in child language):

(30) cat : cats = child : X
      X = childs

Or, as actually occurred in the history of English, given *ston–stones* 'ston–stones,' *shoe–shoen* 'shoe–shoes' was analogized to the form now used in PDE:

(31) ston : stones = shoe : X
      X = shoes

The difficulty with the formula of proportion is that it gives no account of why one member of the pair is selected as the model. Since Meillet's time, a wide range of analogical processes has been identified (see Anttila 1977, and, for a summary, Kiparsky 1992). Kuryłowicz (1945–9) pointed to some tendencies regarding selection of the model, for example, the tendency to replace a more constrained with a more general form, not vice versa. Two decades later Kiparsky (1968) sought to redefine analogy in phonology as rule extension, thereby giving a formal account of the fact that analogy is not random in language change. He views analogy as generalization or optimization of a rule from a relatively limited domain to a far broader one.[9] Of course, neither analogy as originally conceived nor rule generalization are required to go to completion: we still have *foot–feet*, *mouse–mice*, and also *run–ran* alongside of *love–loved*.

Only reanalysis can create new grammatical structures. However, the role of analogy should not be underestimated in the study of grammaticalization.[10] For one, the workings of analogy, since they are overt, are in many cases the prime evidence both for speaker of a language (and also for linguists!) that a change has taken place. Consider the development of the Romance perfect again. In (25) (repeated and reglossed here for convenience as (32)), accusative plural agreement is overt and determinable (*vos . . . fatigatos*):

> (32) Metuo   enim ne ibi   vos   habebam fatigatos.
>   fear-1SG for lest there you:ACC:PL have-1SG tired-ACC:PL
>   'For I fear that I have tired you.'

However, in (24a, b) there is indeterminacy whether there is or is not agreement, since neuter singular (*nihil* 'nothing' in (24a), *satis* 'enough' in (24b)) is the "default" gender/number marker in Latin. With these constructions there is potential for reanalysis, but we recognize that the perfect has arisen only when there is overt and therefore determinable lack of agreement between object and participle (PART) as in:

> (33) Haec   omnia   probatum   habemus.
>   those:ACC:PL all-ACC-PL tried-PART(?) have-1PL
>   'We have tried all those things.'
>   (sixth century, Oribasius: cited in Fleischman 1982: 120)

So long as constructions occurred which were ambiguous between adjectival participials and perfects, e.g., (32), it was not possible to tell whether reanalysis had occurred or not, except perhaps by inference from the context. Specifically, the agreeing participial, which originated in a passive adjectival form, permits the understood subject of the participial to be the subject of either the sentence or of some other entity. For example, in (32) the agent of the act of tiring could either be the subject 'I', as the translation suggests, or some other, unspecified, individual(s), as in 'I fear I have/see you tired.' By contrast, the perfect requires that the understood subject of the participle is the subject of the sentence (Vincent 1982). It is only when clear instances of non-agreement, e.g., (33), occur, that we can find definitive overt evidence for the structure change. These unambiguously non-agreeing forms presumably arose by analogy (= rule generalization) from neuter singular contexts to other contexts.

A well-known example of the cyclical interaction of reanalysis, analogy (= generalization), and reanalysis is the development of negation in French. The process must have been as follows (Hock 1991 [1986]: 194; Schwegler 1988):

    I.   Negation was accomplished by placing the negative particle *ne* before the verb.

    II.   A verb of motion negated by *ne* could optionally be reinforced by the pseudo-object noun *pas* 'step' in the context of verbs of movement:

(34) Il ne va   (pas).
       he not goes (step)
       'He doesn't go (a step).'

    III.   The word *pas* was reanalyzed as a negator particle in a structure of the type *ne Vmovement (pas)*.

    IV.   *Pas* was extended analogically to new verbs having nothing to do with movement; i.e., the structure was now *ne V (pas)*:

(35) Il ne sait   pas.
       he not knows not
       'He doesn't know.'

    V.   The particle *pas* was reanalyzed as an obligatory concomitant of *ne* for general negation: *ne V pas*.

    VI.   In the spoken vernacular *pas* came to replace *ne* via two stages: *(ne) V pas* (reanalysis of *ne* as optional), *V pas* (reanalysis by loss of *ne*), resulting in:

(36) Il sait   pas.
       he knows not
       'He doesn't know.'

In the case of the French negator *pas*, we would not know that reanalysis had taken place at stage III without the evidence of the working of generalization at stage IV. The reanalysis at stage VI would not have been possible without the generalization, since *pas* would have been too constrained by its original semantics of 'step.'

Although analogy is best viewed as rule generalization, in practice it is often useful to maintain the term "analogy" when referring to certain local surface developments. For example, Mikola (1975: 170–2) describes the development in Samoyedic (Uralic) of locative postpositions out of older locational nouns, which were themselves preceded by a noun in the genitive, as in:

(37) Proto-Samoyedic   *mäto-n + în
                                tent-GEN + top
                                'the top of the tent'

The suffixed -*n* of the Uralic genitive came to be reanalyzed as an initial consonant on certain postpositions which were being grammaticalized out of nouns with meanings such as 'upper surface':

(38) mäto + nîn
      tent + onto
      'onto the tent'

This change began as a typical case of reanalysis of morpheme boundaries: [mäto-#n##în] > [mäto-##nîn]. The reanalysis in turn yielded entire families of postpositions with an initial *n*-, the cognates of which may have initial vowels in other Uralic languages. We may speak of the generalization of *n*- here, but it is not a case of rule generalization, only of spread of *n*- in word formation (for a similar example from Maori, see Section 6.2.4).

So far we have considered analogy from the point of view of generalization of types of linguistic structure. There is, however, another important perspective on analogy: that of generalization through patterns of usage, as reflected by the frequency with which tokens of these structures may occur across time. We will be citing several recent examples of studies of frequency in subsequent chapters. Here we discuss an older, well-known example to introduce the method: Fries's (1940) study of word order change in English in which the establishment of verb–object word order was traced through text counts at intervals of one hundred years. Among the relevant statistics concerning the position of the accusative object for the period AD 1000 to 1500 as presented by Fries are the figures in Table 3.1. This method

Table 3.1 *Grammaticalization of VO word order in English between AD 1000 and AD 1500*

	*c.*1000	*c.*1200	*c.*1300	*c.*1400	*c.*1500
Accusative object before verb	52.5%	52.7%	40+%	14.3%	1.87%
Accusative object after verb	47.5%	46.3%	60−%	85.7%	98.13%

Source: based on Fries (1940: 201)

of analysis is a quantitative one. Quantitative analyses can be done taking various variables into account, such as spread across communities, or styles, or genres. The analysis by Fries that we have quoted, however, addresses only the variable of object before verb versus verb before object. In any quantitative analysis the linguist ideally takes a representative sample of texts at regular intervals over several centuries and traces the changes in form and meaning of a particular construction as a function of frequency of use in discourse. The kind of change characterized by the formula A > A/B > B is viewed not from the point of view of types of construction (e.g., OV > VO, or periphrastic future > affixal future), but from the point of view of tokens (how often are OV and VO used over time, how often are periphrastic and affixal future used over time). The quantitative diachronic method captures the progressive aggregation of instances of the newer B construction at the expense of the older A construction. In the case of Old English word order, the A construction is verb-final word order and the B construction is verb–initial word order. Typically, as here, the initial stage is already one of variation, and the final exemplified stage may still be in variation. Such quantitative studies highlight the gradualness of the spread of changes.

It should be mentioned that the gross numbers resulting from simple counts of pre- and post-verbal objects such as are illustrated by Fries's figures conceal complex word order adjustments involving differences such as those between pronoun and noun, definite and indefinite NP, heavy and light NP, independent and dependent clause, and so forth. A more complete explanation of word order change in Old and Middle English would include accounts of the structure of the clause as a whole, including the kinds of subjects that occur in the clause and where, the kinds of object that occur after or before the verb, whether the verb in pre-object position happens also to be in V2 position or not, and so forth (see Canale 1976 and discussion of Canale's paper in the same volume, and Bean 1983 for some representative studies).

3.7 The differential effects of reanalysis and analogy

In conclusion, reanalysis and analogy (generalization) have different effects. Reanalysis essentially involves linear, syntagmatic, often local, reorganization and rule change. It is not directly observable. On the other hand, analogy essentially involves paradigmatic organization, change in surface collocations, and in patterns of use. Analogy makes the unobservable changes of reanalysis observable. The interaction of reanalysis and analogy can be represented for the development of *be going to* from directional phrase to future as in Figure 3.2. Stage I is the stage of the progressive with the directional verb and a purposive clause. Stage II is that of the future auxiliary with a verb of activity; it is the result of reanalysis. Stage III is that of the extension via analogy of the directional class of verbs to all verbs, including stative verbs. And Stage IV is the stage arising out of reanalysis of the complex auxiliary to a single morpheme *gonna*. Stages I, III and IV all still coexist in PDE. In the next chapter we will discuss some further extensions of the distinctions between reanalysis and analogy, specifically with respect to meaning changes.

Reanalysis and analogy are the major mechanisms in language change. They do not define grammaticalization, nor are they coextensive with it, but

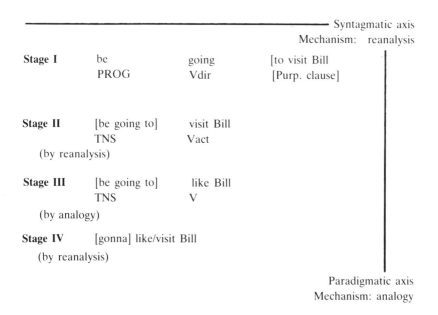

Figure 3.2 Schema of the development of auxiliary *be going to*

grammaticalization does not occur without them. The subset of processes that are particular to grammaticalization are those that over time render more independent elements less independent. We will discuss this unidirectionality of change more fully in Chapter 5, but first we turn to motivations for the changes characteristic of grammaticalization.

4
Pragmatic inferencing

4.1 Introduction

Although it is possible to describe change in terms of the operation of successive strategies of reanalysis (rule change) and analogy (rule generalization), the important question remains why these strategies come about – in other words, what enables the mechanisms we have outlined, most especially those involved in grammaticalization.[1] It is tempting to think in terms of "causes" and even of "explanations" in the sense of "predictions." However, the phenomena that give rise to language change are so complex that they will perhaps never be understood in enough detail for us to state precisely why a specific change occurred in the past or to predict when one will occur and if it does what it will be (Lass 1980). Rather than referring to "causes" or "explanations," we speak more cautiously of motivations or enabling factors, understanding always that we are referring to potential not absolute factors (see, among many others, Langacker 1977, Greenberg 1978b, Romaine 1982, M. Harris 1982, Givón 1989, Croft 1991).

Among motivations for change three have been widely discussed in recent years. Of greatest interest within generative linguistics has been the role of language acquisition, especially child language acquisition. Sociolinguists, by contrast, have tended to focus attention on the role of communities and different types of contact within them. Of special interest to those working on grammaticalization has been the role of speakers and hearers negotiating meaning in communicative situations. We will touch on some of the issues in transmission via language acquisition and contact in Chapter 8; here we consider speaker-hearer roles.

Different linguists have paid attention to different aspects of speaker-hearer roles, and have held different views on their relationships to "grammar" and "rule" (see, e.g., Bever and Langendoen 1972; Slobin 1977, 1985; Langacker 1977; Horn 1984; Haiman 1983, 1985a; Du Bois 1985; among others). We will not attempt to summarize the literature here.

Rather, we will put forward arguments for the view that there are a number of competing motivations which can all in some sense be said to be examples of maximization of economy or "simplicity": basically they can be summarized as maximization of efficiency via minimal differentiation on the one hand, and maximization of informativeness (Langacker 1977: 101–6) on the other. On this view, hearers play a major role in change because they process input in ways that may not match the speaker's intentions. But speakers also play a major role in enabling change, because in producing speech they have communication as their goal, and therefore are always in search of ways to guide the hearer in interpretation. In an ideal communicative situation, speakers take responsibility for success in communication and seek to meet hearers' attempts "to integrate new information with information that is already accessible" (Blakemore 1990). However, differences in what is actually accessible in the communicative situation based on differences in age, social background, culture, attention or other factors may lead cumulatively over time to change. Furthermore, the motivations of simplicity and informativeness are inevitably in competition in the individual language user, and therefore the development of language involves conflict and problem solving (Dressler 1985).

There are great difficulties in defining the notion of economy in anything like rigorous terms. We know very little about what does and does not take "effort" in producing or interpreting utterances, and still less about what would constitute economy of mental effort on either speaker's or hearer's behalf, although we probably know more about simplicity of perception than of production. Nonetheless, there seem to be useful, if sometimes intuitive, notions involved.

In considering the hearer's role, it is usually assumed that the hearer will seek the most unambiguous interpretation, and furthermore that the hearer is actively engaged in interpreting (usually abducing) input, whether as a child or an adult in the process of language acquisition. It is therefore not surprising that work on hearer motivations focuses on perception, and on meanings interpreted from the linguistic data which is the input to the acquisition process. However, it is also possible to think of hearers as the targets of speakers' output. From this perspective, hearers motivate speakers' intent to be informative and clear.

In considering the speaker's role, it has been customary to think of the tendency to reduce the speech signal, e.g., via rapid speech, a process resulting in "signal simplicity." The reduction of *be going to* to *be gonna* is just one example. More striking is the reduction of the Tarahumara third person pronoun. Signal simplification typically results from the routinization (idiomatization) of expressions. Rather than find different ways of saying approximately the same thing, speakers will repeat expressions they have heard before, even if they are in competition with other expressions, perhaps in the interest of sounding "with it." Well-known recent examples include the use of *you know*, *like*, etc. Such routinized, or idiomatized, expressions can be stored and used as simple units. Naturally they are more frequent in discourse than expressions created and used "on the fly," which may indeed be novel, once.

Idiomatization of expressions tends to lead to reduction and simplification of the signal. With this process in mind, Langacker has said: "It would not be entirely inappropriate to regard languages in their diachronic aspect as gigantic expression-compacting machines" (1977: 106). However, compacting, obliteration of boundaries, and reduction of redundancy is balanced in normal language situations by the introduction of new and innovative ways of saying approximately the same thing. These new and innovative ways of saying things are brought about by speakers seeking to enhance expressivity. This is typically done through "deroutinizing" of constructions, in other words, through finding new ways to say old things. Expressivity serves the dual function of improving informativeness for the hearer and at the same time allowing the speaker to convey attitudes toward the situation, including the speech situation. This very process of innovation is itself typically based on a principle of economy, specificially the economy of reusing extant forms for new purposes (Werner and Kaplan 1963, Slobin 1977). To return to our example of the extension of *be going to* to the intentional future: the directional phrase has been reused; it is more substantive (phonologically longer) and therefore more accessible to hearers than, e.g., *'ll* or even *will*. As a future it is also more based in the speaker's subjective attitude and perspective on what is being talked about than is its locational counterpart.

While the competition between motivations has been a major topic of research for some linguists (e.g., Du Bois 1985, Haiman 1985a), most linguists have been interested in different subaspects of the complex balance between creativity on the one hand and routinization on the other. Therefore studies of grammaticalization have taken different paths. A focus on hearers' tendency to reanalyze abductively correlates with a focus on morphosyntactic changes in grammaticalization (Langacker 1977). A focus on speakers' expressive use of language to get a point across correlates with a focus on lexical origins of grammaticalization, especially on pragmatic enrichment of lexical items in the early stages of grammaticalization (Heine, Claudi, and Hünnemeyer 1991a, 1991b; Traugott and König 1991). A focus

on speakers' tendency to economize correlates with a focus on routinization, semantic loss, and frequency (Givón 1979, 1991b; Hopper 1987).
These approaches are, of course, not necessarily contradictory, although
they do sometimes lead to different views of what should or should not be
considered a case of grammaticalization. Any comprehensive study of a
grammaticalization process that lasts over long periods of time and involves
continued grammaticalization must ideally take cognizance of all the kinds
of approaches mentioned above.

Before concluding this section, we should note that the claim that
grammaticalization (and indeed language change in general) is motivated by
speaker-hearer interactions and communicative strategies is a claim that
change is goal-directed. Such claims are known as "teleological" claims, and
have been the subject of much controversy in recent years. There has been a
tendency in American linguistics to distrust teleological arguments, partly
on the grounds that they cannot be empirically proven, partly because the
important research question has been considered to be how language is
understood out of context. Arguments based on mechanisms for change,
and on (passive) capacities for language, have been privileged over arguments based on purposes to which language is put. However, this view is for
the most part not coherent with a functional view of language, in which such
purposes are of crucial importance, nor is it coherent with the view that
language is always in flux, although it may be seen as a fixed system at any
one moment when caught so to speak on the fly by the analyst (for some
overviews defending various aspects of teleological approaches, see Anttila
1988, Shapiro 1991).

We take the position here that languages clearly are not goal-oriented,
but that their users may be, consciously or unconsciously. We agree that
"the view which ascribes language a will of its own, a sort of conscious
control over its own future, seems to us gratuitous and untenable. It remains
true, however, that language is a communicative tool at the disposal of its
speakers, to whom the attribution of an independent will and volition is
considerably less controversial" (Vincent 1978: 414).

Many, perhaps most, researchers working within the framework of
grammaticalization would take a similar position regarding the goal orien-
tedness of change. However, such a position is not necessary for research on
grammaticalization. For example, Bybee sees the development of morphology as spurred on by spontaneous processes whereby semantic functions
that are similar are subsumed under closely related grammatical functions
(Bybee 1985: 204). These processes are in her view cognitive rather than
communicative. In particular, she rejects hypotheses that grammaticaliza-

66

tion is motivated by communicative need. We agree with Bybee that communicative "need" is not a plausible motivation in most cases of grammaticalization, since not all languages express the same grammatical functions, and even less do they express the same grammatical functions in the same way. Furthermore, to assume that as an older system becomes eroded it may cease to function at an adequate level of communicative coherence and therefore must be revitalized (as suggested by Givón 1982: 117, cited in Bybee 1985: 202) is to posit an incoherent stage of language such as is unknown (i.e., it violates the uniformitarian principle), and is not empirically supported by the data. In speaking of communicative strategies and problem solving in the course of speaker-hearer interaction, we refer not to filling gaps, but rather to strategies used by speakers and hearers in producing and understanding the flow of speech as it is created. In our view, these strategies draw upon general cognitive processes such as are referred to in Bybee's work.

4.2 Inferencing and meaning change

The discussion in the preceding section has made reference to various motivations such as economy, efficiency, clarity, expressivity, and routinization. Such motivations are issues of usage and speaker–hearer purposes, and can be called "pragmatic," that is, they have to do with the relationship between language and the contexts in which it is used (including other instances of language), most especially the meanings that arise from this relationship (Levinson 1983).

Since pragmatics by definition deals with meanings beyond structure, many linguists working in the tradition of formal grammars have excluded pragmatics from consideration in accounting for motivations for change. Many have also excluded the meanings usually treated by lexical semantics, that is, components of sense and their relation to the objects to which they refer. For example, in discussing the syntactic changes involved in the development of the modals, Lightfoot (1979) argued that syntactic change was autonomous, i.e., independent of semantic or pragmatic motivations. He attempted to show that the modals "underwent very many changes in their syntax and in their meaning but . . . these changes seem to have proceeded quite independently of each other" (p. 100). Indeed, he went on to say: "it does not seem possible to define a class of modals (and therefore of preterite-presents) on semantic grounds" (p. 103). And in his most recent book (Lightfoot 1991), he continues to argue that meaning changes result from structural changes, not vice versa. This approach is a natural conse-quence of the claim that significant change arises from processes of language acquisition and interpretation of inputs, in other words, from hearers' perception processes, rather than from speakers' production processes.

The approach from "autonomous syntax" has been called into question by most linguists working on grammaticalization. This follows inevitably from the interest in changes whereby a lexical item becomes a grammatical one, because a lexical item by definition has semantic as well as syntactic, morphological, and phonological properties. But it also follows from the concern that a theory which regards semantic change as independent of morphosyntactic change provides no reasoned account for the extensive evidence that grammaticalization affects similar classes of lexical items in similar ways across a wide number of languages. This point has been made especially cogently by Bybee and her colleagues in various studies of verbal morphology (e.g., Bybee 1985, Bybee and Dahl 1989) and by Heine and his colleagues in various studies of nominal morphology (e.g., Heine, Claudi, and Hünnemeyer 1991a).

Indeed, much work on grammaticalization since the early eighties has focused extensively on the kinds of meaning changes involved in grammaticalization and the cognitive motivations behind them. For some, the meaning changes are "semantic," e.g., "semantic change leads to the development of grammatical meaning" (Bybee and Pagliuca 1985: 59). For others it is mainly pragmatic (Traugott and König 1991). For some it is thought to be motivated primarily by metaphorical processes (Claudi and Heine 1986, Sweetser 1990), for others it is thought to be motivated by associative or "metonymic" as well as metaphorical processes (e.g., Traugott and König 1991, Heine, Claudi, and Hünnemeyer 1991a). The position we take here and will elaborate on in subsequent chapters is that meaning changes and the cognitive strategies that motivate them are central in the early stages of grammaticalization and are crucially linked to expressivity. Furthermore, the meaning changes are initially pragmatic and associative, arising in the context of the flow of speech. At later stages, as grammaticalization continues and forms become routinized, meaning loss or "bleaching" typically occurs, but even so, older meanings may still continue to constrain newer, "emptier" ones.

Before we proceed, a few words about some of the widely accepted ideas concerning semantics and pragmatics may be helpful.

4.2.1 *Semantics versus pragmatics*

There is a vast literature on semantics and pragmatics but as yet little consensus on exactly where the boundaries between the two areas lie, or even whether there are indeed boundaries. Nevertheless, there is a pre-theoretical sense in which it is clear that a distinction needs to be made between the sentence (semantic) meaning of *Can you pass the salt?* (= 'Are you able/willing to pass the salt?'), the expected response to which would be *Yes* or *No*, and the utterance (pragmatic) meaning (= 'Please pass the salt'), the expected response to which is the non-linguistic action of passing the salt. For purposes of this chapter, it must suffice to note that we believe that linguistic theory should eventually provide an integrated account of semantics and pragmatics.

It is useful to distinguish between that part of semantics that concerns lexical, phrase, and sentence meaning, and that part of pragmatics that concerns inferences about linguistic meaning based on contextual assumptions such as the cooperativeness of participants in a conversation. A standard view of the relationship between semantics and pragmatics would be something like the following (Levinson 1983, Green 1989). Semantics is primarily concerned with meanings that are relatively stable out of context, typically arbitrary, and analyzable in terms of the logical conditions under which they would be true. Pragmatics, by contrast, is primarily concerned with the beliefs and inferences about the nature of the assumptions made by participants and the purposes for which utterances are used in the context of communicative language use. It concerns both speakers' indirect meaning, beyond what is said, and also hearers' interpretations, which tend to enrich what is said in order to interpret it as relevant to the context of discourse (Sperber and Wilson 1986). Many of the beliefs and inferences which are the subject of pragmatics are thought to be cognitively "natural," that is, not learned or arbitrary. Furthermore, they are rarely if ever subject to analysis in terms of truth.

4.2.2   *Relationships between senses of a form: homonymy and polysemy*

Another issue on which there is little agreement is exactly how to characterize the relationship between the various senses of a form. For example, rejecting the traditional literary practice of grouping together all related meanings that can be associated with a single phonological form, McCawley (1968: 126) suggests that there is no a priori reason for grouping items together in a dictionary: one could take the notion "lexical item" to mean the combination of a single semantic reading with a single underlying phonological shape, a single syntactic category, and a single set of specifications of exceptional behavior with respect to rules. Under this conception, the form *bachelor* would express four separate lexical items pronounced [bæčələr] rather than a single four-ways ambiguous lexical item. In other words, they would be "homonyms" exhibiting conceptual unrelatedness despite sameness of form. The four meanings he is referring to are:

(1) a. a young knight serving under the standard of another knight
    b. one who possesses the lowest academic degree
    c. a man who has never married
    d. a young male fur seal when without a mate during the breeding time

(Katz and J. A. Fodor 1963: 185)

Most linguists these days would probably agree that there are four homonyms here, but might have some difficulty with McCawley's next example: the distinction of *sad* meaning 'experiencing sadness, said of a living being' and *sad* meaning 'evoking sadness, said of an esthetic object.' As our knowledge of linguistic structures becomes more fine-grained, and as semantic and pragmatic factors have come to be seen as central to linguistics, there has been a return to interest in meaning, but with a difference: the focus is on the relationship of meaning to syntax, and to discourse functions. In this context, linguists of quite different persuasions have argued for or at least assumed a theory of semantics that allows for polysemy wherever some common semantic factor (e.g., sadness) is present (see discussion in J. D. Fodor 1977; G. Lakoff and Johnson 1980). From this perspective, any two or more conceptually related senses with the same form are regarded as one item. Bybee and Pagliuca (1987), for example, suggest that there is one form *will* in PDE with various related, i.e., polysemous, meanings. Such meanings include:

(2) a. Prediction: e.g., Most of this year's students will go into law.
    b. Willingness: e.g., Give them the name of someone who will sign for it and take it in if you are not at home.
    c. Intention: e.g., I'll put them in the mail today.

To put it another way, it is now widely recognized that one form can be ambiguous either because it has two or more unrelated meanings associated with it (homonymy), or because it has two or more related meanings associated with it (polysemy).

In addition, it is sometimes argued that the fine, sometimes minimally discrete, meaning distinctions between various stages of grammaticalization or between focal clusters on a cline call for a theory in which different meanings may be closer or more distant (see G. Lakoff 1987 on the concept of "networks" of polysemies; and, from a different perspective, Kemmer, forthcoming b, on semantic maps of related terms within the domain of voice). For example, willingness and intention are more closely related to each other than to prediction, among the polysemies of *will*.

In general, from the perspective of grammaticalization it is methodologically essential to assume polysemy if there is a plausible semantic relationship, whether or not the forms belong to the same syntactic category, because otherwise relationships between more and less grammaticalized variants of the same form cannot be established, either diachronically or synchronically. What constitutes a "plausible semantic relationship" has until fairly recently been a matter of considerable debate. However, important strides have been made toward answering this question. In the area of lexical semantics there is work on "lexical fields", characterized by such works as Berlin and Kay (1969), Lehrer (1974), Brown (1976), Wierzbicka (1980, 1988, 1989), Brown and Witkowski (1983), Talmy (1985), Wilkins (forthcoming). In the area of grammaticalization there has been extensive work on cross-linguistic evidence for recurrence of polysemies. Drawing on Haiman, especially (1985a), Croft (1990) discusses the distinction between the homonymy of *two, to, too* (all [tu]), and the polysemy of the directional and recipient meanings of *to* in *I drove to Chicago, I told the story to my brother*. He suggests that a major criterion is evidence from cross-typological comparison: "if many diverse languages independently have the same pattern of "homonymy," then the meanings are closely related" (p. 166). *Two, to, too* do not tend to be expressed by the same form cross-linguistically; this, in addition to their lack of historical relatedness, provides evidence that they are homonymous in English. However, directional and recipient *to* are frequently, indeed typically, expressed by the same form cross-linguistically. This, together with their historical relatedness, provides evidence that they are polysemous in English.

There has been a history in linguistics of concern about the notion of polysemy. For example, Bolinger has said: "the natural condition of language is to preserve one form for one meaning, and one meaning for one form" (Bolinger 1977: x, cited in Haiman 1985a: 21). This concern presumably stems from the "scientific" approach to language which is the foundation of linguistics. To oversimplify, from this point of view the optimal language would be one in which every meaning was distinct, just as every numeral is distinct (the "idealized language" we referred to in Section 3.3). However, such "optimality" would clearly in actual fact be dysfunctional since there are far too many meanings for the brain to remember individual expressions for them. "One form – one meaning" is an ideal on one dimension, the dimension of choice of form. It is balanced and offset by another optimality, that of associating like forms with like meanings, in other words, of developing polysemies (Haiman 1985a). Grammaticalization is in some sense the process *par excellence* whereby structural relationships and associations among them are given grammatical expression. It is therefore not surprising that it typically involves polysemy.

4.2.3 Conversational and conventional inferencing

With regard to pragmatics, we are particularly interested in those inferences that are made in linguistic contexts from one clause or constituent to another, or even from one utterance to another. These are in principle implicational inferences (in the linguistic jargon called "implicatures") of the type characterized by Grice (1975) as "conversational." Such inferences are computable on the basis not of lexical meanings alone, but of lexical meanings together with implicatures arising from speech act maxims such as "Make your contribution as informative as is required (for the current purposes of the exchange)" (the first maxim of Quantity), "Do not make your contribution more informative than is required" (the second maxim of Quantity), "Try to make your contribution one that is true" (the maxim of Quality), "Be relevant" (the maxim of Relation), and "Be perspicuous" (the maxim of Manner) (Grice 1975: 45–7). There is considerable debate whether this is the right set of maxims. Indeed, it has been suggested that a maxim of Relevance alone, defined in such a way as to include informativeness, is sufficient to account for pragmatic meaning (Sperber and Wilson 1986; for other views, see Atlas and Levinson 1981, Horn 1984). As we will show, processes of grammaticalization seem to draw primarily on Relevance.

Most conversational implicatures are strictly speaking abductive (given an utterance, hearers may relate it to a general maxim, and guess the speaker's intent). The guess may be wrong because the maxims can always be flouted, e.g., it is possible for speakers to be uninformative or to lie. Furthermore, implicatures are "cancelable" either by the speaker (in which case an explanation is given), or by hearers' inferences from the situation. An example from Levinson (1983: 115) is:

(3)　a.　John has three cows.

The implicature from the second maxim of Quantity is that

(3)　b.　John has three cows and no more.

But this can be canceled by a vague statement such as

(3)　c.　John has three cows, if not more.

and even denied:

   (3)   d.   John has three cows, in fact ten.

The pragmatic effect of conversational implicatures across utterances and their cancelability can be illustrated by the example of conjoined clauses without any connective, that is, without any structural marker of coherence. These are likely to be interpretively enriched as having some coherence, that is, relevance to each other, simply because they are uttered in sequence.

   (4)   a.   The earthquake hit at 8 a.m. A four-car crash occurred.

Typically the relationship inferred will be that of temporal sequence and even causal connection if the clauses are action/event clauses and connectable in terms of encyclopedic or world knowledge, as in (4a), but no such relationship is likely to be inferred if the sequence is incoherent in terms of world knowledge, as in (4b), where inference of a causal connection is unlikely, and even close temporal connection may be in doubt:

   (4)   b.   A four-car crash occurred. The earthquake hit at 8 a.m.

If a grammatical form is present, e.g., *and, because, you see*, this element will further "constrain the relevance of the proposition it introduces" (Blakemore 1987: 130). But this constraint is not absolute. For example, the presence of *and* in (5a) implies only that a connection is intended by the speaker and that the hearer should compute one; it does not require that the implicature is a causal one, though that is what hearers would typically assume unless causality is canceled, as it is in (5b):

   (5)   a.   The earthquake hit at 8 a.m. and a four-car crash occurred.
           b.   The earthquake hit and a four-car crash occurred, but actually the cause was the fog, not the earthquake.

Conversational implicatures are typically contrasted with "conventional" ones (in the next section we will show that conventional implicatures typically arise out of conversational ones). Conventional implicatures are unpredictable and arbitrary, that is, they must be learned as part of the polysemies of the word, and are not cancelable. Thus in (6a) the verb *manage* conventionally implicates (6b):

   (6)   a.   John managed to solve the problem.
           b.   John solved the problem.

Neither (6a) nor (6b) are cancelable by, e.g.:

   (6)   c.   but he didn't solve it.

Since they must be specially learned along with the phonological and syntactic characteristics for the item in question, conventional meanings can, at least for our purposes, be included among the semantic polysemies of a form. For a classic case consider the temporal and causal meanings of *since*, as in (7):

> (7) a. I have done quite a bit of writing since we last got together. (temporal)
>
> b. Since I have a final exam tomorrow, I won't be able to go out tonight. (causal)

With *since*, when both clauses refer to events, especially events in the past, the reading is typically temporal, as in (7a). When one clause refers to a non-past event or to a state, the reading is typically causal, as in (7b). The causal meaning is conventional and not cancelable, as illustrated by (7c):

> (7) c. *Since I have a final exam tomorrow, I won't be able to go out tonight, but don't assume a causal connection!

In (7a) the first clause contains a past tense. In (7b) neither clause does. In other words, different meanings of *since* can be associated with different syntactic contexts. The difference between these meanings is sometimes syntactically obscured, and then there can be ambiguity, as in (7d):

> (7) d. Since Susan left him, John has been very miserable. (temporal or causal)

These facts allow us to conclude that *since* is semantically ambiguous (polysemous).

We turn now to the question of whether there are pragmatic as well as semantic polysemies. Consider, for example, *after* in (8a):

> (8) a. After we read your novel we felt greatly inspired.

This may be interpreted as a literal statement of temporal sequence, or it may implicate:

> (8) b. Because we read your novel we felt greatly inspired.

The implicature in (8b) is relevance-based, and strengthens informativeness because it enriches the relation between *After we read your novel* and the rest of the utterance, thus providing an interpretation of why the speaker thought it was relevant to include these temporal facts. However, there is no regular syntactic correlate for this relationship, and there are no regularly associated, conventional, implicatures. Rather, example (8a)

74

suggests that there can be pragmatic ambiguities/polysemies as well as semantic ambiguities/polysemies. (For fuller discussion of the importance of recognizing both pragmatic and semantic ambiguities, see Horn 1989, Sweetser 1990.)

4.3   The role of pragmatic inferencing in grammaticalization

With regard to the question of what role pragmatic inferencing has in grammaticalization, toward the end of his seminal article "Logic and conversation," Grice tentatively stated: "it may not be impossible for what starts life, so to speak, as a conversational implicature to become conventionalized" (1975: 58). This idea had been explored earlier in Geis and Zwicky (1971) in connection with the development of causal *since*, and was explicitly followed up in Cole (1975) in connection with *let's*. Dahl hypothesizes that many of what he calls "the secondary meanings" of tense and aspect, e.g., the "present relevance" of the perfect, are derived by conventionalization of implicatures. Below we will show that in early stages of grammaticalization conversational implicatures frequently become "semanticized,"[2] that is, become part of the semantic polysemies of a form. Dahl's characterization of the process is as follows: "if some condition happens to be fulfilled frequently when a certain category is used, a stronger association may develop between the condition and the category in such a way that the condition comes to be understood as an integral part of the meaning of the category" (Dahl 1985: 11). For the present, it should suffice to note that for inferences to play a significant role in grammaticalization, they must be frequently occurring, since only standard inferences can plausibly be assumed to have a lasting impact on the meaning of an expression or to function cross-linguistically. Among stereotypical inferences we may include the inferences of causality from temporal sequence that we have already discussed in connection with *since* and *after*, the well-known logical fallacy (abduction) characterized as *post hoc ergo propter hoc*. By contrast, we would not expect grammaticalization of such strictly local and idiosyncratic, highly contextualized, inferences as are exemplified by:

(9)   a.   What on earth has happened to the roast beef?
　　　b.   The dog is looking very happy. (understood to implicate that perhaps the dog has eaten the roast beef)

　　　　　　　　　　　　　　　　　　　　　　　　(Levinson 1983: 126)

One question is when we can recognize conventionalization to have occurred. A brief look before we proceed at some early examples of the contexts in which the change of *since* (originally *siþþan*) came about will be useful in serving as a methodological caution, and show that it is essential to look beyond individual sentences to larger contexts before reaching too hasty conclusions that change has occurred. In OE texts before AD 1050 *siþþan* as a preposition was used almost exclusively to mean 'from the time that, after.' The standard causal was *for þæm þe* 'for that that,' originally a deictic expression. As a connective *siþþan* meant 'from the time that,' that is, it marked the lower temporal boundary of the event in the main clause, and signaled an overlap with some point in an earlier event.

In certain contexts, however, the modern reader may detect a causal implicature. For example, Mitchell (1986 (2): 352) cites (10) as a putative example of causal *siþþan*:

(10) Þa, siþþan   he irre   wæs &   gewundod, he ofslog
     then, after/since he angry was and wounded,   he slaughtered
     micel þæs   folces.
     much of-that troop

(c. 880, Orosius 4 1.156.11)

When we read this sentence out of its larger context, the participle *gewundod*, being perfective and involving change of state, seems to favor a temporal reading, but the adjective *irre* favors a causal one, since it appears to express state. Nevertheless, a temporal reading with the adjective is plausible if we assume that *wæs* is inceptive-resultative or perfective, i.e., 'had come to be' rather than 'was.' In other words, the adjective in this context can be interpreted as expressing a contingent rather than a general state (the latter would more probably have been expressed by *bið*). Indeed we find that this sentence occurs in the context of a narrative concerning the legendary Pyrrhic victory. In the battle a Roman soldier wounds an elephant in the navel; this elephant, having become enraged, wreaks mayhem on the army. *Siþþan* in (10), then, is best interpreted as a temporal (indeed it partially translates the Latin adverbial *postquam* 'afterward'), and is not a conclusive example of the conventionalizing of causative inference in OE.

A more convincing example is:

(11) Ac ic þe   wille nu   giet getæcan þone weg siþþan ðu   ongitst
     but I thee will   now still teach   that way since   thou seest
     þurh   mine lare   hwæt sio soðe gesælð   bið, &
     through my   teaching what that true happiness is,   and

hwær hio bið.

where it   is

'But still I will now teach you the way since you see that true
happiness comes through my teaching, and where it is.'

(*c.* 880, Boethius 36 104.26)

Here *siþþan* translates the Latin causative *quoniam* 'because.' But even
without the Latin original we can assume it is causative since the context is
non-narrative: the stative perception-mental verb 'see, understand' introduces an aspectual generic clause signaled by the verb *bið* instead of the
contingency verb *is*. Although the causal inference is detectable in OE in
examples such as (11), so many other examples are undecidable that we
cannot establish that the causal inference had truly become conventionalized at this period. The change appears to have occurred in the fifteenth
century, when the form is attested frequently in stative and other non-
completive environments where the temporal reading is blocked, as in (11).

A second question is what types of inferences are most characteristic of
these early stages. Two different kinds, metaphorical processes and metonymic processes, have been much discussed in the literature, and it is to these
that we now turn.

4.3.1   *Metaphorical processes*

Metaphor is one of the most widely recognized processes in
meaning change. Standard examples of metaphor include such utterances as
(12) and (13):

(12)   Sally is a block of ice.

(Searle 1979: 97)

(13)   The sentence was filled with emotion.

(Reddy 1979: 288)

Although definitions of metaphor vary, most have certain concepts in
common, especially understanding and experiencing one kind of thing in
terms of another, and directionality of transfer from a basic, usually
concrete, meaning to one more abstract (see, for example, J. D. Sapir 1977;
J. G. Lakoff and Johnson 1980; Claudi and Heine 1986; Heine, Claudi, and
Hünnemeyer 1991a, 1991b). Metaphorical processes are processes of inference across conceptual boundaries, and are typically referred to in terms of
"mappings," or "associative leaps," from one domain to another. The
mapping is not random, but motivated by analogy and iconic relationships.

These relationships tend to be observable cross-linguistically. Some have been thought of as "image schemata" with very concrete sources that are mapped onto abstract concepts (Sweetser 1988). In the lexical domain one image schema that is well known is that of seeing and knowing, grasping and understanding (as in *I see/grasp the point of your argument*). In this particular case the relatively concrete concept has been said to be mapped onto the relatively abstract one in a relationship called the "mind-as-body metaphor": bodily experience is a source of vocabulary for psychological states (Sweetser 1990: 28–48). Another well-known relationship is "force dynamics" (Talmy 1988, Jackendoff 1990, Sweetser 1990), the relationship of forces and barriers found in such expressions as (14) and (15):

(14)   The crack in the stone let the water flow through.

(15)   I have a mental block about sports.

Metaphoric processes have traditionally been regarded as semantic. Recently, however, it has been suggested that, not being truth conditional, but rather being based in communicative use, they are more appropriately considered pragmatic (e.g., Levinson 1983, Sperber and Wilson 1986, Green 1989). We accept the view that metaphor is pragmatic, and argue below that in so far as metaphor is primarily analogical in character, it is different from the kinds of conversational processes based on maxims mentioned above, which operate primarily in linear, syntagmatic ways. A further difference identified by Green (1989: 122) is that, at a superficial level, metaphors often involve propositions that are intended to be recognized as literally false (for example, it is false that a person can be a block of ice), but conversational implicatures do not.

Most examples of metaphorical processes in language change have been discussed with respect to the lexicon. However, recently arguments have been put forward that early grammaticalization is also strongly motivated by metaphoric processes. Typical of early claims along these lines is: "Rather than subscribe to the idea that grammatical evolution is driven by communicative necessity, we suggest that human language users have a natural propensity for making metaphorical extensions that lead to the increased use of certain items" (Bybee and Pagliuca 1985: 75).

Probably the most appealing examples of metaphoric processes in grammaticalization are provided by the development of spatiotemporal terms. Claudi and Heine (1986) and Heine, Claudi and Hünnemeyer (1991a, 1991b) discuss the development of body part terms into locatives, of spatials into temporals, etc. in terms of metaphors such as SPACE IS AN OBJECT,

TIME IS SPACE (capitals indicate abstract, cross-linguistic meanings, as opposed to language-specific lexical items). For example, spatial terms such as BEHIND can be derived metaphorically from a body part (an example of the shift from OBJECT > SPACE), and subsequently temporal terms can be derived metaphorically from the spatial term (via SPACE > TIME), e.g., *We are behind in paying our bills*. Spatial terms abound cross-linguistically as temporal particles, auxiliaries, etc. (see Traugott 1978, 1985a; Bybee and Dahl 1989; Bybee, Pagliuca, and Perkins 1991 on expressions of the future). A few examples from English which have been regarded as metaphorical in origin include *be going to* (future), *in the years ahead* (future), *drink something up/down* (completive), *drink on* (continuative), *come to believe that . . .* (ingressive). Extensive examples from African languages can be found in Heine, Claudi, and Hünnemeyer (1991a and 1991b), and from Oceanic languages in Lichtenberk (1991b) (e.g., GO for continuative and future, COME for ingressive and future).

Another domain of meaning change among grammatical categories that has been widely regarded as metaphoric is the development of modal meanings, particularly the development of meanings relating to obligation into meanings relating to possibility and probability (known as "epistemic" meanings). For example: "The obligation sense of *have to* predicates certain conditions on a willful agent: X is obliged to Y. The epistemic sense is a metaphorical extension of obligation to apply to the truth of a proposition: X (a proposition) is obliged to be true" (Bybee and Pagliuca 1985: 73). In this view (modified in Bybee 1990), the process envisioned appears to be strictly speaking the schematic mapping of one concept onto another. Building on Talmy (1976, 1988), Sweetser takes a different approach to the modals, that of "sociophysical concepts of forces and barriers" (1990: 52). The *may* of permission is, according to Sweetser, understood in terms of "a potential but absent barrier," obligative *must* in terms of "a compelling force directing the subject towards an act." The force of *must* is "directly applied and irresistible," whereas that of *have to* is resistible under certain circumstances, cf.:

> (16) I have to/??must get this paper in, but I guess I'll go to the movies instead.
>
> (Sweetser 1990: 54)

Sweetser regards the epistemic meanings of these modals as deriving from the tendency to experience the physical, social, and epistemic worlds in partially similar ways. This similarity in experience, she suggests, allows the mapping of sociophysical potentiality onto the world of reasoning. For example, with respect to *may*, she says: "In both the sociophysical and the epistemic world, *nothing prevents* the occurrence of whatever is modally marked with *may*; the chain of events is not obstructed" (p. 60). With respect to *must*, she gives the following analysis (p. 61):

(17) a. You must come home by ten. (Mom said so.)
          'The direct force (of Mom's authority) compels you to come home by ten.'
      b. You must have been home last night.
          'The available (direct) evidence compels me to the conclusion that you were home.'

She goes on to show that yet another metaphorical mapping is possible: of potential barriers to the conversational world (what is often called meta-linguistic expression). Thus, in a hypothetical situation where Mondale's advisor is giving directions to a speech writer, the following might be imagined (p. 71):

(18) Reagan will/must be a nice guy (as far as the content of the speech is concerned, even if we criticize his policies).

In other words, "the interlocutor is being allowed to treat a certain statement as appropriate or reasonable."

Can any metaphor occur in the process of grammaticalization? The answer appears to be no. Talmy (1983, 1988) has suggested that only certain types of spatial concepts are used cross-linguistically in grammatical items: specifically, topological concepts. Thus precise distances between points on a scale, or precise angles, do not grammaticalize. Indeed, angles in general (e.g., *corner in time*) do not appear to grammaticalize.[3] However, topological relations on a linear parameter frequently do so, e.g., *front–back*, *up–down*.

Sweetser has suggested that when a lexical item expressing a spatial concept is grammaticalized, only the topological concept is transferred. The concrete image associated with the lexical item is replaced by a more schematic one, and the meaning transfer "is to a fairly abstract, topological domain . . . so there is less fleshing-out of meaning" (Sweetser 1988: 393).

4.3.2 *Metonymic processes*

There is little doubt that metaphor is one process at work in grammaticalization. However, since reanalysis, not analogy, has for long been recognized as the major process in grammaticalization at the structural, morphosyntactic level, it would be surprising if metaphor, which is analogical, were the prime process at work pragmatically and semantically. In this section we show that other processes, which depend on contiguity and reanalysis, also play a major part, and that some instances of grammaticalization that have heretofore been regarded as metaphorical can be seen to arise out of contiguity rather than or as well as out of analogy.

The overriding importance that metaphor has been given in many discussions of grammaticalization seems to derive from the tendency to think in terms of "lexical item > grammatical item," i.e., in terms of form, relatively independently of context rather than in terms of "use of lexical item in discourse > grammatical item," i.e., in terms of form in utterance contexts.[4] For example, when the lexical item *go* is considered out of context and is said to grammaticalize to an auxiliary, metaphor is naturally invoked with respect to its spatial properties. But in fact it was not *go* that grammaticalized; the phrase *be going to* did, presumably only in very local contexts, e.g., that of *be going in order to V*. The contiguity with *to* in the purposive sense must have been a major factor in the development of the future meaning in *be going to* as an auxiliary. We discuss this point more fully below.

The meaning changes arising out of contiguity in linguistic (including pragmatic) contexts are known as "associative" or conceptual "metonymic" changes. We will use the term "(conceptual) metonymy" here. "Metonymy" does, however, have some disadvantages for our purposes. For one, the term has been used primarily for changes arising out of contiguity in the non-linguistic world, cf. such examples as Lat. *coxa* 'hip' > Fr. *cuisse* 'thigh' (the parts of the body are spatially contiguous in the physical world), and *boor* 'farmer' > 'crude person' (association of behavior with a certain person or class of persons). One of the most famous examples is the transfer by association of the term for 'prayer' (OE *gebed*) to the objects by which a series of prayers was counted, the *beads* of a rosary (and ultimately, by generalization, to any beads). However, contiguity in the utterance, often resulting in ellipsis, has also been used as an example of metonymy, cf. French *foie* 'liver' < Latin *iecur ficatum* 'liver-fig-stuffed.' Neither of these senses of metonymy is useful for us. Rather, we use the term in the restrictive sense of conceptual association. This sense can be found in Stern, who, in speaking of "permutation," says it results from "a word [being] used in a phrase where a notion in some way connected with its meaning is liable to form an element of the context" (1931: 353). He goes on to list under examples of permutation the development of the logical meanings of *considering, supposing,* and of concessive *while.* More recently, Brinton (1988) has argued that the development of the English aspect markers, including *have,* is metonymically rather than metaphorically motivated.

A second reason why the term "metonymy" may not be ideal is that some linguists include it along with other figures of speech under metaphor (e.g., Hock 1991 [1986]). Or, if it is differentiated, it is assigned an insignificant place among the types of semantic change. For example, Dirven speaks of metaphor as a "major associative leap" but of metonymy as a "minor process" (1985: 98). Furthermore, in the tradition deriving from Jakobson and Halle's (1956) classic distinction between metaphor as choice functioning on the paradigmatic axis versus metonymy as association and sequence functioning primarily on the syntagmatic axis, metaphor is thought to lead to homogeneity and coherence, metonymy to juxtaposition and potential incoherence (J. D. Sapir 1977: 4). Nevertheless, there are other views of the difference between metaphor and metonymy that are more useful to us. For example, Anttila suggests that "Metaphor is semantic transfer through a similarity of sense perceptions," and is analogical and iconic, while metonymy is semantic transfer through contiguity and "indexical" (1989 [1972]: 141–2). In other words, metonymy points to ("indexes") relations in contexts. From this perspective, metaphor operates across conceptual domains, while metonymy operates across interdependent (morpho)syntactic constituents.

In an utterance such as (19) the verb *go* invites the conversational inference that the subject arrived at a later time at the destination, and the purposive *to,* introducing a subordinate clause, invites the conversational inference that someone intended the marriage to occur:

(19) I was/am going to be married. (in the sense 'I was/am going for the purpose of getting married')

However, this implicature can be canceled:

(20) I was going/on my way to be married, but on the plane I changed my mind and decided to join the Army.

We hypothesize that the future meaning of *be going to* was derived by the semanticization of the dual inferences of later time indexed by *go* and purposive *to,* not from *go* alone. Indeed, we hypothesize that the inference from purposive *to* must have played a significant role in the grammaticalization of *be going to* given that the major syntactic change involved in the development of the auxiliary is the rebracketing of [[. . . be going] [to S]] as [. . . be going to V] (Section 1.1). The progressive *be-ing* indexed activity in process, and so motivated the tendency for *be going to* to be interpreted as a purposive that was relevant to the reference time of the clause and likely to be imminent (see Bybee and Pagliuca 1987, Pérez 1990, who differ from the analysis presented here mainly in treating the change as a case of metaphorization).

To appreciate the importance of the relationship between *to* and *go*, in the development of auxiliary *be going to*, consider the following possible early instance:

> (21) Thys onhappy sowle . . . was goyng to be broughte into helle
>   for the synne and onleful lustys of her body.
>
> (1482, Monk of Evesham [OED go 47b])

This can be understood as an expression of motion in the context of the belief that after death the soul goes on a journey with the purpose of being rewarded or punished for actions in life. Note that in this example the passive demotes the inference that the subject of *go* is volitional or responsible with respect to the purposive clause. Because the destination of the journey (hell) is an adjunct not of *goyng to* but of *broughte*, the directionality of *going* is also demoted, and the inference of imminent future resulting from the purposes of the judges of the dead is promoted.

Similarly, in the passage in (22) the answer to *whither away* is (*to*) *a messenger*, and *I am going to deliver them* seems best understood as answering the question (*why*) *so fast?*, in other words, it seems more informative if it is inferred to answer the question in terms of purposes rather than directions:

> (22) *Duke* Sir Valentine, whither away so fast?
>   *Val.*   Please it your grace, there is a messenger
>   That stays to bear my letters to my friends,
>   And I am going to deliver them.
>
> (c. 1595, Shakespeare, Two Gentlemen of Verona III.i.51)

The full semanticization (and grammaticalization) of *be going to* is evidenced when the following subject and/or the verb is incompatible with purposiveness, for example, an inanimate subject or a verb of mental experience such as *hear*, or *like*. Once the semanticization of later time/ future had occurred, the *will* future could no longer be used with *be going to*, presumably because it had become partially redundant, and did not fit the auxiliary verb structure into which the construction had been absorbed. (Note, however, that the *will*-future can still occur in the main verb construction *be going to*, as in *I will be going to visit Aunt Mildred tomorrow.*)

The metaphor account, whereby a trajectory through space is mapped onto a trajectory in time, does not give adequate insight into why the progressive and most especially *to* are involved in the English expression *be going to*. This becomes particularly clear when we compare the cross-linguistic grammaticalization of the verb with the abstract meaning GO to future markers, each of which seems to have a slightly different history. Sometimes, for example, there is no overt purposive, in which case the future inference arises out of the directional verb and its associated aspect alone, as in French. Sometimes, however, GO may be grammaticalized into either a purposive or a temporal marker of imminence, as occurred to *bang* 'go' in Rama:

(23) a. Tiiskama ni-tanang-bang.
    baby   I-look-at-ASP
    'I am going to look at the baby.'
  b. Tiiskama ni-sung-bang taak-i.
    baby   I-see-SUB   go-TNS
    'I am going in order to see the baby.'

(Craig 1991: 457)

In each case inferences from the highly local contexts of the verb in its linear position within the clause appear to be the immediately motivating factors for change, though the capacity to create metaphors of time from space may well provide a cognitive framework that supports the changes.

We have suggested that semanticization of conversational inferences played a major role in the development of *be going to*. Another example is provided by the development of *while* (see Traugott and König 1991, on which the following discussion is based). This connective originated in OE in an adverbial phrase translatable as 'at the time that' consisting of the accusative distal demonstrative, the accusative noun *hwile* 'time,' and the invariant subordinator *þe*, a highly explicit coding of simultaneity,

(24) & wicode þær þa   hwile   þe man þa burg
    and lived there that:DAT time:DAT that one that fortress
    worhte   & getimbrode.
    worked-on and built
    'And camped there at the time that/while the fortress was worked on and built.'

(Chron A [Plummer] 913.3)

This phrasal expression was reduced by late OE to the simple conjunction *wile*:

(25) Ðæt lastede þa [xix] winttre wile Stephne was king.
      'That lasted those 19 winters while Stephen was king.'

                                        (ChronE [Plummer] 1137.36)

In the process, the precise specification of simultaneity signaled by the demonstrative was lost, allowing for other, less precise, conversational inferences to play a part. One such inference is that the conditions specified in the subordinate clause serve not only as the temporal frame of reference for those in the main clause, but also as the grounds for the situation (the disasters lasted nineteen years because Stephen was king). Such an inference to grounds for the situation is dominant over temporality in some examples dating from the later fourteenth century:

(26) Thar mycht succed na female, Quhill foundyn mycht be ony male.
      'No female was able to succeed while any male could be found.'

                              (1375, Barbours Bruce 1.60 [*OED* **while** 2a])

The causal inference from *while* did not become semanticized in English. However, in some languages this inference to the grounds for the situation has become the main extension of WHILE. For example, in German the temporal meaning of *weil* 'during' has become obsolete and the causal has become the main meaning.

In English a different inference came to dominate, that of surprise concerning the overlap in time or the relations between event and ground. This led to the adversative, concessive meaning (cf. similar developments for *as long as, at the same time as*). Probable instances of the semanticization of surprise and hence concessivity appear in the early seventeenth century, among them:

(27) Whill others aime at greatnes boght with blod,
      Not to bee great thou stryves, bot to bee good.
      'While others aim at greatness that is bought with blood, you strive to be not great but good.'

                              (1617, Sir W. Mure, *Misc. Poems* xxi.23 [*OED* **while** 2b])

This could be interpreted as a statement about simultaneous behaviors. However, there is a strong inference, reinforced by the inversion in the second line, that it is unusual not to be bloodthirsty. Unambiguous examples of concessive meanings appear later, typically with present tense stative verbs, e.g., *While you like peaches, I like nectarines*. The overall shift of *while* is from reference to a relatively concrete state of affairs (a particular time) to expression of the speaker's assessment of the relevance of simultaneity in describing events, to assessment of contrast between propositions. In other words, it demonstrates a shift to a relatively abstract and subjective construal of the world in terms of language.

A similar development to increased subjectivity is evidenced by *be going to*; the motion verb requires that the direction of motion be anchored in the subject as well as in the speaker's viewpoint.[5] But the auxiliary can be anchored in the speaker's subjective viewpoint alone, not in that of the subject:

(28)   An earthquake is going to destroy that town.

(Langacker 1990: 23)

An earlier example is:

(29)   It seems as if it were going to rain.

(1890, Cham. Jrnl. [*OED* **go** V.b])

Other examples of subjectification include the development of epistemic modals, for example the development of *must* in the sense of 'I conclude that' as in (17b) from *must* in the sense of 'ought' as in (17a) (Traugott 1989, Langacker 1990).

4.4   Metaphor and metonymy as problem solving

In discussing the principle of exploiting old means for novel functions, and the recruitment of concrete for more abstract terms, Heine, Claudi, and Hünnemeyer suggest that:

> grammaticalization can be interpreted as the result of a process which has **problem-solving** as its main goal, its primary function being conceptualization by expressing one thing in terms of another. This function is not confined to grammaticalization, it is the main characteristic of metaphor in general.

(1991b: 150–1)

In other words, semantic change in general, not just grammaticalization, can be interpreted as problem solving (see also C. Lehmann 1985). One problem to be solved is that of representing members of one semantic domain in terms of another, and metaphoric strategies serve this purpose. The second problem is the search for ways to regulate communication and negotiate speaker-hearer interaction. We have shown that this is a kind of metonymic change, indexing or pointing to meanings that might otherwise be only covert, but are a natural part of conversational practice. The main direction of both types of problem solving is toward informativeness, but the two types correlate with shifts along different axes. Metaphorical change involves specifying one, usually more complex, thing in terms of another not present in the context. Metonymic change, on the other hand, involves specifying one meaning in terms of another that is present, even if only covertly, in the context. It is largely correlated with shifts to meanings situated in the subjective belief state or attitude toward the situation, including the linguistic one. While metaphor is correlated primarily with solving the problem of representation, metonymy and lexicalizing of conversational meanings are correlated with solving the problem of expressing speaker attitudes.

In summary, metonymic and metaphorical inferencing are complementary, not mutually exclusive, processes at the pragmatic level that result from the dual mechanisms of reanalysis linked with the cognitive process of metonymy, and analogy linked with the cognitive process of metaphor. Being a widespread process, broad cross-domain metaphorical analogizing is one of the contexts within which grammaticalization operates, but many actual instances of grammaticalization show that the more local, syntagmatic and structure changing process of metonymy predominates in the early stages. We can now refine the model for *be going to* outlined in Figure 3.2. to specify that syntagmatic reanalysis is accompanied by metonymic strategies, and paradigmatic, analogical change by metaphorical ones. The revised model is presented in Figure 4.1.

The competing motivations of expressivity (which underlies metonymic and metaphorical inferencing) and routinization, together with the mechanisms of reanalysis and analogy discussed in Chapter 3, will be shown in the next chapter to motivate the unidirectionality typical of grammaticalization.

4.5   Pragmatic enrichment versus "bleaching"

From very early times researchers on issues related to grammaticalization have observed that it involves a process of loss of semantic content. This has been described by the metaphor of "fading" or "bleaching" (Gabelentz spoke of "verbleichen" 'grow pale,' Meillet of "affaiblissement" 'weakening'). More recently, Heine and Reh characterized grammaticalization as: "an evolution whereby linguistic units lose in semantic complexity, pragmatic significance, syntactic freedom, and phonetic substance" (Heine and Reh 1984: 15). Readers will have noted that in this chapter we have, however, spoken of pragmatic enrichment, strengthening,

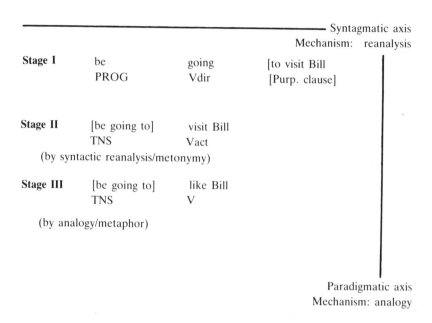

Figure 4.1 Revised schema of the development of auxiliary *be going to*

and so forth. This is because we have been discussing the beginnings of grammaticalization, that is, the motivations that permit the process to begin, rather than its outcomes. There is no doubt that over time, meanings tend to become weakened during the process of grammaticalization. Nevertheless, all the evidence for early stages is that initially there is a redistribution or shift, not a loss, of meaning.

For example, with reference to the development of future *go*, Sweetser says: "we lose the sense of physical motion (together with all its likely background inferences). We gain, however, a new meaning of future prediction or intention – together with *its* likely background inferences" (Sweetser 1988: 392). In speaking of the subjectification of *be going to*, Langacker draws attention to the loss of objective locational reference points that movement entails, and suggests that this loss is replaced by realignment to the speaker's temporal perspective (1990: 23). In other words, one meaning is demoted, another promoted.

As grammaticalized forms become increasingly syntacticized or morphologized they unquestionably cease over time to carry significant semantic or pragmatic meaning. This can most clearly be seen when former lexical items become empty syntactic elements, as in the case of *do*, or when formerly separate morphemes become bound and serve primarily as "morphological detritus" after repeated fusion (see Chapter 6). An excellent example is provided by the development of French *ça* 'that,' a form which is the worn-down relic of several stages of expressive reinforcement:

(30)   hoc 'that' > (ecce) hoc 'behold that' > eccehoc > ço > ce > ce(la) 'that there' > cela > ça

(Lüdtke 1980: 212)

The individual meanings of *hoc, ecce* and *la* have been lost, as has the form's distal demonstrative function (M. Harris 1978: Chapter 4).

Two general working principles arise out of our understanding of the processes of inferencing in grammaticalization. One is that the meanings will always be derivable from the original lexical meaning by either metaphorical or conceptual metonymic inferencing. Therefore meaning changes in grammaticalization are not arbitrary. Secondly, since the initial phase of grammaticalization involves a shift in meaning, but not loss of meaning, it is unlikely that any instance of grammaticalization will involve a sudden loss of meaning.

One of the most well-known examples of grammaticalization in English, the development of "empty" *do*, has been treated mainly as an example of syntactic change, and might be regarded as a counterexample. There has been considerable speculation about its origins. Causative *do*, as in (31), has been thought to be one source (Ellegård 1953):

(31)   Þe king sende efter him & dide him gyuen up ðat abbotrice of Burch.
'The king sent for him and made him give up the abbey of (Peter)brough.'

(Peterb. Chron 1132 [*MED* **don** 4a])

Denison (1985) and more recently Stein (1990a) have suggested that grammaticalization occurred not directly via loss of causative meaning, but via a perfective meaning, which arises particularly in past tense causative contexts. This perfective meaning demotes the issue of who undertook the action (in the causative, this is typically not the speaker), and permits the inference that what occurred and its relevance to the current discourse is the significant issue. This is particularly likely to occur in constructions without an overt subject of the infinitive clause. For example, in (32) the subject ('they') may have caused the women to be mocked, but the absence of an intermediary party between the mockers and their victims demotes the causality and promotes the accomplishment (perfectivity) of the action:

89

(32) And so thei dede bothe deseiue ladies and gentilwomen, and
      bere forthe diuerse langages on hem.
      'And so they both mocked ladies and gentlewomen, and made
      various allegations against them.'

$\qquad\qquad\qquad$ (*c.* 1450, Knt. Tour-L, 2.24; cited in Denison 1985: 50)

There are some problems with the causative analysis, among them the fact
that many instances of *do* in Middle English in the area in which it
developed (Southwest England) were and continue to be habitual in
meaning (Andrew Garrett, p.c.[6]). Garrett cites several modern examples
such as this one from Somerset:

(33) The surplus milk they did make into cheese and then the
      cheese did go to the different markets, that's how that did
      work.

$\qquad\qquad\qquad\qquad\qquad\qquad\qquad\qquad$ (Ihalainen 1976: 615)

Whatever the final analysis turns out to be, the point is that sudden
emptying of meaning is not expected. Furthermore, it is incumbent on the
researcher to seek a plausible set of inferences that enable changes to occur.

   Perhaps the most damaging evidence against the automatic association of
bleaching and sudden emptying of meaning with grammaticalization comes
from evidence that later constraints on structure or meaning can only be
understood in the light of earlier meanings. In other words, when a form
undergoes grammaticalization from a lexical to a grammatical item, some
traces of its original lexical meanings tend to adhere to it, and details of its
lexical history may be reflected in constraints on its grammatical distribution. This phenomenon has been called "persistence" (Hopper 1991).

   An example is provided by Lord's discussion of the development in West
African languages of object markers ("accusative cases") out of former
serialized verbs like 'take.' In Gã (a Benue-Kwa language of West Africa),
the form *kɛ̀* is an accusative case marker in sentences such as:

(34) È kɛ   wòlò ŋmè-sĩ.
      she ACC book lay-down
      'She put down a book.'

$\qquad\qquad\qquad\qquad\qquad\qquad\qquad\qquad\qquad$ (Lord 1982: 287)

It was originally a verb meaning 'take,' which has become grammaticalized
as an accusative case marker, and sentences such as these are historically of
the type 'He took a book [and] laid [it] down.' Certain restrictions on the
distribution of this case marker can only be understood from the point of

view of its origin in the meaning 'take.' Let us for a moment consider a language which has a fully developed accusative case marker, Latin. In Latin, accusative is a general marker of direct objects. The Latin accusative case occurs (to a large extent) irrespective of the semantic relationship between the verb and its object. Accusative objects in Latin may be perceived, produced, ordered, imagined, and so on. With a few exceptions, any noun which has the role of an object is marked as an accusative.

Gã is quite different from Latin in this respect. Consider, for example, (35a) and its ungrammatical counterpart (35b):

(35) a. È ŋmè wɔlɔ̀.
           she lay egg
           'She laid an egg.'
     b. *È kè   wɔlɔ̀ ŋmè.
          *she ACC egg lay '

                                          (Lord 1982: 288)

The semantic relationship between verb and object in 'laid down the book' is quite different from that in 'laid an egg.' In the first, the object is changed (moved, grasped, etc.) through the action of the verb; the object is "affected" (Lord 1982, Hopper 1986a). In the second, the object is produced or brought about by the action of the verb; the object is "effected." The accusative case marker in Gã can only be used if the object is "affected." For this same reason, the accusative case marker *kè* is inappropriate if the verb is one of experiencing:

(36) a. Tètè nà Kɔkɔ́.
           Tete saw Koko
           'Tete saw Koko.'
     b. *Tètè kè   Kɔkɔ́ nà.
          *Tete ACC Koko saw

                                             (ibid.)

These kinds of constraints exist because Gã retains the restriction on accusative case marking which derives from the historical antecedent of this grammatical morpheme in the lexical verb 'to take': only objects which can be 'taken' are marked morphologically as accusatives.

Persistence of old meanings is not restricted to African languages. Some differences in the meanings of the Present Day English tense/modal auxiliaries reflect possibilities of meaning which have existed for over a thousand years. Bybee and Pagliuca show that: "the differences in the uses of these future markers [i.e., *will, shall, be going to*, PH and ET] can be understood as continuations of their original lexical meanings" (Bybee and Pagliuca 1987: 117). As mentioned in connection with example (2), there are several polysemies of the "future" *will*. These include prediction (the "pure" future), willingness, and intention. Bybee and Pagliuca show that two of these meanings were already found in Old English. (37) exemplifies willingness, (38) intention:

> (37)   Gif he us geunnan wile, þæt we hine swa godne   gretan
>   if   he us grant   will, that him   so   generous greet
>   moton . . .
>   should . . .
>   'If he will/is willing to grant that we should greet him who is
>   so gracious . . . '
>
>   (*Beowulf* 346–7[7]; cited in Bybee and Pagliuca 1987: 113)

> (38)   Wen' ic þæt he wille, gif he wealdon mot, in þæm guðsele
>   think I that he will, if he prevail may, in the war-hall
>   Geotena leode etan unforhte.
>   of-Geats men eat unafraid
>   'I believe that he will, if he should prevail, devour the people
>   of the Geats without fear in their war-hall.'
>
>   (*Beowulf* 442–4; cited in Bybee and Pagliuca 1987: 113)

The "predictive" future has developed out of the intention/promise use of *will*. Bybee and Pagliuca show that the future meaning becomes established in the Middle English period when inanimates incapable of volition begin to appear as the subjects of *will*. When this happened, it did not result in an across-the-board re-semanticization of *will*; the predictive future remains only one of several distinct meanings of *will* in PDE. All that happened was that a new meaning was added to an already polysemous form, and thus new distributional possibilities were opened up for the form. Furthermore, the fact that *will* and *be going to* do not mean the same thing (*be going to* expresses present orientation and goal-directed plan), is attributable to the fact that the latter had progressive and directional origins while the former did not.

The process of demotion of some lexical meanings and promotion of others can be hypothesized to be typical of grammaticalization. Those that are promoted tend to be relatively abstract, and particularly relevant to expression of temporality, role relationships, etc. (i.e., "grammatical meanings"). Furthermore, they tend to be the ones most salient in the original contexts/formulae within which grammaticalization takes place (e.g., intention regarding the future is salient in the contexts relevant to the grammaticalization of *be going to*). These originally salient meanings tend to persist over time and to constrain the later uses of the grammaticalized form. "Bleaching" must therefore be taken to be a very relative notion, and one that pertains almost exclusively to late stages of grammaticalization. An important question for future research is what exactly constitutes bleaching, when it can be said to set in, and how it correlates with morphosyntactic generalization. It is to such generalization that we now turn.

5
The hypothesis of unidirectionality

5.1 Introduction

Grammaticalization as viewed from the diachronic perspective is hypothesized to be prototypically a unidirectional phonemenon. In this chapter we elaborate further on some general principles of unidirectionality, with particular attention to such diachronic issues as generalization, decategorialization, increase in grammatical status, and renewal. We will also discuss synchronic issues such as the resultant variability and "layering" arising from those diachronic processes. And we will also briefly touch on counterexamples to unidirectionality. In Chapter 6 we will discuss in more detail some well-known kinds of unidirectionality found in morphological change, that is, in the later stages of grammaticalization. In Chapter 7 we will suggest that similar types of unidirectionality also occur in morphosyntactic change, especially the development of complex clauses.

Once grammaticalization has set in, there are certain likely paths along which it proceeds. One path discussed by Meillet is that whereby a lexical item becomes a grammatical item, summarized as:

lexical item > morphology

As mentioned in Section 2.2, one of Meillet's examples was the Modern Greek future particle *tha*, as in:

(1) Tha têlephônêsô tou patéra mou.
     '[I] will telephone my father.'

The source of *tha* is the Classical Greek *thelô ina* 'I wish that.' In the preceding chapters we have discussed examples that suggest this formulation of the path of grammaticalization is not quite right. The path is not directly from lexical item to morphology. Rather, lexical items or phrases come through use in certain highly constrained local contexts to be reanalyzed as having syntactic and morphological functions. Schematically, this can be characterized as:

lexical item used in specific linguistic contexts > syntax >
morphology

The lexical items that become grammaticalized must first serve commonly
needed discourse functions. They then become syntactically fixed (they
become constructions), and may eventually amalgamate morphologically,
say, as stem and affix. The basic assumption is that there is a relationship
between two stages A and B, such that A occurs before B, but not vice
versa. This is what is meant by unidirectionality.

As has been stated frequently in previous chapters, there is nothing
deterministic about grammaticalization and unidirectionality. Changes do
not have to occur. They do not have to go to completion, in other words,
they do not have to move all the way along a cline. A particular
grammaticalization process may be, and often is, arrested before it is fully
"implemented," and the "outcome" of grammaticalization is quite often a
ragged and incomplete subsystem that is not evidently moving in some
identifiable direction. One example of a deterministic argument is: "Before
a change is manifested little by little, its end result is already given in the
underlying representations" (Andersen 1973: 788). Taken in its strong sense
as presupposing a predetermined outcome, even a "goal" for grammaticalization, this suggests that once a change has started, its progress is
inexorable. However, this hypothesis is not empirically supported. What is
supported is the fact that there are strong constraints on how a change may
occur and on the directionality of the change, even though we do not yet
fully understand all the factors that motivate this directionality (for some
earlier discussion, see Section 4.1).

Before proceeding, it should be mentioned that the unidirectionality in
question is not the same as what E. Sapir called "drift," although it has some
similarities. In a famous statement, Sapir said: "Language moves down time
in a current of its own making. It has a drift" (1921: 150). Even if we were to
emend this statement to acknowledge that it is not language that changes,
but rather the rules of grammar (see Section 3.2), there would still be a
fundamental difference from what is meant by the unidirectionality of
grammaticalization. Sapir was interested in the fact that English is losing
case inflections on its pronouns (e.g., the *who/whom* distinction is losing
ground), and English is also becoming more periphrastic, for example,
possessive genitive is being replaced by *of*. While Sapir was thinking of
language-specific changes, and, within languages, of highly specific phenomena, other linguists later showed how the separate phenomena he
discussed for English were in fact part of the same thing (case loss and

95

periphrasis go hand in hand), and indeed part of larger typological shifts. R. Lakoff, for example, focused on drift "defined . . . very loosely as historical fluctuation between syntheticity and analyticity" (1972: 179), that is, on fluctuation between bondedness and periphrasis, while Vennemann (1975) focused on shifts from OV to VO order. Lakoff's summary of Sapir's notion of drift as "a metacondition on the way in which the grammar of a language **as a whole** will change" (R. Lakoff 1972: 178) serves well to differentiate "drift" from unidirectionality. Drift has to do with regularization of construction types within a language (see also Malkiel 1981), unidirectionality with changes affecting particular types of construction. Unidirectionality is a metacondition on how particular grammatical constructions will change.

5.2 Generalization

Among characterizations of grammaticalization, the following statement is typical: "It is often observed that grammatical meaning develops out of lexical meaning by a process of generalization or weakening of semantic content [Givón 1973, Fleischman 1982, and many others]. It can be further hypothesized that . . . this semantic change is paralleled over a long period of time by phonetic erosion" (Bybee and Pagliuca 1985: 59–60). As we showed in Section 4.5, early stages of grammaticalization do not show bleaching. Rather there is a balance between loss of older, typically more concrete, meanings, and development of newer, more abstract ones that at a minimum cancel out the loss. Many are the result of pragmatic strengthening, and increase in informativeness. We will not repeat these arguments here. Instead, we will focus on the notion of generalization. Generalization is a process which can be characterized, in part, as an increase in the polysemies of a form, and in part as: "an increase of the range of a morpheme advancing from a lexical to a grammatical or from a less grammatical to a more grammatical status" (Kuryłowicz 1965: 52).

5.2.1 Generalization of meaning

We start with issues of generalization of meaning. Here the question is not whether the meanings become less distinct in the process of grammaticalization (as the hypothesis of bleaching suggests), but whether there are constraints on what meanings are subject to grammaticalization, on how the meanings of lexical items that become grammatical may change.

When we think of the lexicon, we assume that it includes not only syntactic and phonological characterizations, but also characterization of

96

such semantic relations as take part in fields (e.g., color terms, or verbs of saying: *say, tell, claim, assert*), relational terms (e.g., kinship terms), taxonomies (hierarchies such as *creature, animal, dog, spaniel,* including part-whole hierarchies, such as *finger–arm–hand–body, keel–boat*), complementaries (non-gradable pairs, with excluded middle, e.g., *true–false*), antonyms (gradable pairs, e.g., *slow–fast*), directional oppositions (e.g., *go–come, teach–learn*), synonyms (e.g., *fiddle–violin*), polysemies (e.g., *mug* [of tea, usually with a handle] and *mug* [of beer, often without a handle]), and so forth. General accounts of lexical semantics can be found in Ullman (1964), Lyons (1977) and Cruse (1986), and the reader is referred to them for details.

As we have noted in previous chapters, the lexical meanings subject to grammaticalization are usually quite general. For example, verbs which grammaticalize, whether to case markers or to complementizers, tend to be superordinate terms (also known as "hyponyms") in lexical fields, for example, *say, move, go.* They are typically not selected from more specialized terms such as *whisper, chortle, assert, squirm, writhe.* Likewise, if a nominal from a taxonomic field grammaticalizes into a numeral classifier, it is likely to be selected from the following taxonomic levels: beginner (e.g., *creature, plant*), life form (e.g., *mammal, bush*), and generic (e.g., *dog, rose*), but not from specific (e.g., *spaniel, hybrid tea*), or varietal (e.g., *Cocker, Peace*) (Adams and Conklin 1973). In other words, the lexical items that grammaticalize are typically what are known as "basic words." In some cases, a formerly fairly specific term can be grammaticalized, but only after it has become more general. An example is provided by Latin *ambulare* 'walk' > French *aller* 'go' > future auxiliary. As these already general lexical items take on grammatical functions, they are generalized in so far as they come to be used in more and more contexts, that is, they gain wider distribution and more polysemies. This follows naturally from the fact that former inferences are semanticized.

To the extent that there is a difference between lexical and grammatical meaning changes, grammatical meaning changes are a subset of lexical ones. Most notably, grammaticalization does not provide evidence of narrowing of meaning. By contrast, although many lexical changes involve broadening (generalization) of meanings, there are also well-known cases of narrowing, typically of a higher to a lower taxonomic level.

Examples of narrowing in lexical change include the restriction of *hound* to a special type of dog, in an avoidance of synonymy (the generic OE *hund* became narrowed to specific rank when Scandinavian *dog* was borrowed). Other well-known examples include the narrowing of OE *cwen* 'woman' to 'woman of royal rank' as the competing form *wifman* 'woman' (lit. 'female person') took over. Occasionally, narrowing may involve the restriction to a subtype, in which case the integrity of the lexical item and its components may become blurred. Examples include *raspberry, strawberry*, where *rasp* and *straw* have virtually lost their independent meaning, but together with *berry* identify different varietals of berries. One lexical domain in which narrowing is particularly likely to occur is the domain of terms for dispreferred entities, especially those associated with taboo, social prejudice, or unpleasantness, however these are defined in a particular culture. Examples include *stink* (originally 'to smell/have an odor'), *cock* (now restricted in some registers to 'penis,' with the term for the bird replaced by *rooster*), *mistress* (originally 'head of household,' now restricted to female lover, or 'kept woman') (for a fuller study, see Allan and Burridge 1991).

Narrowing appears to be absent in grammaticalization. What is particularly interesting is that this absence predicts constraints on possible developments not only in the meanings of grammatical items but also in morphology (Horn 1972, 1989). Horn (as cited in Levinson 1983: 163-4) is concerned with the absence of the starred forms in:

(2) | **negative phrase** | **negative incorporation** |
|---|---|
| not possible | impossible |
| not necessary | *innecessary |
| not some | none |
| not all | *nall |
| not sometimes | never |
| not always | *nalways |
| not or | nor |
| not and | *nand |

The suggestion is that the non-existence of the starred forms can be explained on the following grounds. In each pair, *necessary–possible, all–some, always–sometimes, and–or*, the extant negative form is the negation of the weaker member of the pair. This weaker member can be strengthened by an implicature cancelable upward to the stronger meaning, e.g.:

(3) a. It was possible, in fact necessary.
     b. Some boys fled, in fact all.

By contrast, the stronger member cannot be weakened (canceled downward to a weaker meaning), since such statements would be redundant (uninformative):

(4) a. *It was necessary, in fact possible.
     b. *All boys fled, in fact some.

Horn's hypothesis is that by lexically asserting the negation of the weaker member of the pair, one implicates that the stronger member does not apply. Since this lexical item already exists, there is no need for a separate item that would assert that the stronger item does not apply. In other words, **innecessary* in the logical sense *necessary that not* would be no more informative than *impossible*, **nall* no more informative than *none*; hence the absence of *innecessary, nall,* etc. Similar asymmetries exist not only in most European languages, but also in many other languages: "Thus, for example, Malagasy *tsy* 'not' and *misy* [miš] 'some' combine to form [tsiš] 'no,' literally 'not some'; there is no corresponding lexicalization of 'not all' or 'some not'" (Horn 1989: 254). Such constraints follow naturally from the claim developed in Chapter 4 that grammaticalization typically involves increasing the range of informativeness.

One constraint on lexical change that is often noted in the literature is "avoidance of homonymic clash," in other words, avoidance of what might be dysfunctional ambiguity from the perspective of "one meaning – one form" (see especially Geeraerts 1986). Well-known examples are the loss and replacement of one lexical item by another when two or more formerly distinct lexical items undergo regular phonological changes that make them potentially homonymous. Probably the most famous case is that of the replacement of the term for 'rooster' in Southwestern France by forms such as *faisan* 'pheasant' when Latin *gallus* 'rooster' and *cattus* 'cat' fell together as *gat* due to regular sound change (Gilliéron 1902–10). In England OE *lætan* 'prevent' and *lettan* 'permit' fell together in ME as *let*. The first was replaced by *forbid* and *prevent*, and the potential problems of ambiguity between opposite meanings were avoided (Anttila 1989 [1972]: 182).

The majority of examples of avoidance of homonymic clash are lexical, and even in the lexical domain they are infrequent. They are even more infrequent in the grammatical domain. If they do occur, they do so almost exclusively in connection with relatively independent morphemes. For example, it has been suggested that the idiosyncratic development of the Oscan prepositions *faza* 'toward' (< Latin *facie ad* 'with one's face to') and *(f)ata* 'until' (< Arabic *hatta* 'until') into Middle Spanish *(h)acia* and *fasta* respectively may be attributed to "the powerful urge to differentiate homonyms despite semantic similarity" (Malkiel 1979: 1). Similarly, the borrowing in Middle English of the Northern English feminine pronoun form *she* and of the Scandinavian plural pronoun *they* have been attributed in part to the falling together in ME of OE *he* 'masc.sg.pro.,' *heo* 'fem.sg.pro.,' *hie* 'pl.pro.' (For a detailed study, including possible evidence for regulation of a new homonymic clash that developed between *þai* 'they' and the less frequent *þai* 'though,' see Samuels 1972.) However, as we have seen, grammatical items are characteristically polysemous, and so avoidance of homonymic clash would not be expected to have any systematic effect on the development of grammatical markers, especially in their later stages. This is particularly true of inflections. We need only think of the English *-s* inflections: nominal plural, third person singular verbal marker,[1] and the *-d* inflections: past tense, past participle. Indeed, it is difficult to predict what grammatical properties will or will not be distinguished in any one language. Although English contrasts *he, she, it*, Chinese does not. Although OE contrasted past singular and past plural forms of the verb (e.g., *he rad* 'he rode,' *hie ridon* 'they rode'), PDE does not except in the verb *be*, where we find *she is/they were*.

In sum, in the process of grammaticalization, meanings expand their range through the development of various polysemies. Depending on one's analysis, these polysemies may be regarded as quite fine-grained. It is only collectively that they may seem like weakening of meaning. The important claim should not be that bleaching follows from generalization, but rather that meaning changes leading to narrowing of meaning will typically not occur in grammaticalization.

5.2.2 *Generalization of grammatical function*

It follows from the preceding discussion that, in so far as grammatical forms have meanings, they will come to serve a larger and larger range of meaningful morphosyntactic purposes. Bybee and Pagliuca (1985) refer to the development of progressives into imperfects. A clear example in English is the spread of an originally highly constrained progressive structure *be V-ing*, that was restricted to agentive constructions, first to passives (*the house was being built* is a later eighteenth-century construction, replacing the earlier *the house was building*), and later to stative contexts, where it serves a "contingency" function, as in *There are statues standing in the park*.

Another example is the development in Finnish of the genitive case morpheme to signal the underlying subject of a non-finite clause, for example, a clause introduced by a verb of cognition such as *uskoa* 'think, believe' (Timberlake 1977: 144–57). What is at issue here can perhaps best be explained through an English example. In a sentence such as (5) there is a certain ambiguity at the surface level in the function of the word *Jane*:

(5) a. We watched Jane dancing/dance.

From one point of view, *Jane* is the person we are watching, and is therefore the object of *watch*. From another perspective, the event (Jane's dancing) is the object of *watch*. From yet another perspective, *Jane* is the subject of the verb *dance*. For example, we say:

(5) b. What we watched was Jane dancing/dance.

    c. Who we watched was Jane dancing/dance.

However, in a language that has a system of cases that overtly distinguish between subjects and objects, it is possible to resolve the potential surface ambiguity in different ways, and there may be a diachronic shift from the one to the other. This is essentially the kind of change that occurred in Finnish.

In Finnish, in both older and modern periods, there is no single case for objects; instead, objects are indicated in several different ways (Comrie 1981b: 125–36):

(a) with the accusative case if there is an overt subject, and the matrix verb is active

(b) with the nominative if there is no overt subject

(c) with the partitive if the verb is negated, or if the object is partially affected.

Subjects in non-finite clauses in Modern Finnish are indicated with the genitive case:

(6) Näen poikien   menevän.
    I-see boy:GEN:PLUR go:PART
    'I see the boys going.' (lit. 'I see the going of the boys.')
                                 (Anttila 1989: 104)

The genitive case for subjects of non-finite clauses in the modern language replaces an earlier case marking system in which other cases were used. The following examples are from older Finnish texts:

(7) a. **Accusative**
    Seurakunnan   hen lupasi   psysyueisen   oleuan.
    congregation:ACC he promised long-lasting:ACC being:ACC
    'He promised that the congregation would be long-lasting.'

    b. **Nominative**
    Homaitan se tauara   ia   Jumalan   Lahia
    observed it goods:NOM and God:GEN gift:NOM

poiseleua.
being-lacking:NOM
'It is observed that the goods and the gift of God are lacking.'

c. **Partitive**

Eike lwle site   syndi oleuan.
Not think this:PARTIT sin   being:PART
'Nor does one think this to be a sin.'[2]

(Timberlake 1977: 145)

These three cases, of course, comprise the set of cases that signal objects. Therefore the change to constructions such as are illustrated by (6) has been one of reanalysis whereby a noun that was once construed as the object of a main clause verb comes to be construed as the subject of a subordinate clause verb. The participle in the non-finite clause has also changed: in the earlier type of sentence it is inflected and agrees with the object case (partitive, nominative, or accusative) of the noun. But in the later type of sentence the participle is not inflected – it remains invariant. While it has not assumed any new verbal properties such as tense, it has shed its noun-like properties of inflection (that is, it has become de-categorialized; see next section).

How did this come about? Timberlake (1977), following Anttila (1972: 103–4), suggests that the reanalysis originated in those constructions in which the case morpheme was ambiguous. The original accusative *-m* and the genitive *-n* of singular nouns became homophonous as a result of a phonological change in which word-final nasals merged as *n*. As a consequence, those constructions with singular nouns (e.g., 'boy') serving as objects with participal attributes could be reanalyzed as partitive attributes of a verbal noun (that is, as surface subjects of non-finite verbs).[3]

It appears that a reanalysis that occurred in one very local construction (with singular agentive nouns) was then generalized through a number of new environments via the following historical stages: first singular NPs and pronouns; then, in addition, plural pronouns and plural agentive NPs; and finally plural non-agentive NPs. Timberlake suggests that among other things these stages reflect a spread along a functional hierarchy from noun phrases that are more subject-like to less subject-like noun phrases. The highest on the hierarchy are entities that are agentive, and individuated (a singular noun or pronoun), and therefore are prime candidates for being subjects. Next come those that, if not singular, are most likely to initiate actions, that is, personal pronouns and nouns denoting an agent. Finally come non-singular nouns that are less likely to be subjects or to initiate actions, such as inanimates. The syntactic reanalysis is therefore driven by a hierarchy of semantic contexts rather than by strictly syntactic structure.

It would be remarkable to find a hierarchy of this kind reversed. We are unlikely to find, for example, that subjects of verbs (whether finite or non-finite) could originally comprise a broad class of all nouns and pronouns, but that the class of possible subjects of verbs progressively narrowed to exclude, first, inanimate plural nouns, then plural pronouns and animate nouns, and so finally became restricted to singular pronouns and nouns. Nor would we expect to find subject case marking beginning with abstract, inanimate, and plural nouns and only later spreading to animate, anaphoric pronouns.

5.3 Decategorialization

Another perspective on unidirectionality presents it as a spread of grammaticalization along a path or cline of structural properties, from a morphologically "heavier" unit to one that is lighter, that is, from one that tends to be phonologically longer and more distinct (e.g., with stressed vowels) to one that tends to be less distinct and shorter. It is from this structural perspective that we approach unidirectionality in this section, with particular attention to the issue of the correlation between increased grammatical status and decategorialization. One important factor in our discusson will be the tendency for less grammatical items to become more grammatical. Another will be frequency: the more frequently a form occurs in texts, the more grammatical it is assumed to be. Frequency demonstrates a kind of generalization in use patterns.

In the standard view of grammatical categories, linguistic forms are classified in advance according to criteria that may vary quite widely from language to language. If morphological criteria are available, these usually play a role in the assignment of a form to a category. In the Indo-European languages, for example, "nouns" are typically identified through properties such as case, number, and gender, and "verbs" through properties such as tense, aspect, and person/number agreement. If morphology is lacking, as in Chinese, categories are usually identified through functions such as (for "nouns") ability to be a topic (e.g., ability to be referential, unavailability for questioning), or (for "verbs") ability to serve as certain kinds of predicates.

When a form undergoes grammaticalization from a lexical to a grammatical form, however, it tends to lose the morphological and syntactic properties that would identify it as a full member of a major grammatical category such as noun or verb. In its most extreme form such a change is manifested as a cline of categoriality, statable as:

major category (> adjective/adverb) > minor category

In this schema the major categories are noun and verb (categories that are relatively "open" lexically), and minor categories include preposition, conjunction, auxiliary verb, pronoun, and demonstrative (relatively "closed" categories). Adjectives and adverbs comprise an intermediate degree between the major and minor categories and can often be shown to derive straightforwardly from (participial) verbs and (locative, manner, etc.) nouns respectively. At least two major categories – noun and verb – are identifiable in almost all languages (see Hopper and Thompson 1984, 1985) with some consistency (Croft 1991 argues for three major categories: noun, verb and adjective), whereas the minor categories vary from language to language, being manifested often only as affixes. Given the theory of unidirectionality, it can be hypothesized that diachronically all minor categories have their origins in major categories.

A clear case of shift from major to minor category is seen in the conjunction *while*, as in *while we were sleeping*. As mentioned in 4.3.2., historically, *while* was a noun (OE *hwil*) meaning a length of time; this meaning is still preserved in PDE (*we stayed there for a while*). As a conjunction, however, *while* has diverged from this original lexical function as a noun, and is grammaticalized as a signal of temporal organization in the discourse. Among the changes involved in the grammaticalization of *while* to a conjunction is a loss of those grammatical features that identify *while* as a noun. When it is used as a conjunction, *while*:

(a) cannot take articles or quantifiers
(b) cannot be modified by adjectives or demonstratives
(c) cannot serve as a subject or as any other argument of the verb
(d) can only appear in the initial position in its clause, and
(e) cannot subsequently be referred to by an anaphoric pronoun.

It will be noted that these categorial changes are here presented as negative qualities or losses. This structural characterization contrasts with the pragmatic one in Chapter 4, which focuses on the fact that *while* has "gained" an ability to link clauses and indicate temporal relationships in discourse in a way that was not possible for it as an ordinary noun. In ascribing "decategorialization" to a form we are not tracing the decay or deterioration of that form, but its functional shift from one kind of role to another in the organization of discourse. Because this new role is one that does not require the trappings associated with discourse reference, such as articles and adjectives, these trappings are naturally discarded, but this should not be identified with simple loss, as if somehow a conjunction were a "degenerate" noun.

Similarly, as they become grammaticalized, verbs may lose such verb-like attributes as the ability to show variation in tense, aspect, modality, and person–number marking. In the following pair of sentences, the initial participial "verb" can still show some verb-like features when it is understood literally as in (8), but loses this ability when it is understood as a conjunction, as in (9):

(8) Carefully considering/Having carefully considered all the evidence, the panel delivered its verdict.

(9) Considering (*having carefully considered) you are so short, your skill at basketball is unexpected.

In (8), the participle *considering* can take an adverbial modifier, can have a present or past tense form, and must have an understood subject that is identical with the main clause subject; it therefore in a sense has a (recoverable) subject, like a verb. In (9), none of these verb-like attributes are available to *considering*.

Two typical paths of development have been much discussed in the literature. One is a path for nominal categories, another for verbal. These are "grammatical clines," in the sense that they make reference to hierarchical categories relevant to constituent structure. They are also clines of decategorialization, in that the starting point for the cline is a full category (noun or verb) and the intermediate points are characterized by a loss of morphological trappings associated with the full category.

Some caveats should be noted in any discussion of unidirectionality along a cline. Firstly, as mentioned in 1.2.2, clines should not be thought of as continua strictly speaking. Rather, they are paths along which certain grammatical properties cluster around constructions with "family resemblances" (Heine, forthcoming) (e.g., constructions resembling auxiliaries, or articles, or prepositions). But these clustering points should not be thought of as rigid "resting spots." A metaphor for linguistic forms in these clusters might be chips in a magnetic field; over time fewer or more of the chips in the clusters may be pulled magnetically to another field.

Secondly, because there is always a period of overlap between older and newer forms and/or functions of a morpheme, the cline should not be thought of as a line in which everything is in sequence. As we indicated in

Chapter 1, Heine and his colleagues use the term "chaining" to emphasize the non-linearity of relations on a cline. We prefer the term "layering" (see 5.5.1 below) because that metaphor allows more readily for multiple origins of a grammatical form. But here as in other matters, the metaphors are only partially helpful.

A further caveat is that because the particular course of events in any cline that is presented is not predetermined, once the "slippery slope" is embarked upon, continued grammaticalization is not inevitable, but may be suspended indefinitely at any point. Indeed, it is typically suspended at the pre-affixal stage in situations of language death (Dressler 1988). Furthermore, we cannot logically work backwards from some given point to a unique antecedent on the same cline. Absent a historical record, we cannot, for example, uniquely conclude from a cline on which prepositions occur (see the next section) that any given preposition must once have been a certain noun, although we can state that it might have been. This is because other sources for prepositions, such as verbs, are possible. For example, the preposition *during* was once the *-ing* form of an obsolete verb meaning 'to last, endure.'

Last but not least, it is both difficult and unnecessary to illustrate the whole of any one cline with a single form. It is difficult because historical records are rarely long enough to permit the recovery of the entire sequence of events, and so usually we must either posit reconstructed forms for past stages, or else indulge in speculation about future stages. And it is unnecessary because what is at issue is the directionality between adjacent forms on the cline, not the demonstration of the complete sequence of events for a given form. Furthermore, at any one stage of a language, the historical unidirectionality may be obscured by synchronic evidence of renewal of old forms (see 5.4.3 below). And, very importantly, different languages tend to exemplify different clusterings on a cline. In other words, not each position on a cline is likely to be equally elaborated at any particular stage. Thus English and Romance languages have fairly elaborated clitic structures, and minimally elaborated inflectional structures, while some other languages, such as Slavic languages, have highly elaborated inflectional structures.

5.3.1 A noun-to-affix cline

We will first consider one cline the starting point of which is a full noun, specifically a relational noun (to be defined below). The cline has been presented as follows (C. Lehmann 1985: 304):

> relational noun >
> secondary adposition >
> primary adposition >
> agglutinative case affix >
> fusional case affix

These five points should not be taken as strictly discrete categories, but as marking, somewhat arbitrarily, cluster points on a continuous trajectory. In other words, most forms that are locatable on this cline will not fit unambiguously into one or the other of the named categories, but will be seen as moving toward or away from one of them in a direction that we can call "from top to bottom," following the writing conventions adopted above.

A relational noun is one the meaning of which is a location or direction potentially in relation to some other noun. *Top, way*, and *side*, and many body parts such as *foot, head* and *back* often assume a relational meaning, and in doing so may enter this cline (Heine, Claudi, and Hünnemeyer 1991b). The relational noun usually appears as the head noun of a phrase, such as *side* in *by the side of* (> *beside*), or as an inflected noun, such as German *Wegen* 'ways [dative plural]',' > *wegen* 'because of,' as in *wegen des Wetters* 'because of the weather.'

The term "adposition" is a cover term for prepositions and postpositions. Secondary adpositions are usually forms (words or short phrases) that define concrete rather than grammatical relationships. They are typically derived from relational nouns, e.g., *beside the sofa, ahead of the column*. Primary adpositions are thought of as the restricted set of adpositions, often monosyllabic, that indicate purely grammatical relationships, such as *of, by*, and *to*. However, primary adpositions may themselves be characterized by a cline in meaning in so far as some may have a relatively concrete spatial meaning, for example, *by* in *a hotel by the railway station*, while others do not, for example, *by* in *arrested by a plain clothes policeman*. While the distinction between concrete and grammatical meaning is often not easy to define, the spatial meanings of primary adpositions are always very general. The spatial meanings are moreover likely to be recovered by some kind of reinforcement, e.g., *by the railway station* > *down by the railway station*; *in the house* > *within/inside the house.*

Primary adpositions are easily cliticized, and may go one step further to become affixes. Locative suffixes of various kinds can often be traced back to earlier postpositions (and, still further back, to nouns). In Hungarian the suffix *-ban*, as in *házban* 'house-inessive/in the house,' was once the locative case of a relational noun meaning 'interior.' Similarly, the elative, meaning 'away from,' as in *házból* 'from the house,' shows a suffix *-ból* that goes back to a different case of the same word. The final segments *n/l* of the two suffixes are themselves relics of the two case endings on the relational noun (Comrie 1981b: 119).

The Hungarian suffixes *-ban* and *-ból* are examples of agglutinative suffixes: they are joined to the stem with a minimum of phonological adjustments, and the boundary between stem and suffix is quite obvious. By contrast, fusional affixes show a blurring not only of the stem/affix boundary, but also of the boundaries among the affixes themselves. In Latin *militibus* 'to/from the soldiers,' *-ibus* is a dative/ablative plural suffix which cannot be further analyzed, and in *miles* 'soldier:NOM:SG' the *-t-* of the stem **milet-* has been lost through assimilation to the nominative singular suffix *-s*.

5.3.2 A verb-to-affix cline

A parallel cline has a lexical verb as its starting point which develops into an auxiliary and eventually an affix (verbal clines have been the subject of several cross-linguistic studies, most notably Bybee 1985, Bybee and Dahl 1989). Some of the points on this cline are as follows (the parenthetical line indicates that the position on the cline is optional in many languages):

> full verb >
> (vector verb >)
> auxiliary >
> clitic >
> affix

On this cline, we typically find that verbs having a full lexical meaning and a grammatical status as the only verb in their clause come to be used as auxiliaries to another verb. Auxiliary verbs tend to be finite, that is, to carry tense, mood or aspect markers, to have semantic properties of tense, aspect or mood, and to show specialized syntactic behavior (e.g., in English, auxiliary *will* cannot occur in certain temporal and infinitival clauses; hence the following are ungrammatical: **Let's wait till she will join us*, **I would like her to will join us*). There are numerous examples of the shift from main to auxiliary verb. From PDE we have cited *go* in *be going to*. Other examples include *have*, which is a full verb in *have a book*, but a quasi-(partial) auxiliary in *have a book to read* and *have to read a book* (Brinton, forthcoming), and a full auxiliary in *have had a book*. Another example is *keep*, which is a full lexical verb in *she keeps indoors on cold days*, but an auxiliary in *she keeps watering the tomatoes*. Auxiliaries may become clitics, like English *have* in *we've built a new garage*. And such clitics may become affixes. As discussed in 3.4.1, this happened in the French future tense paradigm, as in *ils passeront* 'they will pass,' where *-ont* reflects a former cliticized auxiliary 'have.'

The category "vector verb" represents one of several intermediate stages that can be posited between full verb and auxiliary. The term is owed to Hook (1974, 1991), who presents data from Hindi and other Indo-Aryan languages in which a clause may contain a complex of two verbs known as a "compound verb." One of these verbs, the "main" or "primary" verb, carries the main semantic verbal meaning of the clause, and is non-finite. The other, the "vector" verb, is a quasi-auxiliary which is finite, and therefore carries markers of tense, aspect, and mood. Semantically, it adds nuances of aspect, direction, and benefaction to the clause. The compound verb as a whole may occur with true auxiliaries indicating grammatical distinctions of tense, person, and number. In modern Indo-Aryan languages the vector verbs include: '*go*,' '*give*,' '*take*,' '*throw*,' '*strike*,' '*let go*,' '*get up*,' '*come*,' '*sit*,' '*fall*,' and others (Hook 1991). The size and diversity of the set, that is, the low degree of specialization as auxiliaries displayed by its members, is one factor that points to the need to think of them as intermediate between full verbs and auxiliaries.

Hindi being a verb-final language, the order of the two verbs in the "compound" construction is main–vector:

(10) mAI ne das baje   aap ko   fon   kar liyaa.
     I   AGT 10 o'clock you DAT phone make AUX
     'I telephoned you at 10 o'clock.'

(11) mAI ne use   paise de   diye.
     I   AGT him:DAT money give AUX
     'I gave him the money.'

(Hook 1974: 166–7)

The elements here glossed AUX are the vector verbs. They are in the past tense, and are in fact homophonous with past tenses of verbs meaning 'to bring' (*lenaa*) and 'to give' (*denaa*). The main verb in (10) is *kar* 'make,' and in (11) *de* 'give.' In (11), then, 'give' appears as both the main verb (*de*) and the vector verb (*diye*). The semantic force of the auxiliary (the vector verb) is hard to specify, but in general it expresses perfectivity. Both of the sentences could be phrased with the main verb alone, as in:

(12) mAI ne   das baje   aap ko   fon   kiyaa.
     I   AGT 10 o'clock you DAT phone make
     'I telephoned you at 10 o'clock.'

(13) mAI ne   use   paise   diye.
     I   AGT him:DAT money give
     'I gave him (the) money.'

However, (12) leaves open the question of whether the call was successfully put through, while (10) would definitely suggest that the call was completed. (11) implies that all the money was given, while again (13) leaves this open. In other words, the compound verb has all of the semantic complexities of perfective aspect, such as emphasis on completion, full affectedness of the verb's object, and involvement of an agent. It should also be noted that there are certain types of construction where it is mandatory.

We have here a movement toward grammaticalization of a set of verbs which are becoming specialized as auxiliary verbs. It is interesting to trace the trajectory of this grammaticalization by looking both at earlier texts and at other Indo-Aryan languages closely related to Hindi in which the grammaticalization has not proceeded so far. This latter strategy is a highly convenient one because the languages are fully accessible and texts in the various cognate languages are available which are thematically similar or identical. Consider first the relative textual frequency of simple versus compound verbs in Hindi and some of the related languages (Hook 1991: 65). The following figures are the approximate proportions of compound verbs in texts among various languages of the group:

Shina (Gilgit)	0
Kashmiri	1
Marathi	3
Gujarati	6
Bengali	7
Marwari	8
Hindi-Urdu	9

That is to say, in comparable texts there are about nine times as many compound verbs in Hindi-Urdu as in Kashmiri, and twice as many in Gujarati as in Marathi. The sheer textual frequency is prima facie evidence of degree of grammaticalization.

Textual frequency is accompanied by differences in the kinds of main verbs which may be accompanied by one of the vector verbs. In Marathi, which represents a less advanced stage from the point of view of the grammaticalization of vector verbs as auxiliaries, there is a preference for a vector verb to be used only when the main verb is inherently unspecified according to completedness; in other words, they add aspectual information. In Hindi-Urdu, where vector verbs are more frequent, they have spread to environments in which they are redundant, that is, to inherently completive verbs, including communication verbs, which, in context, tend to be completive (as, for example, *she said*) (Hook 1991: 69–70). Table 5.1. shows the difference between Marathi and Hindi-Urdu with regard to the ratio of compound verbs to the total verb forms for certain classes of main verbs. In other words, as grammaticalization proceeds, the semantic range of the emergent grammatical morpheme expands or generalizes. The difference between Hindi and Marathi is a statistical one, not a categorical one. There still is no category of auxiliary verb in Hindi as distinct from Marathi, and there may never be. We may not be able to define auxiliary verb in such a way as to include the Hindi phenomena but exclude the Marathi ones. This "messiness" is in fact typical of languages.

Table 5.1 *Ratio of compound verbs in Marathi and Hindi-Urdu according to semantic class of main verb*

Semantic class of main verb	Marathi	Hindi-Urdu
Displacement or disposal	10%	44%
Creation/change of state	8%	30%
Change of psychic state	8%	8%
Sensation or perception	4%	8%
Mental action	4%	10%
Communication	2%	20%

Source: based on Hook (1991: 69)

One is reminded here of Lehmann's distinction between "primary" and "secondary" adpositions discussed above in connection with nominals. The vector verbs, being more numerous, semantically concrete, and more verb-like, are analogous to secondary adpositions. The true auxiliaries, being fewer in number and more general in meaning, are analogous to primary adpositions. As with adpositions, clear categorial discreteness is not in evidence, only a cluster of relationships on a cline from lexical to grammatical form.

Statistical evidence is a valuable tool in providing empirical evidence for unidirectionality. For diachronic studies access to texts of comparable genres over a fairly long period is needed. It is only in a few languages that we are fortunate enough to have this kind of textual history. And it is for only a small subset of these languages that we have any statistical studies at all of the development of grammatical items. There is an urgent need for additional reliable statistical studies of a variety of phenomena in which early grammaticalization appears to be involved. Among such studies, in addition to Hook (1991), there are Givón (1991a) on the development of relativizers, complementizers, and adverbial clause markers in Biblical Hebrew; Hopper and Martin (1987) on the development of the indefinite article in English, and Kytö (1991) on the development of auxiliaries *may/might* and *can/could* in English. Statistical work on a case where grammaticalization is already so far advanced as to be unmistakable may be illustrated by Kroch (1989a, 1989b) and Stein (1990a) on the history of English *do*. Statistical studies of changes that appear to be occurring in current speech situations include Givón (1991b) on verb serialization in four languages of Papua New Guinea, and Thompson and Mulac (1991) on parenthetical *I think* in English (discussed below in Section 7.5.4). More work is necessary to diagnose grammaticalization in its early stages and to develop the kinds of statistical parameters which will reveal it.

5.3.3 Multiple paths

So far our examples in this chapter have been of changes along a single cline. Not all cases of grammaticalization are of this kind, however. Some show development along two or possibly more different clines. Craig has given the name "polygrammaticalization" to such multiple developments, where a single form develops different grammatical functions in different constructions. Her example is from Rama. As alluded to in Section 4.3.2 in connection with example (23), **bang* 'go' in Rama developed into: (i) a temporal marker in the verbal domain; (ii) a purposive adposition in the nominal domain, and then a conjunction in the complex sentence domain (conjunctions are analyzed as adpositions to clauses, see Section 7.3). Givón (1991b) shows that relative clause morphology, specifically Biblical Hebrew *'asher* (probably derived from *'athar* 'place'), later reduced to *she*, spread both into adverbial clause domains such as causatives, and also into complementizer domains. Lord (1976) shows that 'say'-complementizers generalize in different languages to causal clauses in languages such as Yoruba and Telegu, and to conditionals in Gã. Development along such multiple paths into different grammatical domains conforms to unidirectionality in that the later forms are more grammatical (abstract, reduced, generalized) than the earlier ones.

Not all multiple paths show split, however. Just as in phonology we find split and merger or convergence, so in grammaticalization we find that sometimes forms from several slightly different domains may converge on one grammatical domain, provided that there is pragmatic, semantic, and syntactic appropriateness. The phenomenon of convergence from various sub-paths of grammaticalization is often described in terms of the metaphor of convergence in "semantic space." One example is provided by Kemmer (1992, forthcoming b), who charts the domain of reflexives and middle voice. In her characterization of these domains, the reflexive construction expresses situations where the initiator and endpoint of the event refer to the same entity, but are conceived as conceptually different, as in *hit oneself, see oneself*. Middle voice constructions such as *wash (oneself)*, *dress, get angry, think* are similar in that they express situations where initiator and endpoint in the event are the same entity, but they are different in that the conceptual difference is less than that in reflexive situations. Kemmer (1992) shows that the generalization of reflexives into middles is very common cross-linguistically (see also Faltz 1988), but other sources are evidenced too, such as passive and reciprocal (the 'each other' construction). Other semantic maps with multiple sub-paths have been suggested for evidentials (L. Anderson 1986) and conditionals (Traugott 1985b).

5.4 Some processes participating in unidirectionality

Several processes typical of grammaticalization contribute to semantic and/or structural generalization and decategorialization. They may, however, at first glance appear to complexify the process, and to raise questions about it. We will discuss three typical processes: specialization, whereby the choice of grammatical forms becomes reduced as certain ones become generalized in meaning and use; divergence, whereby a less grammatical form may split into two, one variant maintaining its former characteristics, the other becoming more grammatical; and thirdly, renewal, whereby old forms are renewed as more expressive ways are found of saying the same thing.

5.4.1 Specialization

In considering textual frequency and semantic generalization of the sort discussed in connection with Indo-Aryan compound verbs above, we might imagine that this textual frequency and semantic generalization could in theory proceed with exactly the same set of vector verbs at each stage. However, as the semantic range of individual vector verbs becomes greater and more general, the chances of overlap and ambiguity on the fringes are bound to increase, and some of the vector verbs will become redundant. Hook (1991: 75) notes that:

(a)   In both the Hindi-Urdu and the Marathi text samples, the most frequently occurring vector verb was the one meaning GO. But in Hindi-Urdu GO accounted for 44% of all vector verbs in the sample, while in Marathi it accounted for only 32% of all vector verbs.

(b)   The five most frequent vector verbs in the Hindi-Urdu text sample accounted for 92% of the total number of vector verbs; while in Marathi the five most frequent vector verbs accounted for only 82% of the total number.

(c)   In the Hindi-Urdu text sample, only 10 different verbs were used as vector verbs; in the Marathi sample, 14 different verbs were used as vector verbs.

These statistics suggest that in Hindi as some vector verbs become more frequent, others are becoming less so. A handful of verbs is gaining the ascendancy in the competition for auxiliary status. This exemplifies specialization, the process of reducing the variety of formal choices available as the meanings assume greater grammatical generality (Bréal 1991 [1882]: 143; Hopper 1991: 22). Here again we see a major difference between lexical and grammatical items. In any domain of meaning the number of lexical items will vastly exceed the number of grammatical morphemes. Moreover, lexical items form an open class, which can be added to indefinitely, while the inventory of grammatical morphemes is added to only very sparingly, by items originating in the lexical class. If we compare, for example, the number of tense and aspect distinctions which are expressed grammatically in a given language with the number of ways of modifying actions and events available through lexical adverbs, we can see immediately that the process of grammaticalization is a selective one in which only a few lexical forms end up as grammatical morphemes. However, old forms may continue to coexist (see especially 5.5.1 on "layering" below); therefore specialization does not necessarily entail the elimination of alternatives, but may be manifested simply as textual preferences, conditioned by semantic types, sociolinguistic contexts, discourse genres, and other factors.

Another good example of specialization is the Modern French negative construction, which in the written language consists of a negative particle *ne* before the verb and a supportive particle, usually *pas*, after it:

(14) Il ne   boit   pas   de   vin.
      he NEG drinks NEG PARTIT wine
      'He doesn't drink wine.'

As mentioned in Section 3.6, at earlier stages of French, predicate negation
was accomplished by *ne* alone placed before the verb. This *ne* was itself a
proclitic form of Latin *non*, Old French *non*. Already in Old French, a
variety of adverbially used nouns suggesting a least quantity (Gamillscheg
1957: 753) could be placed after the verb in order to reinforce the weakened
negation. These reinforcing forms included; among others:

> *pas* 'step, pace'
> *point* 'dot, point'
> *mie* 'crumb'
> *gote* 'drop'
> *amende* 'almond'
> *areste* 'fish-bone'
> *beloce* 'sloe'
> *eschalope* 'pea-pod'

They seem originally to have functioned to focus attention on the negation
itself, rather than on the verb being negated; without the reinforcer, the
focus of attention would fall on the verb (Gamillscheg 1957: 755). By the
sixteenth century, the only ones still used with negative force were *pas*,
point, *mie* and *goutte*, all of them more general terms than those which were
no longer used. Even in the sixteenth century, *pas* and *point* predominated,
and by the modern period these were the only two which were still in use.
Of the two remaining, there is a clear sense in which *pas* is the only
"umarked" complement to *ne* in negation. It is by far the more frequent in
discourse, it participates in more constructions than *point*, and is semantically more neutral, *point* being an emphatic negator. *Point* today denotes
only emphatic negation contradicting a previous assertion (though there is
some possibility that this semantic distinction between *pas* and *point* was
originally an artifact of French grammarians). In other words, *point* cannot
be relatively negative, perhaps because of the operation of persistence (see
Section 4.5) – a 'point' is not relative. Therefore in a sense *pas* is the only
form which has become fully grammaticalized out of an array of forms
which could reinforce negation in Old French. It has also become a negative
morpheme in its own right in a number of contexts (*pas moi* 'not me,' *pas
plus tard qu'hier* 'not later than yesterday,' etc.), and in the spoken language

the *ne* of ordinary verbal negation is usually dropped (*je sais pas* 'I don't know'), leaving *pas* as the only mark of negation.

This "thinning out" of the field of candidates for grammaticalization as negators is accompanied, as usual, by a shift of meaning, in this case from the lexical meaning 'step, pace' to the grammatical meaning of negation. There is in this instance no phonological change peculiar to the grammaticalized form, and no fusion with neighboring words. The original noun *pas* lives on in its earlier meaning of 'step, pace,' and it remains completely homophonous with the negative particle.

Before leaving the example of French negators, it is worth while to consider its implications for the discourse motivations of grammaticalization. The origins of the use of concrete nouns as reinforcers of negation cannot be documented, but it is reasonable to surmise that they were once linked to specific verbs. Presumably *mie* 'crumb' was once collocated with verbs of eating, i.e., 'he hasn't eaten a crumb,' or perhaps – in a milieu where food was scarce and bread a common means of payment for services rendered – giving, and so on: 'they didn't pay/give me a crumb.' Similarly with *goutte* 'drop': 'he hasn't drunk a drop.' With *pas* 'step,' the verb must have been a verb of motion: 'he hasn't gone a step.' We may compare the vernacular English use of 'drop' and 'spot' in (15), where the context of *drop* has similarly been expanded in a way that suggests incipient grammaticalization:

(15) He didn't get a drop (spot) of applause.

Bit (i.e., a small bite, cf. German *bißchen*) is of course normal in such contexts for all dialects.

There is nothing strictly conceptual (semantic) about nouns such as 'peapod,' 'crumb,' 'step,' and the others which would predict that they would become negators. They are not all intrinsically "minimal quantities" of things, but they assume that meaning when combined in discourse with negators. However much in retrospect we see semantic commonalities in the ways in which forms evolve, it is important to keep in mind that ultimately its roots and motivations are in real speech and real collocations, and that the study of how forms are distributed in discourse is indispensable in understanding grammaticalization.

5.4.2 *Divergence*

When a lexical form undergoes grammaticalization to a clitic or affix, the original lexical form may remain as an autonomous element and undergo the same changes as ordinary lexical items (Hopper 1991: 22). This characteristic of "divergence" is a natural outcome of the process of grammaticalization, which begins as a fixing of a lexical form in a specific potentially grammatical environment, where the form takes on a new meaning (the same phenomenon is called "split" in Heine and Reh 1984: 57–9). Since the context of incipient grammaticalization is only one of the many contexts in which the lexical form may appear, when the form undergoes grammaticalization, it behaves just like any other autonomous form in its other, lexical, contexts, and is subject to semantic and phonological changes and perhaps even to becoming obsolete.

Consider, for example, the English indefinite article *a/an*. In OE this word was *an*. Its vowel was long, the same as the vowel in the word for 'stone,' *stan*. It meant 'one, a certain,' and was not used in the general non-specific sense that we might use it in today, as in *I caught a fish*, but was chiefly used to "present" new items, as in *There was once a prince of Tuscany*.

The normal phonetic development of this word in PDE would have been [own], rhyming with 'stone.' While in Scottish Engish the two words continue to have the same vowel ([eyn/steyn]), in most other dialects a phonological development peculiar to this word occurred yielding the PDE full form [wʌn]. The cliticized form of this same word became de-stressed, and formed a single accentual unit with the following noun or constituent of the noun phrase (adjective, etc.), resulting in its PDE form and distribution: the vowel [ə], and retention of the [n] when followed by a vowel. The divergent histories of the stressed and unstressed forms can be seen in alternations such as the following:

(16)   Would you like *a* Mai Tai? – Yes, I'd love *one*.

We turn now to a more detailed example of divergence, from Malay. Nouns in certain discourse contexts in Malay must be preceded by a classifier (Hopper 1986b). Classifiers occur in many languages in association with number words; they are comparable to the word 'head' in 'ten head of cattle' (see Schachter 1985: 39–40). The following examples are from a Malay narrative text known as the *Hikayat Abdullah*:

(17)   Ada-lah kami lihat tiga   *orang*   budak-budak kena
       happen we   see   three <CL> boy-PL   get
       hukum.
       punishment
       'We happened to see three <CL> boys being punished.'
                                                (Hopper 1986b: 64)

117

(18) Maka pada suatu pagi   kelihatan-lah sa-*buah* kapal
      and   on one morning was:seen-*lah* a-<CL> ship
      rendah.
      low
      'Then one morning a <CL> low ship was sighted.'

(p. 77)

(19) Mati-lah tiga *ekor*   tikus.
      dead-*lah* three <CL> rat
      'Three <CL> rats were killed.'

(p. 144)

The italicized words *orang, buah*, and *ekor* are classifiers. In Malay they indicate that the noun which is classified is new and relatively important to the discourse. They are not interchangeable: *orang* is used before human nouns, *buah* before objects of a bulky size, and *ekor* before nouns which denote animals of any kind. There is in addition a more general classificatory word *suatu* (also found as *satu*), used before singular objects (in the sense of 'things') and competing with *buah*:

(20) Maka di-beri-nya hadiah akan Sultan itu *suatu*   kereta
      and   he-gave   as-gift to Sultan the a:<CL> carriage
      bogi.
      buggy
      'And he gave a <CL> buggy carriage to the Sultan as a gift.'

(p. 166)

The classifiers themselves are preceded, as in these examples, by a number word such as *tiga* 'three,' or the singular clitic *sa-* 'one, a.' However, *suatu* is only singular and is not preceded by *sa-* or any other number word or quantifier; the reason for this, as we shall see, is that the *s-* of *suatu* is itself historically the same singular morpheme *sa-* that is found with the other classifiers when the classified noun is singular.

In Malay, as in other classifier languages, most of the classifiers double as autonomous nouns. *Buah* means 'fruit,' *orang* 'person, man,' and *ekor* 'tail.' There is thus a divergence between a lexical meaning and a grammaticalized meaning. On occasions when the two come together, a sort of haplology (contraction of adjacent identical material) occurs; while the word for a Malay person is *orang Malayu*, one instance of *orang* stands duty for both the classifier *orang* and the head noun *orang*. Consequently, 'five Malay men' is:

(21) lima *orang*   Malayu
      five \<CL\>/men Malay

rather than

(22) *lima *orang* orang Malayu

Similarly, with *buah*: a pomegranate is *buah delima*, but if the expression is classified, in place of *sa-buah buah delima* 'a pomegranate,' *sa-buah delima* is used.[4] The constraint against *orang*, *buah*, etc. occurring with homophonous lexical items shows that grammaticalization has not proceeded so far that these classifiers and their cognate lexical noun are sensed as being formally unrelated.

With *suatu* the situation is quite different. While this form competes with *sa-buah* as the classifier for bulky inanimate objects, it is often used with abstract nouns in contexts where *sa-buah* would not be appropriate, e.g., *suatu khabar* 'a piece of news,' *suatu akhtiar* 'an idea.' The form *suatu* is in the modern language somewhat archaic and literary; it is generally pronounced and written *satu*, and has, significantly, become something like a strong indefinite article. It is also the numeral 'one' when counting 'one, two, three, etc.,' and in this sense often corresponds in the texts to English 'one' in 'one day, one morning,' etc. The older form with *u* (*suatu*) suggests a reconstruction *sa watu 'one stone,' with a noun *watu 'stone' having cognates in Javanese *watu* 'stone' and Malay *batu* 'stone.' The phonological change from initial *w* to initial *b* before *a* has several parallels in Malay. However, *batu* does not serve as a classifier in modern Malay, although it would not be at all strange if it did. There is a classifier *biji* whose corresponding lexical noun means 'seed,' and which is used for smallish round objects; larger objects, as we have seen, are classified with *buah*. Presumably *watu as a classifier once covered a similar range, classifying three-dimensional objects of an indeterminate size. The older form *watu 'stone' continues as a frozen classifier embedded in an indefinite article-like quantifier meaning roughly 'a, one.' It is distributed in the texts much like the complex *sa-* + classifier, referring to new and prominent things in the discourse, but it occurs preferentially with nouns which do not belong in an "obvious" category for one of the established classifiers. Interestingly, in the texts it is often used with abstract nouns, many of them of Arabic origin, and with nouns denoting concrete objects not in the traditional Malay cultural registry.

The evolution represented by *watu 'stone' > *sa watu 'a (classifier for smallish objects?)' > *sa watu 'a (classifier for every kind of ob-

ject)' > *suatu* 'one/a (with abstract or non-traditional objects)' > *satu* 'one/
a (with any noun)' is a paradigm case of grammaticalization. It exemplifies
persistence, that is, the grammaticalized construction is constrained by its
origins: a real classifier is not also used if a noun is quantified with *s(u)atu*,
e.g., *suatu buah rumah 'one house' is excluded: only *suatu rumah* or
sa-buah rumah are permitted. This constraint against *suatu buah rumah
can be explained by the fact that *suatu* itself historically already contains a
classifier. It is also an example of divergence. A form assumes two distinct
functions (lexical noun and classifier). One of these functions (that of lexical
noun) is found in an environment where it is exposed to a phonological
process (initial *w-* > *b-* before *a*) from which the other function is insulated
(when protected from initial position by the proclitic *sa-*, *w-* did not undergo
the change). The result is that the two forms *satu* and *batu* are no longer felt
as cognate by speakers of the language. For example, *satu batu* 'a/one
stone ~ a/one mile' is unobjectionable, whereas, as we have seen, *sa-orang
orang* 'a/one person,' or *sa-buah buah* 'a/one fruit' are avoided.

It should be added that phonological (allomorphic) split of the kind we
have described for Malay *batu/suatu* is not necessary for this kind of
divergence to occur, nor is it a required outcome of the process. In many
instances the autonomous lexical item and its grammaticalized counterpart
may cooccur quite happily in the same construction; e.g., the English
auxiliary verb *do* frequently occurs with *do* as main verb (*do do it!*; *they do
do that*).

As mentioned in 3.2, there has in the past been a tendency to think of
change in terms of "A uniformly > B." Given such an approach, divergence might seem to be an unlikely characteristic. However, as we have
noted, change must always be seen in terms of variation, and the formula
for change should therefore be A > A/B > B. Even so, it still needs to be
stated that it is by no means inevitable that A will disappear. A and B may
instead each go their own ways and continue to coexist as divergent reflexes
of a historically single form over many centuries, even millennia. An
example is the development and persistence from ME on of constructions of
the type *The more he complains, the angrier he gets.* This construction
originated in a comparative introduced by *þy,* the instrumental form of the
demonstrative. The new form has coexisted with the demonstrative *that*
from which it derives, and with the article *the* which it resembles in form,
but does not have the syntax of either. The formula should ideally therefore
be further modified to A > B/A (> B).

5.4.3   Renewal

In divergence existing forms take on new meaning in certain contexts, while retaining old meanings in other contexts. We turn now to a process whereby existing meanings may take on new forms: renewal.

If all grammaticalization leads to decategorialization and ultimately to minimal, compacted forms, how is it that language users can ensure that languages continue to serve their purposes of organizing cognition and achieving communication? This question is in part answered by the hypothesis of competing motivations of increasing informativeness versus routinization. But does this mean that unidirectionality is a chimera? The answer is that new structures keep being grammaticalized through the process that Meillet termed "renouvellement" or "renewal," and that instances of renewal consistently show evidence of unidirectionality once the renewal has set in.

A vivid example of renewal is the recent history of English intensifiers (words such as *very* in *very dangerous*). At different times in the last two centuries the following among others have been fashionable: *awfully, frightfully, fearfully, terribly, incredibly, really, pretty, truly* (cf. *very*, which is cognate with French *vrai* 'true') (Stoffel 1901). Even in the written language, *very* often alternates with such words as *most, surprisingly, extremely, highly, extraordinarily*. Over time, however, we can expect the choices to be reduced, owing to specialization.

Intensifiers are especially subject to renewal, presumably because of their markedly emotional function. They are unusual in undergoing renewal especially frequently. But certain other categories, although not as short-lived as intensifiers, are also renewed with some degree of predictability. Negative constructions are one example. In spoken English expressions such as *no way* (cf. *No way we're taking this stuff*) are replacing simple *n't*, from *not*, itself a contraction of *na wiht* 'no thing.' Schwegler (1988) writes of a "psycholinguistic proclivity" for the development of negative emphasizers, and shows how they have their starting point in contexts of contradiction, in other words, in emotionally loaded contexts. Coordinators, too, seem often to undergo renewal; for example, in the Indo-European languages the commonest sentence linker, corresponding to English *and*, rarely has a cognate with the same function in another branch of the family.

The example of negative renewal shows that sometimes old forms (in this case *n-*) may be involved in the new structure (but not in exactly the same way as before). Another example is provided by the reinforcement in

Surselvan (Rhaeto-Romance) of reflexive *se* by the form *sesez* (Kemmer 1992). In most Romance languages the reflexive *se* serves both reflexive and middle functions. However, in Surselvan the reflexive has been reinforced by an emphatic version of itself while the original *se* now serves only middle functions.

The renewal of one form by another may or may not occur in the same constituent position. English intensifiers such as *awfully* and Surselvan *sesez* are simply substitutes, involving no new syntactic or phonological strategy. But sometimes renewal may involve a more strategic overhaul. The spoken English negator *no way* has little in common syntactically with the *n't* with which it competes. The French negative reinforcer *pas*, which is assuming the role of general negator, occurs after rather than before the verb, reflecting a change that could be represented over several centuries as:

ne va 'doesn't go' > *ne va pas* > *va pas*

Similarly in English the original negator *ne* preceded the verb, as in (23):

(23)   Ne canst þu huntian   butan mid nettum?
       not know you hunt-INF except with nets
       'Do you not know how to hunt with anything but nets?'

(c. 1000, Ælfr Coll. 62)

Being subject to reduction through rapid speech, it could even combine with some verbs, e.g., *ne wæs* 'not was' > *næs, ne wolde* 'not wanted' > *nolde*. But the new, phonologically fuller, *not* that replaced it followed the verb, as in (24):

(24)   . . . that moves not him: though that be sick, it dies not.

(c. 1600, Shakespeare, *Henry IV* Part 2.*II*.ii.113)

Such differences in syntax between older forms and their replacements or renewals are often subject to word order changes that are on going in the language, or may even contribute to them.

Renewal by a non-cognate item to effect semantic expressiveness probably underlies most examples of the development of innovative periphrasis in the process of word order changes. This appears to be true of the development of periphrastic markers of modality, such as *will*, *shall*, and *must*, which convey more precise differences of meaning than the older subjunctive inflection, and the development of phrasal case markers such as *to* and *of*, which also tend to convey more differences than the earlier inflectional cases. Langacker has called periphrasis "the major mechanism for achieving perceptual optimality in syntax" (1977: 105). One way of defining periphrasis is to characterize it as fulfilling the following criteria (cited in Vincent, forthcoming b; based on Dietrich 1973): the meaning of the periphrasis is not deducible from the constituent elements; the periphrastic construction shows syntactic unity at some level of analysis, where it did not do so before; the new periphrasis competes paradigmatically with other morphologically relevant categories.

Once renewal occurs, the new form may itself be subject to grammaticalization and reduction, through rapid speech and routinization, as in the case of *not* > *n't*. This is one factor that makes grammaticalization a continuously occurring phenomenon. The question is when this renewal is understood to occur. When the same structure is renewed, some speak of "recursive cycles" of grammaticalization. Some think of the cycle as starting with reduction of a form, in extreme cases to zero, followed by replacement with a more expressive form (e.g., Heine and Reh 1984: 17; Lightfoot 1991: 171). This kind of model is extremely problematic, because it suggests that a stage of language can exist when it is difficult or even impossible to express some concept.

Rather than replace a lost or almost lost distinction, newly innovated forms compete with older ones because they are felt to be more expressive than what was available before. This competition allows, even encourages, the recession or loss of older forms. Textual evidence provides strong support for this view of coexisting competing forms and constructions, rather than a cycle of loss and renewal. The periphrastic future form existed in Late Latin long before the eventual loss of future *-b-* and its replacement by *-r-*. In contemporary French and other Romance languages, the inflectional *-r-*future is itself in competition with a more "expressive" periphrastic construction with *aller*, cf. *j'irai* 'I will go,' and *je vais aller* 'I will/plan to go.' Furthermore, when the syntactic structures of the older and newer forms differ, they may be used side by side in the same utterance (cf. French *ne va pas*, and Middle English *ne might not*). When the syntactic structure is the same, but the lexical items are different, alternate usages coexist, as in the case of *very* and *awfully*.

5.5   A synchronic result of unidirectionality

As we have seen in the context of discussion of persistence and divergence, old forms may persist for a long period of time. Renewal results primarily in alternate ways of saying approximately the same thing, or alternate ways of organizing linguistic material. The persistence of older forms and meanings alongside newer forms and meanings, whether derived by divergence from the same source or by renewal from different sources, leads to an effect that can be called "layering" or "variability" at any one synchronic moment in time. We turn now to some comments about this characteristic of grammaticalization.

5.5.1 *Layering*

Within a broad functional domain, new layers are continually emerging; in the process the older layers are not necessarily discarded, but may remain to coexist with and interact with new layers (Hopper 1991: 22). Layering is the synchronic result of successive grammaticalization of forms which contribute to the same domain.

In any single language there is always considerable synchronic diversity within one domain. Some of the most obvious cases are those where a full and a reduced form coexist, with related forms and only minimally different functions. An example is the coexistence in Classical Armenian of three demonstratives: *ays* 'close to first person,' *ayd* 'close to second person,' *ayn* 'close to third person,' and three articles -*s*, -*d*, -*n* (Greenberg 1985: 277). In such cases it is a reasonable hypothesis that the reduced form is the later form. In other cases a variety of different forms and constructions may coexist that serve similar (though not identical) functional purposes. A small fragment of the PDE repertoire of tense-aspect-modal indicators suggests the potential range involved:

(25) a. Vowel changes in the verb stem: *take, took*
     b. (Weak) alveolar suffix: *look/looked*
     c. Modal auxiliaries: *will take/shall take*
     d. Have V-en: *has taken*
     e. Be V-ing: *is taking*
     f. Keep on V-ing: *kept on eating*
     g. Keep V-ing: *kept eating*
     h. Be going to V: *is going to take*

(There are, of course, many more.) In cases like this is it a reasonable hypothesis that the most bonded forms have the longest histories in their present grammatical functions, and that the least bonded are the most recent.

Yet another example given comes from Estonian. Relative clauses in Estonian may be formed in two ways, one being a construction with a relative pronoun and a finite verb (26a) and the other with a participial verb and no pronoun (26b):

(26) a. Vanake silmitse-s   kaua   inimes-t
          old-man observe-PAST:3SG for-a-long-time person-PARTIT
          kes sammu-s   üle   õue   elumaja
          REL go-PAST:3SG across courtyard:GEN residential
          poole.
          building:ILL
          'For a long time the old man observed the person who was
          going across the courtyard to the residential building.'

     b. Vanake silmitses   kaua   üle
          old-man observe:PAST-3SG for-a-long-time across
          õue   elumaja   poole   sammu-vat
          courtyard:GEN residential building:ILL go-PRES:PART
          inimes-t.
          person-PARTIT

                                        (Comrie 1981b: 123–4)

The second type in (26b), the relative clause of which is constructed around
a present participle, i.e., a non-finite verb, is literally something like 'The
old man watched for a long time the across the courtyard of the residential
building going person.' Such clauses are characteristic of a learned or
archaic style (Comrie 1981b: 134); the more usual way of forming relative
clauses in Estonian is with a relative pronoun and a finite verb, as in (26a).

Typically, grammaticalization does not result in the filling of any obvious
functional gap. On the contrary, the forms that have been grammaticalized
compete with existing constructions so similar in function that any explanation involving "filling a gap" seems out of the question – there is no obvious
gap to be filled. We saw that in Ewe, verbs of saying evolved into new
complementizers at the same time as older complementizers – themselves
grammaticalized verbs of saying – were still available. Latin periphrastic
futures of the kind *cantare habet* "he has to sing > he will sing" coexisted at
one stage with morphological futures of the type *cantabit* "he will sing," and
eventually replaced them.

During any phase of coexistence there are some contexts in which the two
(or more) types in question involve a clear pragmatic difference. There are
other contexts in which the choice between them is less clear with respect to
pragmatic difference. Frequently we find that one of the competing forms
predominates (specialization), and eventually extends its range of meanings
to include those of the construction which it replaces. In this way,
historically continuous speech communities may, through repeated

                                                               125

renewals, retain categories (such as the future tense) for a considerable length of time while other speech communities have never developed them.

Quite often the newer layers of functionally similar constructions are symptomatic of more global adjustments. Estonian (like the other members of the Balto-Finnic branch of Uralic) is a language historically of the OV type which has become thoroughly permeated with VO features from its Germanic and Slavic neighbors. The two different ways of forming relative clauses exemplified in (26) are part of this change in type. The older type, in which a participial clause precedes the head noun, is characteristic of OV languages. The newer type, with a finite verb and a relative pronoun, is characteristic of VO languages.

5.6 Counterexamples to unidirectionality

The strong hypothesis of unidirectionality claims that all grammaticalization involves shifts in specific linguistic contexts from lexical item to grammatical item, or from less to more grammatical item, and that grammaticalization clines are irreversible. Change proceeds from higher to lower, never from lower to higher on the cline. Extensive though the evidence of unidirectionality is, it cannot be regarded as an absolute principle. Some counterexamples do exist. Their existence, and their relative infrequency, in fact help define our notion of what prototypical grammaticalization is.

One putative kind of counterexample to the proposal that grammaticalization involves changes in the degree of grammaticalness of an item has been proposed by Nichols and Timberlake (1991). The authors point out that in the history of Russian there have been changes in the uses to which the instrumental case has been put that are akin to grammaticalization in so far as they involve the coding of grammatical relationships, but are unlike grammaticalization in its prototypical directional sense, in so far as they simply demonstrate a shift in the way relatively stable grammatical networks operate. Thus in Old Russian, the instrumental was allowed only with nouns expressing status or role (e.g., 'tsar,' 'secular leader,' 'nun') that could change over time, and only in contexts of entering that status (inception), or continuing in it for a period of time. Later Russian, however, virtually requires the instrumental with such nouns referring to status or role, and also quasi-status nouns (agentive nouns such as 'bribe-giver,' 'bribe-taker') can now allow the instrumental in contexts of durative aspect. This example certainly shows that grammatical morphemes can remain stable over a very long period of time. There is no case of "more > less grammatical" here. However, as the authors themselves say: "the overall effect has been to fix usage in one domain and develop variation in another" (Nichols and Timberlake 1991: 142). In other words, the history of the Russian instrumental is in fact an example of prototypical rule generalization and spread. Rather than being a counterexample to the unidirectionality of grammaticalization, it is only an example of rule generalization over a lengthy period of time (about 1,500 years). It also illustrates the potential longevity of certain types of grammatical organization, and suggests that persistence is not limited to the meanings of grammatical items, but is also evidenced by purely grammatical inflections.

Probably the most often cited putative counterexamples are those involving the lexicalization of grammatical items, as in *to up the ante, that was a downer, his uppers need dental work*. Similar examples can be found in other languages. For example, in German and French the second person singular familiar pronouns *du* and *tu* are lexicalized as the verbs *duzen* and *tutoyer*, respectively, both meaning "to use the familiar address form." Since lexicalization is a process distinct from grammaticalization, is not unidirectional, and can recruit material of all kinds (including acronyms, e.g., *scuba* < Self-contained Underwater Breathing Apparatus), data of this kind can and, we believe, should be considered examples of the recruitment of linguistic material to enrich the lexicon. In other words, they are not part of grammaticalization as a process, but rather of lexicalization.[5]

Some less clear examples involve the incorporation and fossilization of earlier independent grammatical morphemes into lexical material, for example, the freezing of *to-* in *today*. We have discussed the case of the development of an independent "affirmative adverb" *ep* in Estonian, in connection with reanalysis (Section 3.5). In this language a new question word *es* also appeared as a result of reanalysis of morpheme boundaries, and loss of vowel harmony (Campbell 1991: 291). In many languages what originate as phonologically predictable alternations may eventually be morphologized (e.g., *foot–feet* is the modern reflex of an earlier stage when the plural was *fot-i*; phonetically, the *o* was fronted before the *-i*, and when the *-i* (plural marker) was lost for phonological reasons, the fronted vowel remained as the marker of plurality). These examples and others show that there is a point at which grammaticalization as a unidirectional process and lexicalization as a non-unidirectional one may intersect. We will discuss a further example in connection with subordination strategies in 7.4.

Such counterexamples should caution us against making uncritical inferences about directions of grammaticalization where historical data is not available. Usually such inferences are justified, however, and the rare counterexamples should not be allowed to deprive us of a useful descriptive method and an important source of data. But the possibility of an anomalous development can never be absolutely excluded.

An interesting possible source of counterexamples to unidirectionality is the development of "adaptive rules" (Andersen 1973). A language user who has developed a new rule is likely to find that at certain points Output2 does not match Output1. Therefore the individual may be misunderstood, or ridiculed, etc. Such an individual may develop "cover-up" rules that are not integrated into his or her grammar, but which in essence permit output analogous to that of users of Output1. Hypercorrection (overuse of an item considered to be socially or stylistically salient) is of this kind. For example, the speaker who has not acquired a *who–whom* distinction may attempt to accommodate to users who do make such a distinction and produce utterances such as *Whom did you say was looking for me?* In a study of such rules, Disterheft (1990) suggests that hypercorrections are particularly often found in writing. She cites Stein's (1990b) study of the replacement in the fifteenth century of the third singular present tense marker *-th* by *-s*. The *-s* form spread gradually in different syntactic and phonological environments and increased in frequency until *c.* 1600. However, just before the turn of the century, *-th* increased in frequency, dropping off again in the seventeenth century. The resurgence of *-th* is evidence, it is argued, for an adaptive rule which led to overuse of the older form in a written Standard developed from Chancery English owing to association of the *-th* with "high style." If so, this (and other sociolinguistic data discussed in Labov 1972) suggests that adaptive rules may for the most part be typical of adult rather than child language users. As Disterheft points out, they make the effects of abductive change (i.e., reanalysis) hard to detect. Hence they may give the impression of greater gradualness of change than was actually the case. Furthermore, they may obscure (or even divert) the natural path of change, and so may lead to counterexamples to unidirectionality.

5.7 An unresolved question[6]

Unidirectionality is a strong hypothesis. The evidence is overwhelming that a vast number of known instances of the development of grammatical structures involved the development of a lexical item or phrase through discourse use into a grammatical item, and then into an even more grammatical item, and that these changes were accompanied by decategorialization from a major to a minor category. Counterexamples are few. All are of a specific type: more grammatical items become less so. To date there is no evidence that grammatical items arise full-fledged, that is, can be innovated without a prior lexical history in a remote (or less remote) past. Some grammatical items show enormous longevity, and we cannot look back into their pre-history. Among the highly stable grammatical items with no known lexical origin is the Indo-European demonstrative *to-*. Given the unidirectionality hypothesis, we must hypothesize that *to-* originated in some currently unknown lexical item. We do not at this stage of our knowledge know what that item was. But neither do we know that there was none, or indeed that there might theoretically have been none. We must leave for future empirical study the question whether grammatical items can arise fully formed, and if so under what circumstances.

6
Clause-internal morphological changes

6.1 Introduction

We turn now to more specific instances of the unidirectionality discussed in the preceding chapter with a focus on the kinds of changes that typically occur clause-internally. In the next chapter we consider cross-clause changes.

In the first part of this chapter we look in some detail at examples of "compacting" – the fusing of erstwhile independent elements with each other, most especially the development of clitics into inflections. This process is often called "morphologization."[1] Then we look in some detail at examples of the development of grammatical forms in two domains: that of the paradigm, and that of argument structure, specifically subject and object marking. Finally we consider the "end" of grammaticalization: loss.

6.2 Morphologization

In French and most other Romance languages adverbial formations such as the following are found:

(1) lentement 'slowly'
     fermement 'firmly'
     doucement 'softly, sweetly'

(Lausberg 1962: III/1, 95–8)

For a large class of adjectives, a corresponding adverb is derived by adding the adverbial suffix *-ment* to the feminine form, e.g., *lent* 'slow (masc.),' *lente* 'slow (fem.),' *lente-ment* 'slowly.' This suffix was originally an autonomous word, Latin *mente* 'mind + ablative case.' Its beginnings as an adverbial suffix are to be sought in such phrases as *clara mente* 'with a clear mind.' However, it is no longer restricted to psychological senses, but is a general adverb formative, as in:

130

(2)   L'eau coule doucement.
      'The water flows softly.'

In Old French (and in Modern Spanish and some other Romance languages) there are still traces of the autonomy of *mente*, in that it tends to appear only once with conjoined adjectives: *humble e doucement* 'humbly and gently' (cf. Spanish *clara y concisamente* 'clearly and concisely').

The history of the French suffix *-ment* is a straightforward instance of grammaticalization: a new grammatical formative has come into existence out of a formerly autonomous word. It has done so in a familiar manner, by ousting its competitors such as *modo* 'manner,' *guise* 'way, fashion' (specialization), and by forming a progressively closer grammatical relationship with the adjective stem. Semantically, too, the Latin word *mente* 'mind + ablative case' has lost its restriction to psychological states. The once independent lexical item *mente* has progressed all the way down the cline that leads to affixation to a stem. An affix such as French *-ment* which was once an independent word and has become a bound morpheme is said to be morphologized, and its historical lexical source (in this case, Latin *mente*) is said to have undergone morphologization.

Where long written histories are available, many bound morphemes can be shown to go back to independent words. Often, too, a historical source in independent words can be assumed through inspection of synchronic divergent forms. For example, in Buryat Mongolian (Comrie 1980: 88) person-number suffixes on the verb are clearly related to independent pronouns in the nominative case, as shown in Table 6.1. But as we have seen in previous chapters, not every instance of grammaticalization involves morphologization. For example, modal auxiliaries in English are grammaticalized out of earlier full verbs, but they have not (yet) become affixes.

The beginnings of morphologization must be sought in repeated use of syntactic constructions. Some linguists, among them Chafe (1970) have

Table 6.1 *Buryat Mongolian pronouns and verb endings*

	Pronoun	V ending
1 singular	bi	-b
2 singular	ši	-š
1 plural	bide	-bdi
2 plural	ta	-t

Source: based on Comrie (1980: 88)

insisted that "syntax" itself is only morphology writ large, and that units of discourse – sentences – are structured with the same kinds of rules as those by which words are internally structured. The study of grammaticalization to some extent supports such a view, in that the conceptual boundaries separating constituents such as sentence, phrase, and word often seem somewhat arbitrary, and there is a continual movement among them. While at any synchronic stage there may sometimes be reasons for setting up such discrete constituent types, from a historical perspective the relationship between a stem and an affix can only be considered in the context of the phrasal and even higher level syntax from which they are derived.

Virtually by definition, morphologization is that part of grammaticalization that primarily involves the second and third parts of the cline:

lexical item > clitic > affix

Such a cline is of course a gross oversimplification of the highly detailed facts of language. For various detailed hypotheses about how to approach some of the historical phenomena encompassed by this cline, see Bybee (1985), Dressler (1985), Bybee and Dahl (1989), and Schwegler (1990). For some synchronic approaches, see Greenberg (1960), Sadock (1991), and papers in Hammond and Noonan (1988).

While there is not always evidence of a clitic pre-stage in the grammaticalization of affixes out of autonomous lexical words, the very loss of lexical autonomy involved in the process presupposes a clitic stage. In the example of French *-ment*, Spanish *-mente* which we discussed above, and in other examples of derivational affixes such as English *-hood*, *-ly*, etc. out of full nouns, it may be assumed that at one stage the eventual affix was attracted to what came to be its future stem and came to form an accentual unit with it. Clitics obviously have a central role in setting up the sorts of structures that undergo morphologization. It is the frequent syntactic collocation of a particular word class, such as a noun, with a particular type of clitic, such as an adposition, that most typically leads to morphologization (e.g., as a noun with a case affix).

6.2.1 Some characteristics of clitics

As mentioned in Chapter 1, the word "clitic" is usually used to refer to a set of unaccented forms that tend to be found attached to a more heavily accented form (known as the "host"). The attachment may be so close that the clitic becomes affix-like, for example, English *n't* in *don't* (see Pullum and Zwicky 1983 for arguments why *n't* behaves in its distribution more like an inflection than like a clitic form of *not*). Or the attachment may be quite loose and more like an autonomous word, such as *however* in *The judge, however, took a different view.*

In many languages there are distinct sets of clitic and "tonic" (stressed) forms of the same word. This is especially true of pronouns; the clearest example in English of such a contrast is in the third person plural *them* (tonic) versus *'em* (clitic), where the clitic and tonic forms actually have different origins (*'em* is from OE *heom*, while *them* is a ME form ultimately of Scandinavian origin). More often the two forms are simply accented (tonic) and unaccented (clitic) varieties of the same word, e.g., *you/ya*. Prepositions and postpositions (the class of "adpositions") are often cliticized variants of adverbs. Again, this is clear in English and some other Indo-European languages, where the difference between an adverb and a preposition resides basically in that prepositions are (pro-)clitic (e.g., prepositional *up* in *up a tree* versus adverbial *up* in *she got up early*). Auxiliary verbs and verbs of having and being are frequently clitics, and may likewise have clitic and tonic variants (e.g., *I'm the head waiter* versus *I AM the head waiter*).

The functional characteristics of clitics are consistent with their status as units that are already in part grammaticalized. Compared with their full forms, clitic forms are more context-dependent and more general in meaning. Often they have functions whose closest counterparts in other languages are clearly grammatical, such as aspect, modality, participant reference (such as to person and number), and case. Other clitics, for instance those which are connectives, pronouns, or interrogative markers, have a syntactic or discourse function.

6.2.2 *Positions of clitics*

Clitics are typically restricted to certain positions in the clause. One of these is next to a specific host; for example, possessive pronouns may form an accentual group with the possessed noun, auxiliaries may be constrained to occurring adjacent to the lexical verb, determiners must be placed next to the noun, and so on. In these examples, the host belongs to a specific word class and the clitic has a functional affinity for just that class and no other (auxiliaries generally do not go with nouns, etc.). Such clitics are called "phrasal clitics," because they have a grammatical affinity for a particular type of phrase.

Other kinds of clitics are not restricted in this way and are known as "sentential clitics." Many of them function as conjunctions, sentential adverbs, complementizers, and question words (Kaisse 1982). Some occupy what can broadly speaking be called the "first slot" in the clause, and are "proclitic," that is, they are attached to the following element or "host." Others occupy what is broadly speaking the "second slot," and are "enclitic," that is they are attached to a host that precedes. In Homeric Greek of the eighth century BC, for example, an unaccented word *de* (appearing as *d'* before vowels) served to link together main clauses, especially in narrative, as in the following passage from the *Iliad*:

(3)   Hōs eipōn proeiéi,   krateròn d'epì   mûthon
      thus saying, sent:forth:he, harsh:ACC *de*-upon word:ACC
      étellen.   Tō   d'aékonte bátēn parà thîn'
      enjoined. they:DUAL *de*-unwilling went along shore
      halòs   atrugétoio, Murmidónōn
      ocean:GEN restless,   Myrmedons:GEN
      d'epí   te   klisías kaì nûas hikésthēn.
      de-upon both tents   and ships came:they
      'Saying this, he sent them forth, adding some harsh injunctions. So they went reluctantly along the shore of the restless ocean and came to the tents and ships of the Myrmedons.'

                                   (Homer, *Iliad* I: 326–8)

In Latin, *-que* served a similar function:

(4)   Omnibus copiis provolaverunt   impetumque in equites
      all:with   forces flew:forward:they attack-*que*   on cavalry
      nostros fecerunt.
      our   made:they
      'They hurled all their forces forward and launched an attack on our cavalry.'

                    (c. 60 BC, Caesar, *De Bello Gallico* II:20)

The last two examples illustrate a common constraint on sentential clitics. It is commonly known as Wackernagel's Law (or Rule), after Jacob Wackernagel, who noted a positional feature of enclitics in Indo-European (Wackernagel 1892); the phenomenon is now known to be widespread and not restricted to Indo-European. Sentential enclitics have a tendency to occur in the second position in the sentence, following the first tonic element. But other clitics may occur in that position too, for example, clitics with auxiliary verb character. The "second position" tendency may be related to the topic–comment structure that spoken sentences typically have: in many utterances there is an initial phrase (the topic) that, as it were, sets the stage for what is to be said about it (the comment). Clitics that are not bound to a particular word class will tend to follow the initial topic; for instance,

English *however* in sentences such as the one previously cited: *The judge, however, took a different view* implies a contrast between *the judge* and some other participant in the event, so that *the judge* is clearly the topic of this sentence. For the same reason, interrogative markers may serve to focus on one item being questioned, as in Indonesian, where *-kah* is a clitic attached to the first word or phrase, and this phrase is the one being questioned:

(5) Menarik-kah   pilim itu?
     interesting-*kah* film   that
     'Was that film interesting?'

Pronouns and even verbs may also favor the second position in the sentence.

Morphologization involves the creation of a bound morpheme (i.e., an affix) out of an independent word by way of cliticization. The final stage of this process, the uniting of the affix with its stem, is referred to as "univerbation." Although univerbation can in theory include the uniting of the two parts of a compound into a single lexical item (e.g., *boat + swain > bo'sun, cup + board > cupboard*), the term is most often used in reference to a later stage of morphologization, as in examples such as Latin *clara mente* 'with a clear mind' > French *clairement* 'clearly,' where the second element has become an inflectional or derivational affix.

Table 6.2 *Polish tonic and clitic forms of the copula*

	Old Polish		Modern Polish
	Tonic	*Clitic*	
1 singular	jeśm	-(e)śm/-(e)m	-(e)m
2 singular	jeś	-(e)ś	-(e)ś
3 singular	jest/jeść/je	-0	-0
1 plural	jesm(y)	-e)smy	-(e)śmy
2 plural	jeśće	-(e)śće	-(e)śće
3 plural	są	-0	-0
1 dual	jeswa	-(e)swa	
2 dual	jesta	-(e)sta	
3 dual	jesta	-(e)sta/-0	

Source: based on Andersen (1987: 24)

A particularly instructive example of univerbation, and of morphologization in general, has been described by Andersen (1987). During the
recorded history of Polish, a copular verb has come to be suffixed to a
participial verb stem to form an inflected past tense. The earliest stage of
the textual record (Polish prior to 1500) shows a copular verb existing in
both clitic and tonic forms. The clitic typically occurs in second (Wackernagel's) position. In Table 6.2, the clitic form of the verb 'to be' in the third
column is the ancestor of the Modern Polish suffixes in the fourth column.
The tonic forms in the second column drop out of use as copulas at an early
date, but the third person singular *jest* lives on as an emphatic marker. In (6)
-*m* is the clitic first person singular form of the copula, and *ogla dała* is the
"verb," historically a past participle:

(6) a. To-m   jest   ogla dała.
        that-1SG EMPH saw
        'That I did see.'
    b. Bo-cie-m   się   cała   darowała.
        for-thee-1SG REFL entire gave
        'For I gave myself wholly to thee.'

(Andersen 1987: 28)

The clitic -*m* and the verb are separated from one another with -*m* in the
second position in the sentence and the verb at the end.

After about 1500, however, changes begin to occur. Sentence stress on
any element in the "comment" part of the sentence may attract the clitic.
Furthermore, the clitic increasingly appears after the verb, regardless of the
verb's position, especially if the verb is an *l*-form preterit. Here it is suffixed
("agglutinated") to the verb. The movement toward suffixal status is
strikingly illustrated by the statistics cited by Andersen (1987: 29). Table 6.3

Table 6.3 *Bonding of clitic copula to verb stem in Polish,*
AD 1500 to the present

Date	Number	Percentage
1500s	130	23
1600s	649	49
1700s	994	68
1800s	1395	80
1900s	2817	84
(expository prose)	525	92

Source: based on Andersen (1987: 29)[2]

shows the percentage of occurrences of the clitic copula that appears as a suffix on the preterit verb (whatever its position in the clause), expressed as a percentage of the overall number of instances of the clitic copula in texts of different centuries from AD 1500 on.

In the modern language, as can be seen from Table 6.3, the morphologization of the copula as a suffix on the verb is still not complete. Although univerbation of the verb and the clitic is very general, there are accentual reflexes in both modern standard Polish and in the modern dialects of the former clitic status of the verbal suffixes. These differences in accent suggest univerbation has progressed at different speeds in various parts of the preterit paradigm and in different dialects. They also suggest relatively fine distinctions among levels or degrees of "compacting." Polish has generalized a "penult" rule for stress which puts stress on the next-to-last syllable in the word. The dialects differ from the standard language in the degree to which they recognize the suffix as part of the word for purposes of assigning stress. In some forms, the stress (marked with ' before the vowel) is where it should be if the "clitic" is a relatively unmorphologized, separate suffix or "word." In these forms the suffix appears in Table 6.4 with a hyphen. But in others it is where it should be if the "clitic" is a fully morphologized suffix, that is, if verb and clitic have undergone univerbation. The left-to-right arrangement of the table reflects the progress of univerbation: it is almost non-existent in the southern dialects, the standard has carried it through in the singular but not in the plural (except for the third person), and it is complete in the northern dialects. The paradigm is that of the verb 'to speak.' It is important to note that the accentual change here is not simply a morphophonemic (phonological) adaptation of a full lexical item to a neighboring clitic; it is the verb, and only the verb in the preterit, that is making the adjustment. Consider the following example (Andersen 1987: 33):

(7) a. Wcz'oraj-em   prz'zysed-ł.
       yesterday-1SG arrived
       'I arrived yesterday.'
    b. Wcz'oraj przysz'edł-em.
       yesterday arrived-1SG
       'I arrived yesterday.'

The verb adapts its stress to the new suffix, whereas the adverb ignores the clitic for purposes of stress. The clitic does not suffix itself to any random sentence element, but specifically to the verb, and it "seeks out" the verb in

Table 6.4 *Differential univerbation of preterit verb and person-number suffix in Polish dialects*

Southern	Standard	Northern
m'ówił-em	mów'iłem	mów'iłem
m'ówił-eś	mów'iłeś	mów'iłeś
m'ówił	m'ówił	m'ówił
mów'ili-śmy	mów'ili-śmy	mówil'iśmy
mów'ili-ście	mów'ili-ście	mówil'iście
mów'ili	mów'ili	mów'i

Source: Andersen (1987: 32)

a way that suggests that the original, verbal nature of the clitic may still be constraining its current use.

The process of morphologization whereby independent words become clitics and eventually affixes results in a fixed order of morphemes with respect to the stem. Whereas the ancestral independent word may have had a certain amount of positional freedom, univerbation removes any flexibility of position with respect to the stem. It has often been suggested (e.g., Givón 1979: 239–45) that morpheme order may reflect earlier word order tendencies of the language at the time when the morphologization in question was occurring. Givón cites data from Amharic, a Semitic language of Ethiopia. In this language the original word order was VO, but through a strong substratum of Cushitic, a non-Semitic language family with OV word order, verb-final patterns have permeated the language. The original VO word order continues to be reflected in the morpheme order in inflected words:

(8) Kassa borsa-w-n   la-Mulu saṭṭa-at.
    Kassa wallet-the-OBJ to-Mulu gave-IOBJ
    'Kassa gave the wallet to Mulu.'

(p. 244)

Assuming that the suffixes -*w*, -*n*, and -*at* were once autonomous words, presumably demonstratives and pronouns, we can derive the suffixed forms from older sequences of noun + demonstrative + pronoun, and verb + indirect object pronoun. Both these word orders are compatible with a VO type of language, and the hypothesis is that Amharic has preserved the original word order in its order of suffixes even though the syntactic word order has radically shifted. On the other hand, French, a modern VO language in which object lexical nouns must follow the verb, shows object pronouns preceding the verb, consistent with its origins in a strongly OV language (Latin):

(9) a. **Lexical nouns**
Le boulanger donne le bijou à la jeune fille.
the baker gives the jewel to the girl
'The baker gives the jewel to the girl.'

    b. **Clitic pronouns**
Il le lui donne.
he it to:her gives
'He gives it to her.'

In Latin the verb would normally have been placed at the end of the sentence in each case. Describing similar phenomena cross-linguistically, Givón coined the memorable phrase "Today's morphology is yesterday's syntax" (Givón 1971: 413). While not a novel insight, the concept has been the subject of much recent discussion. How general is it? Can the synchronic ordering of morphologized affixes be used to reconstruct the prehistoric order of words in the sentence?

Certainly with Amharic and French the reconstructions are in accord with what we either know or can surmise about original word orders on independent evidence. However, it is clear that the order of morphologized affixes can at best only inform us about the order of the clitics at the time their positions became fixed. This fact alone is not sufficient to invalidate Givón's observation, for it is at least theoretically possible that when clitics move toward being affixes they adopt the place that they would have if they were full lexical items. In such a scenario, auxiliaries would follow the verb in OV languages, possessive pronouns would follow the noun in VO languages, and so on.

However, Comrie (1980) shows that in languages with variation in their basic word order (and many seemingly quite rigid languages show such variation) even phrasal clitics may appear in a position with respect to their host that is different from that normally occupied by corresponding lexical items. In Classical Mongolian, for example, an OV language in which one might expect that possessive adjectives would precede the noun, in fact both orders were possible:

(10) a. minü morin
        my horse
    b. morin minü
        horse my

Here, the (a) phrase was more usual, and differed from the (b) phrase in some such nuance as *MY horse* versus *my HORSE*. In later Mongolian dialects it is (10b), the less usual order, that underlies clitics which, eventually, become morphologized as suffixes indicating possession, cf. Kalmyk:

(11) a. möre-m
          horse-1SG
          'my horse'
      b. minī möre-m
          my horse-1SG
          'my horse'

(Comrie 1980: 90)

Comrie suggests three reasons why such a development might occur. One is that if the usual morphological process in a language is suffixation, newly emerging affixes will conform to the general pattern already available. Another possible reason is prosodic: in Mongolian languages the head of a construction is never preceded by an unstressed element. Morphologization of clitics as prefixes would provide exceptions to this otherwise quite general principle. Finally, there may be a syntactic reason. In languages of the OV type, Comrie argues, there is a general principle that the head of a construction can always be separated from one of its attributes by some other word. For example, the object of the verb, which would be considered such an attribute, does not have to stand immediately next to the verb, but there can be adverbs or other words that intervene. For the same reason, in such languages (and in VO languages such as English that place the adjective before the noun) a possessive adjective that precedes a noun can always be separated from the noun by an adjective: *my horse, my strong horse*, etc. But this separation tends not to occur if the possessive follows the noun, i.e., in examples such as Classical Mongolian *morin minü* (horse my) 'my horse' there would almost never be an adjective between the two words (i.e., *'horse strong my'). The position of the cliticized possessive, then, conforms to that order in which the clitic and the host noun were invariably adjacent to one another.

Even more damaging for the hypothesis that morpheme order reflects earlier word order are examples (admittedly rare) of reordering of morphemes within a paradigm. One such example is from Pengo, a Dravidian language. Bybee (1985: 40), citing Burrow and Bhattacharya (1970), shows that in Pengo the perfect was originally formed by addition of auxiliary *na* to the past tense form, after person-number inflections. So, for example, the following older forms can be found:

(12)   vāt   aŋ   'I came'
       vāt-aŋ-na 'I have come'

In other words, the perfect is formed by V:TNS + person/number + *na*. But the more common, and more recent, formation of the perfect is by repeating the person-number inflection after that template, as in (13a), resulting in the structure V:TNS + person/number + *na* + person/number, or even, in more streamlined fashion, simply V:TNS + *na* + person/number, as in (13b):

(13)   a.   huṛtaŋnaŋ ([huṛta-aŋ-na-ŋ]) 'I have seen'
       b.   huṛtanaŋ ([huṛta-na-ŋ]) 'I have seen'

It seems, then, that while morpheme order reflects earlier word order, Givón's principle is of limited usefulness, since we cannot be sure **which** earlier word is reflected, the basic one or a secondary one. Factors of morphological type, prosody, and syntactic typology as well as general tendencies such as verb second may all influence the order in which clitics are placed with respect to the host. A further factor for which Bybee shows overwhelming evidence is relevance to the meaning of the stem. In the Pengo example, person and number, which agree with the arguments of the verb, are less relevant to verb meaning than temporality. We now turn to a brief discussion of Bybee's hypothesis of the significance of "relevance" for understanding the facts of morphological bonding.

6.2.3   *Semantic "relevance" as a factor in fusion and morpheme order*
       It is a truism that in a language which exhibits affixal morphology, not all grammatical categories will be affixally expressed. Some will be relatively free (still lexical, or clitic), others will be tightly bound and inflectional. Some will be expressed by a phrase, others by a word with affixes. If this were a random happenstance of when which form started to change, then no general patterns of relationship between affixal and non-affixal expression would be expected in a language. However, in an exploratory cross-linguistic survey of fifty languages, Bybee (1985) showed that:

(a)   Meaning elements that are directly relevant to verb meaning are more likely to be fused or bound than those that are not.
(b)   The order in which they occur is partly correlated with their degree of relevance to the verb.

(c) Among meanings relevant to the verb, the most general are likely to be expressed inflectionally.

To avoid terminological confusion, it is important to note that Bybee is using the term "relevance" to refer to the extent to which the meaning of a grammatical category (e.g. aspect or tense) affects the inherent meaning of the lexical item with which it is associated. This is different from the pragmatic "relevance" that we discussed as a motivation for meaning change in Chapter 4. The pragmatic maxim of Relevance has to do with relevance to the participants in the communicative act.

Verbs express events or states of being. A causative situation is without question semantically relevant to the verb, since it affects the event or state of being directly. Causative meanings are often signaled by bound morphemes, e.g., *redden*. However, a causal situation is often understood rather differently from the literal combination of V + causal. The relationship between *die* and *kill* ('cause to die') is a classic instance of this kind of difference. Bybee shows that causal relationships are often expressed by derivational forms. These are bound forms, which, although identifiable as separate morphemes, nevertheless combine with a base to add new, rather specific, meanings, or change linguistic categories, and form a stem to which other affixes, such as inflections, can be attached.[3] *Redden* can, for example, have tense attached (e.g., *reddened*). Even more frequently, causal relations are expressed by lexically different forms, that is, totally fused forms, rather than by inflectional forms, because they are at least partially idiosyncratic.[4] By contrast, tense, aspect, and mood tend to be expressed inflectionally because they are highly general and can apply to most event and state types. Of the languages Bybee investigated, 72% had inflectional tense, mood, and aspect. By contrast, only 56% had inflectional person-number-subject agreement (Bybee 1985: 33). Although number can be expressed derivationally and even in lexically different ways, person-number agreement tends to be less frequently bound than either causal relations or tense-aspect-mood. This, she suggests, reflects the lesser relevance of person-number to the verb: its prime function is not to express aspects of the situation, but to express distinctions among arguments of the verb.

Tense, mood, and aspect themselves have different likelihoods of ordering with respect to each other. Aspect refers to the way in which the internal constituency of the event is viewed, that is, according to whether it is seen as a whole from the outside and completed (perfective), or from within and incomplete (Comrie 1976). Tense places the situation in time with respect to an established point in time, either the time of speech (deictic tense), or some other point in time (relational tense). Mood refers to the way the speaker presents the truth of the proposition, whether as probable, possible, or certain (Bybee 1985: 28). Given the hypothesis of relevance, aspect is most relevant to the verb, tense less so, since it relates the time of the situation to some other time, and mood least so since it expresses speaker point of view on the situation. If that which is most relevant is that which is most likely to be close to the verb, then we would expect aspect to be the most likely of the three categories to be ordered next to the stem (or even be part of it, as a derivational form), tense next, and mood last. The relative positions of aspect and tense are well established for languages in which both are prefixes or both suffixes, as illustrated by:

(14) a. **Tiwi** (Australia)
ŋə-ru-untiŋ-apa.
cook-PAST-DUR-eat
'I was eating it.'

      b. **Kewa** (New Guinea)
Íra-paa-ru.
cook-PERF-1SG:PAST
'I finished cooking it.'

(Foley and Van Valin 1984: 210)

As Bybee notes, the claim that the natural order is mood–tense–aspect–V (or, in OV languages, V–aspect–tense–mood), may seem counterintuitive to linguists who speak of T–M–A (tense–mood–aspect) in that order, and are familiar with the earlier work of Chomsky in which it was suggested that Engish constructions such as *would be going* were tense–mood–aspect–V. As she notes, English does not of course have bound forms. However, recent analyses of the same construction in English actually do reflect the order she predicts, since PDE *would* (also *might, could, should*) is best treated as a mood marker. Normally present tense is in zero form after mood, but is expressed in quasi-modals (e.g., *has to*), and past is expressed by *have* after *may, might, can, could*, etc., but inflectionally with quasi-modals: *would have been going, had to be going* (Bybee 1985: 196–200).

Bybee's hypothesis is a provocative and insightful frame of research which she and her colleagues are pursuing. It has provided results that are in keeping with independent studies of other issues in verbal morphology, such as the extent to which predictions can be made about which verbal affixes are likely to be phrasal, which affixal (see Bybee and Dahl 1989). It can be expected to continue to yield fundamental insights into grammaticalization.

But a few cautions should be noted. These include the fact that in so far as the data base is founded on extant grammars, it is subject to the difficulty that different linguists have made different analyses of such basic properties as morpheme boundaries, status as phrase, word, bound morpheme, etc. (for a detailed account of various definitions of tense and aspect, see Binnick 1991). They have also had different definitions in mind of the categories in question (most notably tense and aspect are often confused). As Bybee notes, other difficulties include the fact that languages often have portmanteau morphemes (morphemes combining two or more categories in segmentally undistinguishable ways (see the next section)). Also, the morpheme order predictions naturally do not hold when affixes are not in sequence; for example, mood affixes may be prefixed while tense-aspect affixes are postfixed, as in Cayuga:

(15) a·-yakó·-nyo·-?
      OPTATIVE-FEM:PATIENT-kill-PUNCTUAL
      'she would get killed'

(Mithun 1991: 177)

Furthermore, Bybee's own statistics do not always provide exactly the predicted facts. Given that aspect is the most relevant to the meaning of the verb, mood the least so, once would predict that aspect would be bound most frequently, mood least. Also, one would predict that aspect would be more likely than the other two categories to be expressed derivationally, given that it defines the internal structure of the situation. In Bybee's fifty-language sample, the statistics are as shown in Table 6.5. Aspect and tense follow the predictions. Aspect is most frequently found as a bound form (in 74% of the languages); in 22% of these languages its form is derivational rather than inflectional. Tense is less frequently found as a bound form (in 50% of the languages); only 2% of the occurrences are derivational. Mood, however, does not follow one prediction since it is more frequently inflectional than the other two categories, and more frequently bound than both tense and aspect. However, it is always

Table 6.5 *Affixal aspect-tense-mood forms*

	% bound forms in sample[5]	% inflectional forms in sample
Aspect	74	52
Tense	50	48
Mood	68	68

Source: based on Bybee (1985: 30)

inflectional rather than derivational, as predicted. Perhaps the reason for the higher frequency as an inflection is that it is so general (the category mood includes evidentials and "hear-say" expressions which express the speaker's attitude toward the likeliness of the truth of the proposition).

6.2.4 *Phonological concomitants of morphologization*

The fusion of a lexical item and a clitic as stem and affix that typifies morphologization is accompanied by phonological changes of various sorts. Most often these changes are characterizable as reductions: vowels and consonants are dropped, a stress or tone accent is lost causing an accentual readjustment over the newly formed word, and adjacent phonological segments are assimilated to one another. If the loss of the word boundary that once separated the two elements is included, some phonological adjustment is by definition always involved in morphologization.

Often, as might be expected from the divergence and the resultant coexistence of both unreduced (tonic) and reduced (clitic) forms, the autonomous lexical form will undergo a different set of phonological changes from the bound form. The result is that sometimes the morphologized form actually preserves something closer to the older state of affairs. A good example of this is the vocalism of English affixes that have been protected from the effect of the Great Vowel Shift, which operated on tonic vowels. Thus we have *manly* [-li], beside *like* [layk], and *because* [bi-] compared with *by* [bay]. The divergence of the article *a* [ə] from numeral one [wʌn] has already been mentioned in 5.4.2.

In the process of phonological attrition and selection that accompanies morphologization, we can identify two tendencies:

(a) A quantitative ("syntagmatic") reduction: forms become shorter as the phonemes that comprise them erode.

(b) A qualitative ("paradigmatic") reduction: the remaining phonological segments in the form are drawn from a progressively shrinking set. This smaller set of phonemes tends to reflect the universal set of unmarked segments. They tend especially to be apical (tongue tip) consonants such as [n], [t], and [s], the glottal consonants [ʔ] and [h], and common vowels such as [a], [u], [i], and [ə]. The result is that from a synchronic perspective grammatical morphemes tend to be composed of "unmarked" segments. As will be elaborated on immediately below, "unmarked segments" are those that are textually frequent, found across a wide range of different languages (indeed, may be universal), are learned early by children, and are targets of neutralization of contrast. (The concept of markedness being invoked here was developed by the Prague School phonologists in the 1920s and 30s. Hyman (1975: 143–56) is an excellent general treatment.)

One aspect of the tendency toward unmarked segments is that morphologization is usually accompanied by a reduction in prominence. Prominence is a function of special accentuation, length, or some sort of positional privilege such as initial syllable in the word (Trubetzkoy 1929: 58). In an environment of lessened prominence, there is a general neutralization of segments, that is, a loss in certain of the phonological distinctions found in full lexical items. Haiman (1972) points out that in this loss of phonological contrasts characteristic of non-prominent syllables, there is a movement toward an unmarked set of phonemes, in the sense that we have just presented it. Admittedly this neutralization belongs to non-prominent syllables in general (a point taken up again below). But because a reduction in prominence is characteristic of forms that are becoming morphologized, one outcome of morphologization is morphemes that typically consist of simple, unmarked, phonological sets. In Turkish, Haiman notes, there are strategies for avoiding the vowel [o] in non-prominent syllables; this vowel is marked because it is simultaneously low and rounded. Significantly, the only grammatical suffix that contains [o] is *-yor*, a progressive verbal form which was once an autonomous (copular) verb and "has only recently degenerated to the status of a suffix" (p. 367). (That is, it is newly morphologized. A shift to some less marked vowel can be predicted for the future.)

A second aspect of the appearance of unmarked segments in morphologized forms is that the analogical spread of one allomorph at the expense of others is aided by the sheer textual frequency of the successful allomorph, and textual frequency is associated with unmarked segments (Greenberg 1960). Let us consider a well-known example from the Polynesian language Maori.

In Maori there is a passive suffix *-ia* which has attracted the final consonant of the verb stem, this consonant being dropped when it occurs word-finally (K. Hale 1973). The result is the emergence of at least as many allomorphs of the passive suffix as there are consonants, as shown in the examples in (16):

(16)	**Verb**	**Passive form**	**Allomorph of passive suffix**
	hopu 'catch'	hopukia	-kia
	aru 'follow'	arumia	-mia
	tohu 'point out'	tohuŋia	-ŋia
	maatu 'know'	maaturia	-ria, etc.

Some of these allomorphs have spread to verb forms where they did not originally occur, replacing the historically "correct" allomorph, so that the present day distribution of the allomorphs does not always reflect the historically expected one. Especially *-tia* has fared well, and appears to be on the way to becoming the norm for the passive suffix in all stems (Krupa 1968: 70–1); *-kia* is also well represented. The tendency for these two allomorphs, especially *-tia*, to oust the others reflects the numerical preponderance of the two consonants [t] and [k]. In Maori texts, [t] and [k], which are about equal to each other in frequency, occur considerably more often than other consonants (Krupa 1966: 22). These two factors – textual frequency and the selection of members of the unmarked set as targets of neutralizations – are closely interrelated, and in fact are simply aspects of the same phenomenon of phonological markedness.

Many of the phonological changes that accompany morphologization are not peculiar to this process but are simply part of the same processes of assimilation, attrition, and other kinds of reduction that are found more generally in non-prominent syllables and across junctures (Heine and Reh 1984 give detailed examples of these in grammaticalization in African languages). For instance, the loss of the final *-ns* in the French first person plural future (*nous finirons* 'we will finish,' pronounced [finirɔ̃]), is part of the general loss of final consonants in Modern French, not a peculiarity of the morphologization of the auxiliary from Latin *habere* (see Section 3.4.1). A more complex example is the following. The Sahaptian language Nez Perce can code the goal of a verb of motion either with a locative suffix on the goal noun, or with a transitivizing suffix on the verb that then treats the goal as an object, as in:

(17) a. 'áayato-na   páa-'naxpayk-a   'níit-pe.
          woman-OBJ 3SUBJ:3OBJ-bring-PAST lodge-LOC
          'He brought the woman to [his] lodge.'
      b. 'áayat pà-'naxpayk-óo-ya   miyóoxato-na.
          woman 3SUBJ:3OBJ-bring-LOC-PAST chief-OBJ
          'He brought the woman to the chief.'

(Rude 1991: 188)

For our purposes the significant morphological difference between the two sentences is that (17b) contains in the verb a (transitivizing) locative suffix *-óo-* which consists of the frozen past tense marker *-e-* and the copula *wée*, presumably in the sense of 'be [in a place]'. By a regular Nez Perce phonological process, the resulting sequence becomes first *-úu-* and then, by vowel harmony, *-óo-*. Thus the seemingly arbitrary erosion accompanying the morphologization of the copula verb as a transitivizing suffix, is in fact the result of well-established changes in the general phonology of the language.

The development of Nez Perce *-óo-* described above involves erosion (of *w*) and morpheme boundary loss, or "fusion" of the tense marker and the copula. Erosion is the loss of phonological segments as the process of fusion continues (Heine and Reh 1984: 21–5). This loss typically occurs at boundaries, such as at the end of a word or morpheme. Although examples are citable from virtually any language, French and English are especially striking because of the conservatism of their orthographies, in which spellings with "silent letters" abound (one does, however, have to distinguish between orthography that reflects actual changes from orthography ·that reflects false etymologizing by scribes and grammarians; for example, French *poids* derives from *pensum*, not from *pondus*, as the spelling suggests). Latin *calidum* 'hot' had lost both its suffixes (*-id-um*) by the time of Modern French *chaud* [šo], and even the *l* of its stem, *cal-*, has been absorbed. Erosion may or may not bring about morphemic loss. An example of erosion that has merely reduced a morpheme without eliminating it is the Latin ablative singular suffix *-ō*, e.g., *lupō* 'from the wolf,' from an earlier *lupōd*.

Extreme cases of fusion are easily identified. One is that in which two or more morphemes fuse as a "portmanteau" morph (Hockett 1947 [1966]: 229) without there being a one-to-one semantic/functional match between any morpheme and any set of phonological segments. French *du* [dü] 'of the (masc.),' i.e., *de* + *le*, and *aux* [o] 'to the (masc./fem. plur.)' (*à* + *le*/*la* + *s*) are examples of this. In many tone languages, fusion may result in a portmanteau morph which has segmental material from one morpheme and a tone from another, the tone being all that remains from the second morpheme. Matisoff (1991) picturesquely refers to this process as 'Cheshirization', from Lewis Carroll's Cheshire Cat, which disappeared leaving only its smile. Matisoff (1982: 32–4) gives the following example. In Lahu, a Lolo-Burmese language of Northern Thailand, an original causative prefix, probably **s-*, underlies alternations between voiced and voiceless initials in such pairs as:

(18) a. dɔ̀ 'drink' : tɔ 'give to drink'
     b. dè 'come to rest' : tɛ 'put down'

There is a tonal change, generally from a lower to a mid or high tone, which is phonetically (albeit indirectly) linked to the voicing change. Where the initial consonant is one that does not show a distinction in voicing, such as the nasal [m] or the affricate [c] in the next example, the tonal difference is the only remaining trace of the former prefix:

(19) a. mɔ̀ 'see' : mɔ 'show'
     b. câ 'eat' : cā 'feed'

Many possible examples of fusion depend crucially on unambiguously defining a "phonological unit." Indeed, Heine and Reh define fusion as the disappearance of the boundary separating two morphemes, "these morphemes thus being reduced to one phonological unit" (1984: 25). Affixes normally form a phonological unit with their stem. Yet fusion is something more than mere affixation; it is a stage in which the phonological substance of an affix (or of the subordinate part of a compound) and the stem start to become indistinguishable from one another. There is much current disagreement about the levels resulting from various degrees of fusion, much of it a function of attempting to define a synchronic system in which every item has a distinct structure. From the point of view of grammaticalization, the issue is not so much what the structure is at some moment in time, but what the direction of change is and how far along the continuum some particular form has moved. Fusion, then, is a characteristic of the right-hand side of a continuum at one end of which are discrete morphs and at the other a single morph, possibly with some purely phonological residue of a previous second morph.

In morphologization, as in all grammaticalization, we must ask whether there are any rules characteristic of morphologization that are not part of the general or historical phonology of the language. It will be recalled that this same question arose in semantic change, where there appeared to be no evidence that the meaning shifts that accompanied grammaticalization were anything other than subtypes of meaning shifts affecting lexical items in general. Since morphologization necessarily involves the emergence of new morpheme boundaries and other junctural phenomena, and the juxtaposition of segmental clusters in ways not found internal to words or across "older" morpheme boundaries, and since usually there is a prosodic reduction of the new affix, any special phonological changes are to be attributed to these subtypes of phonological change rather than to any intrinsic change from "lexical" to "grammatical."

All the same, given that grammaticalization occurs in highly local contexts, and in later stages often involves univerbation of a new affix with a stem, unusual, even unprecedented, sequences of segments may occur, which in turn may set things up for special phonological changes. For example, Latin has an imperfect tense formed synchronically from a verbal stem, a suffix *-ba-*, and a personal ending such as *-m* 'first person singular,' e.g., from *ama-* 'love' can be formed *amabam* 'I used to love.' The diachronic source of the imperfect is likely to have been a present participle (in this case **amants*) followed by a form of the copular verb (**bʰwam* 'I was'). The combination **amants bʰwam* presumably gave rise to *amabam* through a rule whereby the combination *-nts* + *bʰw-* eventually yielded *-b-* (see Baldi 1976: 846–7 for a recent discussion of this idea). But, as Baldi notes, such a sequence of events cannot be proved or disproved on purely phonological grounds, since it is only in this very collocation that the combination of segments in question is ever likely to have occurred in Latin across a morpheme boundary.

6.3 The development of paradigms

Sometimes the coalescence of two parts of a periphrastic construction as stem and affix remains isolated, and has no further consequences. Consider, for example, the second person plural *y'all* found in some English dialects. The form is transparently derived from the periphrastic *you* + *all*; yet *-all* has not in these dialects spread as a general plural morpheme to other words, either nouns or pronouns. We do not, that is, see a "paradigm" emerging of the kind shown in (20).

(20) I   *I-all
      you   you-all
      he   *he-all
      she   *she-all

Nor do we see any real signs that *-all* is becoming a plural suffix in English; *y'all* appears at least in PDE to be paradigmatically isolated. Often, however, later stages of grammaticalization involve a process of emergent paradigms, in which a set of related affixes emerges based on a single form. With verbs, this basic form is often the third person singular. With nouns and pronouns it is often a non-nominative case.

We illustrate the "paradigmatization" of a nominal marker with the development of the Old Norse reflexive pronoun *sik* into an affix. Originally

Table 6.6 *Old Norse present indicative reflexive verb forms*

	Singular	Plural
1	finnomk	finnomsk
2	finzk (z=[t+sk])	finnezk
3	finzk	finnask

the accusative of the third person (singular and plural) reflexive, it spread to other persons and cases and came to mark voice as well. In Old Norse *sik* coexisted with its grammaticalized form, the enclitic *-sk*:

(21) a.   Hann bauþ   sik.
          'He   offered himself.'
      b.   Hann bauzk (zk < *þsk).
          'He   offered-himself.'

(Heusler 1921: 142)

The development of this pronoun as a suffix in Old Norse and on into Danish is a classic example of grammaticalization. With cliticization comes:

(a)   Phonological assimilation. The pronoun merges phonologically with the host. For example, if the stem ends in an apical such as *t* or *þ* the combination is pronounced [tsk] (spelled *zk*). The form *bauzk < bauþ* sik cited above is an example of this.

(b)   "Syncretism," the merging of different parts of a paradigm into a single form. This occurs in two ways. One is syncretism of person/number. The other is syncretism of case.

The third person reflexive *sik* spreads to other persons, and is found already in the earliest texts in all forms except the first person. Thus the inflection of *finnask* 'to find oneself' in the present indicative is in the oldest Old Norse manuscripts as shown in Table 6.6. The third person singular/ plural reflexive pronoun *sik* has spread to the second person singular/plural. The first person singular reflexive *mik* (> *-mk*) has spread to the plural. In addition, the first person plural has assumed the third person, yielding a complex suffix *-msk*. Therefore of the five potential possibilities for autonomous reflexive pronouns only two remain.

We turn now to the second kind of syncretism, that of case. The autonomous reflexive corresponding to *-sk* is the accusative *sik*. But *-sk* is found in environments where a genitive or dative would be expected. For example, in (22a) *sér* is in the dative, but its enclitic form is *-sk* in (22b):

151

(22) a. Hann eignaðe   *sér*   ríke.
        he   appropriated to-himself kingdom
        'He appropriated the kingdom to himself.'
     b. Hann eignaðesk   ríke.
        he   appropriated-himself kingdom
        'He appropriated the kingdom to himself.'

(Heusler 1921: 141–2)

Both kinds of syncretism are exemplified in (23a, b):

(23) a. Ér hefneð yðuar   á honom.
        you revenge yourselves:GEN on him
        'You revenge yourselves on him.'
     b. Ér hefnezk   á honom.
        you revenge-yourselves on him

(ibid.)

The object pronoun *yðuar* 'you:gen:pl.' in its autonomous form is in the genitive because the verb *hefna* 'to avenge' requires that case for its object. The clitic version, however, is -*sk*, formerly the third person accusative. The example of *sik* also illustrates semantic generalization (see Section 5.2.1). Cliticization and morphologization of the reflexive *sik* is accompanied by a shift from reflexive to reciprocals, to middle voice and even passive giving meanings such as:

(24) a. **Reciprocal**
        Spyriask   ðeir tíðenda.
        ask:RECIP they of-news
        'They ask one another for news.'
     b. **Passive**
        Skip búask.
        skips build-*sk*
        'The ships are being built.'
     c. **Experiencer**
        Henne   hugnaðesk þat vel.
        her:DAT pleased-*sk* that well
        'She was pleased at that.'

(ibid.)

These and other meanings found as -*sk* grammaticalizers are typical of the development of reflexives (see Kemmer forthcoming a).

The clitic -*sk* became an -*s* suffix in the Eastern Scandinavian languages. Later in the history of Norse, the form -*zk* (i.e., [tsk]) spread in Eastern Scandinavian languages in favour of -*sk* even in stems where there was originally no apical to motivate it. Later still, the -*k* of the suffix dropped and only [ts] remained. By the modern Danish period this -*z* was further simplified to -*s*. In Danish it has occasional passive uses, as in (25a), but its more usual function is to express middle (25b), and reciprocal (25c):

(25) a. **Passive**
        Døren   åbnedes af en tjener.
        door:DEF open-*s* by a   servant
        'The door is opened by a servant.'
  b. **Middle**
        Jeg har længtes efter dig.
        I   have longed-*s* after you
        'I have been longing for you.'
  c. **Reciprocal**
        Vi har mødtes flere   gange.
        we have meet-*s* several times
        'We have met several times.'

The "passive" construction with -*s* is now largely confined to the written language; the more usual passive is formed periphrastically with the verb *blive* 'stay, remain' or with *være* 'to be' and a participle, e.g., *døren blev malet* 'the door was painted.'

The history of Old Norse -*sk*, first building a paradigm and then smoothing out its irregularities, leading to a uniform stem, is a common one. Many examples of this kind of paradigmatization have been cited in the literature. In Pre-Sanskrit the inflection of *vāk* 'voice' contained stem consonants which sometimes were and sometimes were not phonetically motivated, as shown in Table 6.7. In the (italicized) nominative and genitive plural the alternation *c/k* (caused by a still earlier alternation of *$*e/*ō$* in the vowel of the suffix) must have seemed arbitrary and pre-Sanskrit genitive plural *vākām* was replaced in historical Sanskrit by *vācām* (Jeffers and Lehiste 1979: 59–60). The result is a movement toward a single form of the stem in which variation in the stem is either leveled out or, as here, is directly motivated by the phonetic surroundings.

For another example, consider again the Maori passive suffix -*ia* discussed above. Here, it will be recalled, stem-final consonants were reanalyzed as part of the suffix, giving a variety of allomorphs of the suffix; but

Clause-internal morphological changes

Table 6.7 *Pre-Sanskrit noun inflection*

	Singular	Plural
Nominative	vāk	*vācas*
Genitive	vācas	*vākām*
Instrumental	vācā	vāgbhis
Locative	vāci	vāksi

Source: based on Jeffers and Lehiste (1979: 59)

uniformity with other stems is coming about through the generalization of -*t*. Derived verb forms such as the causative (with the prefix *whaka-*) seem to be especially susceptible to this kind of leveling (K. Hale 1973):

(26) a. hopuk-ia 'be caught'
whaka-hopu-tia (<*whaka-hopuk-ia) 'cause to be caught'
b. maur-ia 'be carried'
whaka-mau-tia (<*whaka-maur-ia) 'cause to be carried'

The picture drawn by such examples as these is of ragged and irregular paradigms being pulled into shape by analogy and generalization. Yet there are other forces at work too that lead to dispersal and disintegration. Purely phonological factors may contribute to this, as in the following example from Pali (Hock 1991 [1986]). Between Sanskrit and Pali the copular verb *as-* 'to be' first underwent leveling, as shown by the data in Table 6.8. In Sanskrit a vowel alternation of *a* and zero in the stem characterized singular and plural forms, reflecting the Indo-European full/zero grade of ablaut. In pre-Pali this *as-/s-* alternation was partly leveled, yielding the vowel *a* in all plural forms except the third person. Sound changes in pre-Pali such as assimilation then brought about more irregularity than existed even before

Table 6.8 *Sanskrit and pre-Pali forms of the copula*

	Sanskrit	pre-Pali[6]
1 singular	as-mi	*as-mi
2 singular	asi[7]	*asi
3 singular	as-ti	*as-ti
1 plural	s-maḥ	*as-ma
2 plural	s-tha	*as-tha
3 plural	s-anti	*s-anti

Source: based on Hock (1991[1986]: 171)

the stem leveling, as shown in Table 6.9. The Sanskrit-Pali development of the irregular paradigm of the verb 'to be' can be explained in terms of understood phonological developments. But irregularity may come about in other quite obscure ways. Andersen (1980: 17) shows that in Bulgarian dialects like that of Macedonia the conjugation of the verb 'to see' has undergone an apparently unmotivated shift in its aorist tense. In Table 6.10, dialect A is Western Bulgaria, dialect B is Macedonian, and dialect C is Southern Serbia. Here dialect A has the older vocalic stem *vide-*, while B has taken on the characteristics of a consonantal stem, changing *vide-* to *vid-*. Dialect C has gone even further and in addition to this change has innovated new stems of the participle that destroy the transparency of the relationship to the stem *vid(e)*. Compare the masculine and feminine forms of the participle 'seen' in dialect B (which in this respect is conservative) with those of dialect C, as shown in Table 6.11. The changes in question have one thing in common: they bring the paradigm of the verb 'to see' closer to that of the verb 'to go,' whose forms are uniquely irregular. But what do 'see' and 'go' have in common that would bring about such a development? Why is the perfectly regular vocalic inflection of the verb 'to

Table 6.9 *Pre-Pali and Pali forms of the copula*

	pre-Pali	Pali
1 singular	*as-mi	amhi
2 singular	*asi	asi
3 singular	*as-ti	atthi
1 plural	*as-ma	amha
2 plural	*as-tha	attha
3 plural	*s-anti	santi

Source: based on Hock (1991[1986]: 171)

Table 6.10 *Differential inflection of the aorist in Bulgarian dialects*

	Dialect A	Dialects B and C
1 singular	vide-x	vid-ox
2–3 singular	vide	vid-e
1 plural	vide-xme	vid-oxme
2 plural	vide-xte	vid-oxte
3 plural	vide-xa	vid-oxa

Source: based on Andersen (1980: 17)

Table 6.11 *Differential inflection of past participles in Bulgarian dialects*

	Dialect B	Dialect C
Masculine	vide-l	višel
Feminine	vide-l-a	višl-a

Source: based on Andersen (1980: 17)

see' abandoned in dialects B and C, and re-created along irregular, even suppletive, lines? And why should the change be restricted to past tenses (aorist and participle)? Andersen hypothesizes that the explanation is to be found in the frequent use of certain syntagms in which 'go and see' figured together, such as *idoxme i vidoxme* 'went and saw,' *prišel e i višel* 'he has come and seen.' It is thus not a "paradigmatic" similarity of sound or of meaning that has conditioned the change, but a "syntagmatic" discourse collocation of the two verbs.

The examples presented here show that while the tendency to conform to a paradigm may appear to be a potent formative force in the ongoing grammaticalization of forms, grammaticalization is not reducible to a uniform process of paradigmatization. Rather, it involves the disintegration and dispersal of forms as well as their assembly into regular paradigms. Grammaticalization again tends to undermine the picture of stability, of clear categorial boundaries, and of structured groups of forms, showing these to be at the most temporary way-stations between different kinds of dispersal, emergence, and fragmentation. This is in fact to be expected, given the approach to grammaticalization developed in this book: that it is essentially the product of reanalysis in the syntagmatic domain of language. It is to this domain that we now turn, with particular attention to functional-semantic hierarchies that motivate the development of markers of subject and object argument structure.

6.4 Argument structure marking: functional-semantic hierarchies and morphological generalization

We have discussed some examples of unidirectionality of segmental form as "compacting" occurs. We have also seen how grammaticalization can proceed along other dimensions too, such as generalization of paradigms. In the case of the development of Old Norse *sik* we also saw spread along a functional-semantic hierarchy in the syntagmatic domain (reflexive, reciprocal, passive, etc.). We illustrate this kind of phenomenon in more detail from object marking in Iranian, and then go on to suggest how evidence from such generalizations can be used to develop research questions concerning languages for which we have only synchronic data, such as Sacapultec.

6.4.1 Object marking in Persian

The development of object marking in Persian (also known as Iranian) nicely exemplifies both the unidirectional cline which comprises lexical word > postposition > suffix and generalization along two other dimensions: the animacy hierarchy and the definiteness hierarchy. According to the animacy hierarchy, human nouns are more likely to be included in linguistic rules than animates in general (e.g., animals), and animates are more likely to be included than inanimates:

human < animate < inanimate < abstract

(for the relation of this hierarchy to personal pronouns, proper nouns, common nouns, and other nominal types as well as to case marking and thematic relations, see Greenberg 1974, Silverstein 1976, and Dixon 1979: 85). According to the definiteness hierarchy, definite (referential) nouns are more likely to be included in linguistic rules than indefinite nouns. Given a three-way distinction between referential definites (e.g., *the*), referential indefinites (e.g., *some/a* in *Some/a man came by trying to sell* The Tribune *this morning*), and non-referential indefinites (e.g., *I need a vacation*), the hierarchy is:

+def/+ref > −def/+ref > −def/−ref

(Croft 1990: 116). For example, definite nouns are readily subjects in English, indefinites less readily so. Passive may be used to avoid indefinite subjects (whether referential or not); and a pseudo-definite subject slot filler *there* is used when a referential indefinite is the subject of an existential copula sentence, as in *There is a man at the door*. Greenberg (1978b) discusses how definite articles may become indefinite, but not vice versa.

It has been suggested that the motivation for hierarchies such as these is the fact that people are more likely to talk about humans than other things, about referential things than about non-referential ones, in other words, factors known as "empathy" and "attention flow" (see Kuno and Kaburaki 1977, DeLancey 1981). These hierarchies capture many organizational phenomena in language, ranging from such relatively obvious properties of discourse as the likelihood of certain nouns occurring in subject position to complex phenomena such as interaction with case and aspect. The animacy hierarchy has already been mentioned in connection with the generalization of genitive case marking to non-finite clause subjects in Finnish (see Section 5.2.2). Here we show its operation in the development of object marking. The data and much of the interpretation are taken from Bossong (1985: 58–79).

At issue is the historical background to the Modern Persian suffix *-râ* in sentences such as (27):

> (27) Ketâb-râ   mi-xân-ad.
> book-ACC CONTIN-read-3SG
> 'He's reading the book.'

> (p. 63)

In such sentences, the object of the verb receives a suffix written as *-râ*, but pronounced [(r)å], the [r] being dropped after stem-final consonants (p. 59). The suffix *-râ* is found only on the direct (accusative) object, not on indirect (dative) objects, and only under certain semantic and discourse circumstances, which we discuss below.

The path toward an object marking (i.e., accusative) suffix on the noun began in Old Persian (*c.* 600 BC) with a noun *rādiy* 'goal, purpose' used as a postposition. By the Middle Persian period this form had become reduced to *-rað* and had become a postposition for dative-benefactive objects, only occasionally used for definite accusative objects and never with indefinite ones. The earliest documents of New Persian (from the ninth century AD on) show a suffix *-râ* used as a definite accusative morpheme, but the dative-benefactive use still flourishes. By the Classical Persian period (twelfth–fourteenth centuries AD) the grammaticalization of *-râ* is complete for all types of definite objects: it is used with all dative and dative-like objects (benefactive, possessive, experiencer) as well as with all accusative objects, provided they are definite. The non-accusative uses are illustrated in the following Classical Persian examples in (28):

> (28) a. Hakim-i   pesar-ân-râ   pand hami-dâd.
> wise-man-a son-PL-DAT advice CONTIN-gave
> 'A wise man was giving his sons advice.'
> b. Ma-râ dar šahr dust-ân   besyâr-and.
> I-POSS in town friend-PL many-3:PL
> 'I have many friends in the town.'

> (Bossong 1985: 61; the spelling is modern)

There appear to be, then, three attested stages between the ninth and fourteenth centuries:

Stage I   (Middle Persian): postposition -*râ* used for dative-benefactive objects

Stage II   (Early Classical New Persian): suffix -*râ* used for dative-benefactive and definite accusative objects

Stage III (Classical New Persian): suffix -*râ* used for dative-benefactive objects, and extensions of the dative-benefactive use such as possessor and experiencer and for definite accusative objects

The change starts with highly specific, individuated objects that are most capable of being affected, namely individual humans. It spreads to all kinds of noun and pronoun objects provided they are individuated (referential). Finally it includes human objects that are only indirectly affected by the action of the verb (possessors and experiencers). This is also a hierarchy of discourse topicality: -*râ* spreads to items down a hierarchy of potential discourse topics, from highly animate participants to ordinary inanimate objects, always provided that they are actually present in the discourse context, that is, that they are referential.

We move now to the Modern Persian period, in which -*râ* has on the one hand been extended to a wider range of NPs, determined on pragmatic discourse grounds that have to do with a foregrounding of the referent, but on the other hand has been restricted with respect to its use with thematic roles. The pragmatic use is seen clearly in (29):

(29)   Arabi-0   balad-i?   Torki-râ   balad-i?
       Arabic-ACC familiar-2SG? Turkish-ACC familiar-2SG?
       'Can you speak Arabic? And Turkish – can you speak that?'
                                                    (Bossong 1985: 67)

The range of -*râ* may even be extended to include indefinites:

(30)   Dâlâne derâze târik-i-râ   peymud.
       corridor long   dark-INDEF-ACC passed-through
       'He passed through a long dark corridor.'
                                                    (p. 66)

At this stage, -*râ* functions to focus on a prominent NP that is the object of a verb, regardless of its animacy and definiteness. Such discourse conditioning of a form as it becomes more grammaticalized is a very important general phenomenon.

At the same time as expanding its range on the animacy and definiteness hierarchies, -*râ* has actually contracted its range on another hierarchy to be discussed in Section 7.5.3, that of thematic roles. With the exception of a few relic phrases, it is now never used in anything but a strictly accusative context, that is, it is used for direct objects only, and is no longer used for dative-like indirect objects. The causes of this contraction of range with respect to thematic roles are not completely understood (see Bossong 1985: 58–79), but may possibly have something to do with a tendency to specialize case markers to the most syntactic cases, that is, subject and object (see H. Smith 1992 for discussion of the interaction of case markers and syntactic case).

6.4.2 *Ergative case marking: a statistical perspective*

The study we have just outlined illustrated morphological generalization over time. In some language families historical data is available from which changing frequencies and discourse environments of forms can be documented. Quite often, however, written historical data is lacking, and trajectories and motivations for grammaticalization must be surmised from the study of the synchronic distribution of grammatical forms in discourse. Among a number of well-known studies of this kind are DeLancey's (1981) and Du Bois's (1987) hypotheses about the clausal marking of case roles. Although the specific forms, and the precise way in which they have emerged, cannot be known, this work shows us how to see that grammatical forms do not exist in a functional vacuum, but reflect general strategies by the speakers of languages for putting together discourses.

Languages that mark subjects and objects with case morphology may present a distinction between an "absolutive" case, the category for objects and intransitive subjects, and an "ergative" case, the category for transitive agentive subjects (two thorough recent treatments of this phenomenon are Comrie 1978 and Dixon 1979). In Basque, the absolutive case suffix is zero, and the ergative case suffix is -(e)k:

(31) a. Martin   ethorri da.
          Martin:ABS came   AUX:3SG
          'Martin came.'
      b. Martin-ek   haurra   igorri du.
          Martin-ERG child:ABS sent   AUX:3SG
          'Martin sent the child.'

(Comrie 1978: 333)

Ergative case marking systems like that of Basque are widely distributed among the world's languages. Ergative languages in fact often agree with one another down to such details as marking the absolutive case with a zero morpheme. To a speaker of a standard European-style "nominative-accusative language" such a system of cases may seem unmotivated. Why do not all "subjects," whether transitive or intransitive, behave as a single grammatical class? Why should objects be marked in the same way as some subjects?

In order to answer this question, we may ask what common functions link the object of the verb with the intransitive subject (absolutive), and set these apart from the transitive subject (ergative). Du Bois (1987) investigated texts in an ergative language, the Maya language Sacapultec, and discovered that "new" information, that is, reference to newer things or persons in the discourse, was often presented in the object of the verb if the clause was transitive, and in the subject if the clause was intransitive. Consider the following two clauses in Sacapultec (spoken in succession by a single speaker):

(32) a. Š-e:-pe: e: išeb' al"ʔ-o:m,
          CMP-3PL:ABS-come PL three boy-PL
          'Three boys came,'
      b. š-0-a:-ki=-siky'-aʔ   l   pe:ra
          CMP-3ABS-MVT-3PL:ERG-pick:up-MVT the pear
          '(They came) and picked up the pear.'

                                        (Du Bois 1987: 824)

(Here, CMP is the completive aspect prefix and MVT is a morpheme meaning 'movement.') In (32a), the three boys are introduced into the narrative with the verb 'come.' Since this verb is intransitive, its subject is 'boys' in the absolutive case; the agreement prefix *e:* on the verb reflects this. In (32b), the newer item is the pear; it is the object of the transitive verb *siky'* meaning 'pick up,' and is likewise in the absolutive case. There is a verbal prefix, which happens to be zero, and which reflects the absolutive case of its object, the pear. The verb has, in addition to the zero aspectual prefix and a 'movement' prefix, a second agreement prefix, *ki-*. This *ki-* is a third person plural ergative and agrees with an unexpressed ergative agent (the situation is roughly the same as the English 'Three boys came and __ picked up . . . ').

In these texts (and it turns out in texts from other languages too) agents are introduced as new entities primarily in the role of intransitive agents. New entities in the discourse introduced in the role of transitive agent are much more rare. One telling statistic is the distribution of the three basic roles (transitive agent, intransitive subject, and transitive object) over the appearance of full nouns, since there is obviously a high correlation between newness in the discourse and reference through lexical nouns. In English sentences such as (33a, b), all three roles – transitive agent and transitive object in (a), intransitive subject in (b) – are represented by full lexical nouns:

(33) a. The paper-boy delivered the magazines.
      b. The letter arrived late.

Yet sentences such as (33a) with a lexical noun in the role of transitive agent, are found to be rare in actual discourse. More commonly, transitive agents are represented by a pronoun (i.e., 'He delivered the magazines'). It must be emphasized that the notion of discourse distribution is critical here. It is not that sentences such as (a) are ungrammatical, or sound strange, or are difficult to elicit in isolation from native speakers; quite the contrary. Rather, empirical evidence in the form of actual text counts reveals a marked skewing such that transitive agents are represented in discourse overwhelmingly by pronouns and appear only rarely as lexical nouns.

In Sacapultec discourse, Du Bois found, a total of 56.5% of all lexical mentions were in the absolutive case category, that is, intransitive subject or transitive object (Du Bois 1987: 827). Within the absolutive case, the two roles were fairly evenly distributed: intransitive subjects comprised 32.8% of lexical noun mentions, and transitive objects 23.7%. By contrast, only 3.4% of full lexical nouns referred to transitive agents. (The remainder of the lexical nouns were found in other sentence roles.)

Evidently Sacapultec has grammaticalized in its case marking not some clause level system of roles involving "agency" and "patienthood," nor even a semantic distinction of animacy, as has sometimes been suggested for ergative languages, but a higher level function involving information flow, that is, the different likelihoods that new information will be presented in one position in the clause rather than another.

According to this analysis, ergative case marking systems seem to emerge as a result of some general discourse tendencies. One of these is to have only one piece of significant new information per clause. Transitive clauses, which contain two arguments, must therefore "manage" their argument structure so as to have at the most one of these two arguments as a lexical noun. Another tendency is to keep the transitive agent anaphoric or "old" (what Du Bois calls the "Given Agent Constraint" – Agent being the designation for the transitive agent) and to assign new information preferentially to the object of the verb. In languages that mark the ergative case only on lexical nouns, then, and mark pronouns in some other way, the ergative case can be seen as the case that marks the transitive agent when it is,

contrary to the general tendency, new to the discourse. The grammaticalization of ergative case marking therefore may consist of a spread of the
ergative case to all transitive subjects, both lexical nouns and pronouns.

By contrast, nominative-accusative systems appear to have grammaticalized in their case marking the syntactic argument roles subject and object,
perhaps via a discourse strategy that aligned agents, whatever their status
with respect to transitivity or to old or new information (Du Bois 1985).

Such quantitative studies as Du Bois (1987) of the synchronic relationships between forms and discourse functions have significant implications
for the study of grammaticalization, in that they suggest explanations from
actual usage for the emergence of a grammatical function. It should be
stressed, however, that the question of **which** form or set of forms comes to
express this function is a separate one. While the grammaticalization of
ergative case morphology may "fall out" from discourse pressure to
distribute arguments in certain ways, the source of the forms themselves
varies. In Malay, for example, an agentive-ergative preposition *oleh* seems
to have its origin in a verb of a separate clause; a sentence such as (34)
would then have originated from something like 'The letter was written
(and) the teacher did (it)':

(34) Surat itu ditulis   oleh   Chek guru.
     letter the 3AG:write ERG:PREP(title) teacher
     'The teacher wrote the letter.'

Here the former verb *oleh*, now the ergative case preposition, once had a
range of meanings apparently encompassing 'get,' 'obtain,' 'do,' 'manage,'
'return.' In other languages, ergative constructions emerge from quite
different sources, such as the passive with an agent in the instrumental case
(among historical studies, see Chung 1977 on developments in Polynesian
languages, S. Anderson 1977 on developments in a variety of languages,
including Hindi, and 1988 on general issues, and Shibatani 1991 on
developments in Philippine languages). As we would expect from grammaticalization in general, the type of source is constrained by discourse
strategies operating on pragmatically and semantically relevant structures.

6.5   Loss

As we saw in connection with the Russian instrumental (Section
5.6), and the Iranian object marker (Section 6.4.1), morphemes can often
remain stable for very long periods, shifting their function in broadly
predictable ways but persisting in their shape. Nonetheless, at the extreme
end of the history of a particular form as a grammatical marker we may find

loss, either of form alone or occasionally of both form and function. Examples of the loss of a form alone occur whenever two or more competing forms exist for the same function, and one is eventually selected at the expense of the others. We have cited many examples of this phenomenon, including the specialization of the French negative *pas* from among a wider set of possibilities, or the selection of periphrastic tenses and aspects over inflectional ones in Late Latin and early Romance.

Similarly, whole inflectional paradigms can pass out of general use, as has happened with the French "passé simple" such as *elle s'évanouit* 'she fainted.' The same has almost happened with the German "imperfect" (i.e., preterit), where *er las* 'he read' is fast receding. In both these instances the older paradigm remains in written and formal registers, but is essentially dead in the colloquial registers. "Renewal," that is, the replacement of a dying form by a newer, usually periphrastic, form with a similar meaning, is common in such cases. Thus the French "passé simple" has been replaced as the ordinary past tense of the verb by the periphrastic perfect (*elle s'est évanouie* 'she fainted'), and the German imperfect also is giving way to the perfect (*er hat gelesen* 'he read').

More unusual is loss of both the morphological function that a form once served and loss of the form itself (or absorption into the stem as a meaningless component). In Old English, for example, adjectives still had case, number, and gender suffixes; thus the singular of the adjective meaning 'good' was as shown in Table 6.12. None of these suffixes has survived as a productive morpheme into PDE; however, in the modern adverb *seldom* we find a relic of the dative plural in -*um* of the adjective *seld* 'strange, rare.' The suffix -*um* in PDE *seldom* is said to have become "de-morphologized," that is, to have lost its morphological value (for some discussion of de-morphologization, see Joseph and Janda 1988). From another, more positive, perspective the process of de-morphologization can be seen as one of "phonogenesis" (Hopper 1990, 1992a), whereby "dead" morphemes become sedimented as phonological segments and over long

Table 6.12 *Old English strong[8] adjective singular inflection*

	Masculine	Neuter	Feminine
Nominative	god	god	god
Genitive	godes	godes	godre
Dative	godum	godum	godre
Instrumental	gode	gode	godre
Accusative	godne	god	gode

periods actually create and repair the phonological bulk of words, rather like the way the shells of dead molluscs create geological formations. The Modern Irish verbs in the left-hand column in (35) derive from simple verb stems to which were attached one or more adverbial prefixes with directional or locative meanings:[9]

(35) **Modern Irish**   **Early Old Irish**
  tag- 'come'   to-theig 'to-go'
  imigh 'go, leave'   imb-theg 'about-go'
  friotaigh 'resist'   frith-to-theg 'against-to-go'
  fog- 'leave'   fo-ad-gab 'under-toward-take'
  faigh 'get'   fo-gab 'under-take'
  abair 'say'   ad-ro-ber 'toward-for-bear'

But the Modern Irish forms are no longer synchronically analyzable as having prefixes – the earlier prefixes are now simply part of the phonology of the verb stem. In this way phonological segments can often be seen to consist of old morphemes; the -*nd* of English *friend, fiend* is a relic of the Germanic present participle -*ende* (cf. German *freuende* 'enjoying'), and these two nouns derive from verbal roots meaning, respectively, 'love' and 'hate.'

De-morphologization can have a real effect on phonology because it may bring about phonotactic changes, that is, changes in canonical syllable shape (introducing, e.g., new consonant clusters) and word length, and this in turn may affect tone and stress. An instance of the effect of de-morphologization on phonotactics has been described by Dixon in the Australian language Olgolo (Dixon 1982 [1969]). In Olgolo many word-initial consonants were lost through erosion. As a result, a considerable number of words began with vowels, an "unnatural" situation which speakers of the language appear to be in the process of remedying by creating noun prefixes out of old demonstratives. These ex-demonstratives marked semantic classes; consequently the new initial consonants still roughly reflect such semantic divisions as animals and insects (*nh*-); fish, oysters, and eels (*y*-); and a broad class of inanimates that include trees, grasses, sun, fire, and language (*w*-). The most important effect has been a phonological one: to restore to the language many more instances of word-initial "natural" (i.e., CV) syllables.

The end product of grammaticalization is thus phonology in the very literal sense of phonological segments. Phonogenesis plays the vital role of ensuring that the attrition which occurs in the natural course of change is compensated for by accretion. De-morphologization in its end stages is therefore not reducible to loss, but rather involves a kind of "phonological strengthening." There is an interesting parallel here to the pragmatic strengthening that we saw always accompanies semantic loss in earlier stages of grammaticalization (see Section 4.5).

Sometimes de-morphologization will not be complete, but will result in the emergence of a new grammatical form. Greenberg (1991) has used the term "re-grammaticalization" to refer to this possibility. Among the examples Greenberg cites is a change in demonstratives whereby they frequently become definite articles ("Stage I"), and then expand their range to include all specific nouns, whether definite or indefinite ("Stage II"). At this stage the article often becomes morphologized as a prefix or suffix on the noun, but it retains some of its article-like functions, in, for example, not being used in generic expressions (compare English *at school, on foot*, etc.). In the next stage ("Stage III"), the use of the affix spreads to virtually all nouns, including proper names. This new distribution leads to a situation in which the former demonstrative assumes new functions having to do with a form's "nominality," its status as a member of the category "noun." One such function, for instance, would be nominalization, i.e., creating nouns out of verbs; another, pluralization (Greenberg 1991: 304–5).

"Re-grammaticalization" might at first sight appear to go counter to unidirectionality in that the process of de-morphologization is apparently arrested and reversed. However, as Greenberg notes, all the examples that he cites initially involve grammatical meanings and dispersal of grammatical function. From this perspective, then, the term "re-grammaticalization" is not really an appropriate one. As we noted in Section 5.6, such cases are best seen not as examples of a radical shift in directionality but rather as natural examples of the sort of generalization, spread, and splitting into different functions that accompanies ongoing grammaticalization.

7
Grammaticalization across clauses

7.1 Introduction

Ordinary discourse does not consist of isolated, context-free utterances, but of linked information units comprising reports, orders, comments, descriptions, and other kinds of linguistic activity. These units, usually expressed by clauses, typically consist of a verb and indicators of the arguments of the verb, in the form of lexical nouns, pronouns, or pronominal affixes. All languages have devices for linking clauses together into what are called complex sentences. These tend to be classified in grammars according to functional-semantic principles, for example, whether a clause functions as an NP (complements, or "noun clauses"), modifies an NP (relative clauses), or has adverbial functions (e.g., temporal, causative, or conditional clauses). However, the form of a "complex sentence" may differ quite radically among languages and among speakers and occasions of speech in one and the same language, from fairly simple juxtapositions of relatively independent clauses characteristic of casual speech, such as (1) to complex dependent rhetorical constructions arising in the context of traditions of written grammar, such as (2):

(1)   Within the decade there will be an earthquake. It is likely to destroy the whole town.

(2)   That there will be an earthquake within the decade that will destroy the whole town is likely.

It has been customary to discuss the development of markers of clause linkage such as the two instances of *that* in (2) in terms of grammaticalization. For example, the development of complementizers, conditional conjunctions, relativizers, and so forth are standard topics exemplifying the grammaticalization of lexical items or the increased grammaticalization of already grammatical items in specifc contexts (in this case, the context of clause combining). So are syntactic changes whereby initially separate clauses may become totally interlaced such that the boundaries between clauses may become obscured at the surface level (e.g., (*It*) *seems that he is right* > *He seems to be right*) or at least a clause may become attached to a constituent inside the matrix clause.

Until recently, however, less attention has been paid to the possibility of including the process of clause combining itself within grammaticalization, except notably in the work of Givón. He proposed (1979: 209) a path of grammaticalization of the type:

discourse > syntax > morphology > morphophonemics > zero

By "discourse" here he meant the loose, unplanned, informal mode of communication in language. Givón illustrated the first three stages of the path (discourse > syntax > morphology) by such phenomena as shifts from topic into subject, and topic sentences into relative clauses, finite clauses in concatenated structures into non-finite complementation structures (e.g., the serial type *I want I go* > *I want to go*). If grammaticalization is defined broadly so as to encompass the motivations for and development of grammatical structures in general, then processes of clause combining clearly fall squarely within its domain, as Givón suggested.

In this chapter we show first that clause combining can be considered from the point of view of a unidirectional cline from relatively free juxtaposition to syntactic and morphological bondedness within the framework of grammaticalization broadly construed. We then focus on a few examples of the development of clause combining across time where the theory of grammaticalization may either help us understand the facts of complex sentence structure, or may suggest a different way of thinking about it than has been customary.

7.2 A cline of clause combining constructions

Many studies of complex sentence structure suggest a sharp distinction between coordinate and subordinate clause structure. This tradition has been based in part on evidence from Indo-European languages and especially the written records that give insight into their history. Recently, the distinction has been called into question as a result of the study of non-Indo-European and of spoken languages (see especially Brugman, Macaulay *et al.* 1984, Haiman and Thompson 1984 on the problem of defining subordination cross-linguistically). Here we have space to sketch only one framework for the study of clause combining. More thorough recent treatments suggesting alternative viewpoints are to be found in Foley and Van Valin (1984), Shopen (1985, vol. 2), Haiman and Thompson (1988), and Austin (1988 – on Australian languages).

A complex sentence, syntactically defined, is a unit that consists of more than one clause. A clause that can stand alone can be referred to as a "nucleus" (Longacre 1985). A complex sentence may consist of a nucleus and one or more additional nuclei, or of a nucleus and one or more "margins," relatively dependent clauses that may not stand alone but nevertheless exhibit different degrees of dependency. Among clauses which form margins, three types can be semantically distinguished: "those which function as noun phrases (called complements), those which function as modifiers of nouns (called relative clauses), and those which function as modifiers of verb phrases or entire propositions (called adverbial clauses)" (Thompson and Longacre 1985: 172). As will be discussed below, adverbial and appositive relative clauses may be less dependent than restrictive relative and complement clauses in some languages, or at some stages of a language.

From the point of view of language change, the initial formation of a complex clause involves the combining into one integrated structure of two separate and autonomous nuclei that are mutually relevant. The act of combining the clauses and signaling this combination linguistically is grounded in rhetorical production strategies. The new single structure becomes more complex in the process, because it now consists of two subparts. Thus independent and autonomous S1 and S2 in (3) are combined in (4) ($\Leftrightarrow$ signals mutual relevance):

(3) S1 $\Leftrightarrow$ S2

(4) S1 ⟋ S ⟍ S2

Complex sentences range in type from multiple nuclei that are juxtaposed under one intonation contour but have no segmental (overt morphological or syntactic) indication of a grammatical relationship between them, to combinations of nucleus and margin in which this relationship is highly compressed. To simplify, we can think initially of a cline with three "cluster points" as follows (the cline is based on discussion by Matthiessen and Thompson 1988; C. Lehmann 1988, 1989; and Langacker 1991):

(a) "Parataxis," or relative independence, except as constrained by the pragmatics of "making sense" and relevance.

(b) "Hypotaxis" or interdependency, in which there is a nucleus, and one or more clauses which cannot stand by themselves, and are therefore relatively dependent. However, they are typically not wholly included within any constituent of the nucleus.

(c) "Subordination," or, in its extreme form, "embedding," in other words, complete dependency, in which a margin is wholly included within a constituent of the nucleus.

These cluster points can be characterized by a "cline of clause combining":

parataxis > hypotaxis > subordination

This can further be elaborated by specification in terms of combinations of the features ±dependent, ±embedded:[1]

parataxis	>	hypotaxis	>	subordination
−dependent		+dependent		+dependent
−embedded		−embedded		+embedded

In establishing these three cluster points, we preempt and redefine the terminology of two traditions, and expand two overlapping pairs into a three-way distinction. One pair – parataxis versus hypotaxis – derives from a primarily nineteenth century tradition in which parataxis was understood to include all kinds of juxtaposition, and hypotaxis to include all kinds of dependency. The other pair – coordination versus subordination and especially embedding – derives from more recent traditions, in which coordination and embedding are defined formally in terms of constituent structure.

The minimal process in clause combining is unification and bonding, at least pragmatically. Such bonding is often, most especially in the case of subordination, accompanied by hierarchical downgrading and desententiali-zation (C. Lehmann 1988), hence decategorialization of one member of the complex structure into a margin. A nucleus canonically contains a finite verb. Therefore decategorialization typically entails reduction of the finite-ness of the verb. Of particular interest to us is the extent to which the cline of dependency matches up with a cline of grammatical integration, for example, finiteness on the left and non-finiteness on the right, expressed by clausal remnants such as infinitives and participles. A special case of integration is that in which bonding brings about what C. Lehmann calls "interlacing": the sharing of participants (e.g., same subject), or of tenses and moods, and also the interweaving of originally separate clauses into the surface structure of the matrix (in *She seems to be smart*, *she* appears in the matrix but is actually the subject of the embedded clause, as shown by *It seems that she is smart*).

The question is whether the different types of clause combining are motivated, and if so, by what. Givón has suggested that there is a cognitive form-function parallelism of the following type: "The more two *events/states* are integrated semantically or pragmatically, the more will the clauses that code them be integrated grammatically" (Givón 1990: 826). This is a statement about diagrammatic iconicity as it pertains to the overt form that a clause takes, not its covert, abstract structure, and can be illustrated by the various forms of complementation in English. Under most current syntactic analyses, the four sentences in (5) involve a "matrix" and a "subordinate" clause at some level of syntactic abstraction; however, they also show increasing degrees of overt morphosyntactic integration. From a discourse perspective they can also be seen to represent increasing degrees of connectedness between states of affairs (or, according to Langacker, increased grounding in the subject's immediate experience of the event):

(5) a. We realize that you have to make a profit.
     b. His wife only pretended to believe his implausible story.
     c. Portia really enjoys walking along the beach.
     d. Numerous witnesses heard the bomb explode.

(Langacker 1991: 439)

In other words, the hypothesis is that the more overt and independent devices for signaling clause linkage (e.g., clitics such as *that* in (5a)) are correlated with minimal semantic-pragmatic integration, and the least overt (in some languages an inflectional affix, in others like English no marking at all) are correlated with maximal semantic-pragmatic integration.

In thinking about the cline of clause combining from the point of view of grammaticalization, then, we need to think of the interaction of at least the properties in Figure 7.1.[2]

parataxis	hypotaxis	subordination
(independence)	(interdependence)	(dependence)

nucleus ———————————————————————————— margin

minimal integration ———————————————— maximal integration

maximal overt linking ———————————————— minimal overt linking

Figure 7.1 Properties relevant to the cline of clause combining

We illustrate some correlations, both weak and strong, between the various factors immediately below and then go on to discuss some examples of the development of complex sentence structures that illustrate the properties in Figure 7.1.

7.2.1 Parataxis

The simplest kind of relationship between two clauses is juxtaposition in which two or more nuclei occur next to one another and the semantic relationship between them is by inference only:

(6) Fort Sumter has been fired on. My regiment leaves at dawn.

The nature of the inferential relationship between such juxtaposed clauses has been discussed in connection with examples (4a) and (4b) in 4.2.3. Two juxtaposed clauses of this kind with independent intonation contours and without any overt signal of linking do not constitute a single complex sentence. However, when juxtaposed clauses are linked in some way, such as by intonation, or by virtue of sharing a single lexical noun subject, there is reason to think of the two clauses as united grammatically into one sentence by parataxis. Caesar's putative declaration, already cited in Section 2.3 as an example of diagrammatic iconicity, is a well-known example of parataxis without overt clause linkage:

(7) Veni, vidi, vici.
     'I came, I saw, I conquered.'

(c. 146, Suetonius, Jul. 37)

Each of the three clauses is autonomous. Each constitutes a nucleus. But this is considered to constitute one sentence with multiple nuclei because the punctuation represents a single unit, that is, a single overarching intonation contour.

Parataxis is in many languages a normal way of forming complex sentences. In Chinese, for example, paratactic clauses may function exactly like clauses which in other languages are overtly marked as margin and nucleus:

(8) Ta mei nian shu, ta da qiu le.
     he NEG study book he hit ball ASP
     'He didn't study, he played ball.'

(Thompson and Longacre 1985: 175)

This sentence would be the usual way in Chinese of saying 'Instead of studying, he played ball.' In some registers of English, simple juxtaposition over a single intonation contour is a common way to express conditional sentences:

(9)   You keep smoking those cigarettes, you're gonna start coughing again.

and even for relative clauses:

(10)   That guy just walked out the store, he reminds me of the photo in the post-office window.

Paratactic clauses of this type are often thought not to show any overt linkage markers. If this is so, then there is clear evidence for the independence of parataxis and maximal overt linking as characterized in Figure 7.1. A question that still needs to be resolved is to what extent the different intonation contours involved in paratactic clause combining may function exactly like overt grammatical markers. For example, (9) is interpreted as a conditional only if the first clause ends in a rising intonation. Otherwise, the construction is considered incoherent.[3] It has been customary to treat only explicit connective words such as *and*, *if*, *who*, or segmental morphology such as clitic *-que* 'and' in Latin in discussions of clause combining. However, recent interest in information flow and differences between orality and literacy have led to important developments in understanding the role of intonation as a morphosyntactic phenomenon (see, e.g., Bolinger 1984, and Chafe 1988). We will not discuss this issue further here, however, because insights into changes in such contours are hard if not virtually impossible to achieve.

   Constructions consisting of adjacent nuclei under one sentential intonation contour and having an explicit connective word such as 'and,' are considered to be more "grammaticalized" than those without, that is, they show more overt grammatical morphosyntax. Such clauses are said to be "coordinated":

(11)   I came and I saw and I conquered.

(12)   Emily is training to be a speech therapist, and Joel works for a law firm in Philadelphia.

Overt clause linkage markers in coordinate sentence structures (equivalents of *and*, *but*, *or*) tend to be developed relatively late in languages, or to be borrowed from "high" registers (Mithun 1988). They are unstable and tend to be renewed frequently (Meillet 1915–16 [1958]). The development of *plus* (originally borrowed from Latin, and recently from mathematical discourse) for *and* is an example in contemporary American English.

7.2.2 *Hypotaxis*

The equivalents of the "coordinated clauses" of modern European languages are in many other languages not structured with overt coordinating conjunctions, but are either presented as simple paratactic clauses, as in the case of (9) and (10), or as a margin with a nucleus, as in the following examples from Japanese:

(13) a. Kōto o   nui-de   hangā ni kaketa.
          coat OBJ take-off-*de* hanger on hung
          'I took my coat off and hung it on a hanger.'
      b. Wain o   nomisugi-te   atama ga   itai.
          wine OBJ drink-too-much-*te* headache SUBJ have
          'I drank too much wine and have a headache.'

In (13) the suffix -*te*/-*de* on the verb stem signals that the clause in question is interdependent and more marginal than an independent nucleus. However, it is not fully dependent. In other words, it is hypotactic. In many languages of Africa, the Americas, New Guinea, and Asia a construction similar to the Japanese -*te* construction is used to link clauses together over long stretches of discourse. This phenomenon is known as "clause chaining." In such chains, usually only one of the clauses is a nucleus containing the full range of verbal markers for tense, aspect, mood, and so on. If the language is verb-final (OV), the fully marked verb is the last in the series. Often the verbal inflections in the chained clauses (margins) are restricted to carrying information about the participants, not temporality. This is especially true of New Guinea languages, where the interior verbs (known as "medial" verbs) are suffixed with indicators of the person and number of the subject of the following verb but not for tense, aspect or mood. The following is an example from Hua with a medial (MED) ending -*gana* that signals switch reference (SW) (the subject of the second verb is not the same as that of the first):

(14) Minaroga rmu:gana   baie.
      down-there go-down:MED:SW stay:3SG:NON-FUT
      'I went down there and he stayed; after/because I went down there, he stayed.'

(Haiman 1984: 68)

Hypotaxis is not limited to clause chaining. Among other hypotactic constructions are appositional relatives in English. These are semantically and even syntactically equivalent to appositional (parenthetical, clarificational) structures, and even to coordinate clauses. For example, (15a) is equivalent to (15b):

(15) a. Bill Smith, who is our president, would like to meet with you.
      b. Bill Smith would like to meet with you. By the way, he is our president.

Furthermore, the matrix NP and the relative can be reversed in order, with only minor pragmatic differences:

(15) c. Our president, Bill Smith, would like to meet with you.

Appositive relatives can even carry their own illocutionary force, that is, they can function as speech acts independent of the speech act of the matrix clause. This means that they can function as questions or imperatives within statements, something which canonically embedded clauses cannot do. An example from Latin is:

(16) Perutiles   Xenophontis libri   sunt, quos
      highly-useful Xenophon's books are, which
      legite   quaeso, studiose!
      read-IMP/PL ask-ISG, studiously
      'Highly useful are Xenophon's books; please read them
      thoroughly.'
                (*c.* 40 BC, Cic.Cat.M.59; cited in C. Lehmann 1988: 194)

Other hypotactic constructions include adverbial clauses, including temporals ('when'-clauses), causals ('because'-clauses), conditional ('if'-clauses), and concessives ('although'-clauses). Example (9) contains two nuclei, and is paratactic. In other, more formal or "literate," registers, the same relationship may be indicated with explicit morphology:

(17) If you keep smoking those cigarettes, you're going to start coughing again.

In (17) the *if*-clause cannot stand on its own. Traditional grammars have treated adverbial clauses as subordinate or embedded. But as Matthiessen and Thompson (1988) show, the relationship of dependency is different from that of the prototypical cases of embedding. Specifically, there is a semantic difference. For example, in (18), *before leaving* is equivalent to *before his departure*, a nominalization that presents an event as an entity, not to *before noon*, which is an adverbial phrase with a noun:

> (18) Before leaving Krishnapur, the Collector took a strange decision.
>
> (Matthiessen and Thompson 1988: 180)

As we will see below, adverbial clauses actually arose out of the reanalysis of adverbial phrases as adverbial clauses; however, they have not reached the level of incorporation that, for example, complements have done.

Adverbial clauses themselves show a continuum of looser-to-tighter integration, a continuum that correlates with their function. Thus an explanatory causal can have independent illocutionary force, as in (19a), while a causal giving the grounds for the consequent cannot do so (19b).

> (19) a. The Knicks are going to win, because who on earth can stop Bernard?
>
> (G. Lakoff 1984: 474)
>
> b. *The Knicks are going to win because do they have the best players?

7.2.3 Subordination

Subordinate clauses are dependent on their matrix clauses in various ways. For one, they cannot have different illocutionary force from the matrix. For another, they are equivalent to the constituents they express. In addition, they typically are interlaced in some way. In the following example of an English restrictive relative, *who just walked out of the store* is structurally equivalent to nominal modifiers such as *the*. Furthermore, it is surrounded by material from the matrix clause (*I think the guy . . . resembles the . . .*):

> (20) I think the guy who just walked out of the store resembles the photo in the post-office window.

In the following example of a Latin conjunct participial construction, the predicative adjective phrase *patria pulsum* is equivalent to a modifier of *Aristides*. The event of Aristides' expulsion is expressed as hierarchically dependent on the object arguments (*Aristides*):

> (21) Aristidem   patria   pulsum   viderunt.
> Aristides-ACC country-ABL expelled-ACC saw-3PL
> 'They saw Aristides, who had been exiled.'
>
> (Haiman and Thompson 1984: 515)

(21) contrasts with the considerably more hypotactic ablative absolute construction in (22); here there is no relationship between the absolute clause and the verb:

(22) Aristide   patria   pulso,   Persae
      Aristides-ABL country-ABL expelled-ABL, Persians
      Graecos   aggressi sunt.
      Greeks-ACC attacked AUX
      'Aristides having been exiled, the Persians attacked the Greeks.'

(ibid.)

Subordinate clauses on the right hand side of the clause combining cline function semantically as well as syntactically as expressions of a constituent. This is particularly obvious in late-stage complementation types, where a clause functions as an argument of the matrix. In (23), *that the Titanic sank* is equivalent both to the nominalization *the sinking of the Titanic* and to the noun phrase *the disaster*:

(23)   That the Titanic sank was unexpected.

7.3   The grammaticalization of clause linkers

The world's languages display a wide variety of techniques for linking clauses into tighter amalgamations. These techniques range from forms and expressions that are indistinguishable from lexical items, such as 'time,' 'place,' to affixes indicating subordination whose origins are completely unknown. Still, significant generalizations about the origins of such forms can be made.

We have seen that grammaticalization does not involve special principles that make reference only to morphosyntax, but is a subset of the processes of language change in general. The historical development of connectives tends therefore to be similar to that of other lexical items, though their positional and suprasegmental features may make them subject to special kinds of changes. Clause linkage markers have their sources in nouns, verbs, adverbs, pronouns, case morphemes (including prepositions and postpositions), derivational affixes, and in phrasal combinations of these. Fairly recently, for example, in spoken English the prepositional phrases *on the basis* (*of*) and *in terms of* have come to be used to link clauses together:

(24)   He's asked for the special retirement package *on the basis* he's been with the firm over twenty years.

(25)   They're a general nuisance *in terms of* they harrass people trying
to enjoy the park.

Once they are recruited as clause linkage markers, the originally lexical
constructions typically undergo the same types of changes as they would as
members of a noun-to-affix or of a verb-to-affix cline.

Typical of hypotactic developments (though by no means necessary or
diagnostic of them) is the recruitment to connective function of deictics and
other demonstratives. The motivation here is the extension of deictic
reference from entities referred to in the non-linguistic world to anaphors
and cataphors of NPs and then to anaphors or cataphors of propositions
(clauses). In other words, deictics may be used for metalinguistic functions
involving clause reference in order to achieve overt linking of clauses. For
example, in Gunwinggu, an Australian aboriginal language, we find clauses
occurring where the linkage is signaled by deictics anaphoric to the
preceding clause as well as by a single overarching intonation contour. For
example, in (26) *gunu* 'that' refers back to 'our language we write':

(26)   . . . dja mi:n bu   ŋadman gadbere gunwo:g
. . . and not   in-regard-to ourselves our   language
garibi'bi:mbun, gunu gari'wagan
we-write,   that we-don't-know
'. . . but we don't know at all how to write our own language'
(Berndt and Berndt 1951: 37, cited in Mithun 1984: 498)

Sometimes a more explicit deictic phrase is used containing a lexical noun
rather than simply a pronoun. One example, the development of *while*, has
been discussed in 4.3.2. The major difference from the development of
prepositions discussed in Section 5.3.1 is that clause linkage markers, when
they function in ways similar to prepositions, introduce whole clauses, at
least at first. In so doing they maximize the constituent with which they are
associated.

Clause linkage markers are in their origins motivated by speakers' desire
to be clear and informative, particularly to give directions to hearers for
interpreting clauses in terms of their linguistic environment (see Halliday
and Hasan 1976). Initially they serve to signal the functional relationship of
the combined clauses to each other (as in the case of the deictics illustrated
above), and to mark syntactic boundaries (which may be obscured by later
syntactic interlacing processes). The cross-linguistic study of clause linkage
markers and the observation that they tend to fall into clearly definable
semantic-pragmatic sets has led linguists recently to characterize somewhat
more fully than in the past the function of many types of clause combining.

For example, it has been observed (Haiman 1985a, Traugott 1985b) that conditional connectives derive from sources such as the following (examples are from Traugott 1985b):

(a) Forms for modality, e.g.: *suppose* (often found as the only marker of the "protasis" or *if-* clause in creoles); Mandarin Chinese *yào* 'wish, be necessary, if'; Miangkabau (Sumatra) *kò'* 'perhaps, may be if.'

(b) Interrogatives: Hua *-ve* 'interrogative, topic status, if'; Russian *esli* < *est* 'be' + *li* 'whether.'

(c) Temporals expressing duration, or temporals that are ambiguous between duration and punctuality: Swahili *i-ki-wa* (*-ki-* imperfect); Hittite *mān* 'when, if, potential'; Tagalog (*ka*)*pag*(*ka*), *kung* 'if, then, while'; Indonesian *djika* 'if, when,' *kalau* 'if, when, as for.'

(d) Copula constructions: Swahili *i-ki-wa* 'it being that' (*-w-* 'be'); Japanese *nara* 'be,' Chickasaw (*h*)*oo* 'be.'

(e) Forms signaling something as known or given: English *given that*, Latin and Romance *si* (<*sei* 'so' < *s* 2nd person deictic + *ei* locative); Sanskrit *yád* 'topic, conditional'; Indonesian *kalau* 'if, as for.'

Conditionals raise possibilities and cast doubt on propositions; therefore the presence of modalities and interrogatives among the sources of conditionals seems naturally motivated by the function of conditionals. The fact that conditionals derive from durative temporal relationships and copulas can be seen to reflect the fact that conditionality presupposes an extant (durative) condition. The presence of topic markers among sources for conditionals may seem more surprising, however. The recruitment of such topic markers for conditional marking, as well as other factors such as clause order patterns, have suggested to Haiman (1978) that conditionals are topics. However, the presence of non-topic sources, especially modalities, as well as the pragmatics of certain uses of conditionals, suggests that conditionals are only partially topics in function (for discussion, see Akatsuka 1986).

The point here is essentially that grammaticalization of items, whether lexical or morphological, is constrained by the grammatical function to be expressed, and by the appropriateness of the inferences from the source items for the function in question. With sufficient evidence from cross-linguistic studies, the researcher can extrapolate pragmatic functions from the forms recruited for grammatical purposes. This is especially useful when new areas of grammatical structure are studied.

Once a form has been recruited for a new function, it will itself be subject to new inferences from that function, and these new inferences will in turn permit further grammaticalization. Thus it appears that temporals can be the sources of conditionals (and causals), not vice versa; conditionals can in turn be the source of concessives (as can temporals such as *while* and focus particles such as *even* or universals quantifiers such as *any* as in *anyhow*) (König 1986, M. Harris 1988). Thus we find *if* being used as a concessive in:

(27) This is an interesting, if complicated, solution.

(König 1986: 239)

Concessive meanings develop late in the history of specific clause linkage markers partly because the concessive is more abstract, partly because it is more complex logically.

Once the principle of an extremely close cognitive relationship between the form of a grammatical marker and its function, in other words, its iconicity, has been appreciated, the reasons for both the range and the limitations of the sources for particular clause linkage markers should seem quite natural. We take a more detailed look here at some of the sources of complementizers.

As discussed in Chapter 1, one source of complementizers is verbs of saying. The grammaticalization of a verb of saying as a complementizer, and the generalization to verbs of desiring, fearing, and other mental states, is very widespread, as the numerous examples cited by Lord (1976: 187–9) testify. The origins of 'say' as a complementizer can perhaps be understood from its constant use in discourse in which, for example, wanting, fearing, wondering, etc. are not purely private matters but are to a great extent the result of interactive construction of the object. The Greek New Testament has numerous examples to illustrate this, e.g.:

(28) Hoi de   anthrōpoi ethaumasan legontes potamos   estin
     the then men   wondered   saying   what-kind-of is
     houtos hoti kai hoi anemoi kai hē thalassa hupakouousin
     this   that and the winds   and the sea   obey
     autǭ.
     him
     'And people were amazed, saying: "What kind of man is this,
     that the winds and the sea obey him?" '

(Matthew VIII,27)

Here *legontes* 'saying' is a verbal participle that is virtually a complementizer of *ethaumasan* 'were amazed.' It is as if a person can be generally in an an amazed state of mind, but as soon as the amazement is attributed to something specific, it must be articulated aloud. A modern translation might well be: 'And people wondered to one another what kind of man this was, that the wind and the sea obeyed him.'

Another source of complementizers is closely associated with nominal morphology, hardly a surprising factor when we consider that complements are essentially clauses functioning as NPs. We will discuss the history of pronominal deictic *that* below in Section 7.5.1. Other nominal sources include case morphemes of various types. These may be prepositions or postpositions, including case prefixes and suffixes attached to a verb phrase or nominalized form of the verb. The following is from the Tungusic language Evenki:

(29) ənii-m   əə-ćəə-n   saa-rə   si   tənəwə
     mother-my NEG-PAST-3SG know-(?) you yesterday
     əmə-nəə-wəə-s.
     come-PTPL-ACC-2SG
     'My mother doesn't know that you arrived yesterday.'
                                              (Comrie 1981b: 83)

The accusative case morpheme is added to the resultative participle of the verb *come* and the participle is seen to be nominal from both the case ending and the second singular person possessor suffix. Genetti (1991) provides a detailed account of the development of postpositions into subordinators in Newari, and of cross-linguistic evidence of similar changes in other Tibeto-Burman languages.

Often the parallelism with an ordinary noun phrase is obvious, as in instances such as the Evenki one in (29), and in English:

(30) a. He left without telling the guide.
     b. He left without his compass.

Sometimes the similarity is not so clear because the historical origins have become obscured. For example, in English the infinitive in *to* functions as the object of some complement taking verbs, but the parallelism with the "allative" proposition *to* may not seem obvious:

(31) a. We want *to* ask you a few questions.
     b. We handed the box *to* the Gypsy.

Absent historical data, one might wrongly assume that the two instances of *to* were simply fortuitous homonyms. However, because the reanalysis of a dative-allative particle as a complementizer is widespread, it is methodologically appropriate to assume that there might indeed some motivation for the form. For instance, in Maori *ki* is both a dative and an allative, and is a complementizer with the same kinds of verbs as English *want*, etc.:

(32) a. **Allative**
          E   hoki   ana   au ki te kaainga.
          PRES return PROG I   to the village
          'I am going back to the village.'

      b. **Dative**
          Ka   hoatu te   taurekareka ki te   rangatira.
          AOR given the slave   to the chief
          'The slave was given to the chief.'

      c. **Complementizer**
          E   hiahia ana   raatou ki   te haere.
          PRES want PROG they   COMP the go
          'They want to go.'

(Noonan 1985: 47–8)

Similarly French *à* in (33) has its origins in the Latin preposition *ad* 'to,' which when construed with a verb required the verb to be in the nominalized form known as the "gerund."

(33) La musique contribuait   à épaisser   l'atmosphère.
      the music   contribute-IMPF to thicken-INF the atmosphere
      'The music contributed to thickening the atmosphere.'

(Simenon; cited in Gamillscheg 1957: 462)

From the verb root *viv-* 'live' would be formed the infinitive *vivere* and the gerund *vivendum*, for example:

(34) Ad beate   vivendum virtute   opus est.
      to blessedly live-GER courage-ABL need is
      'To live blessedly there is need of courage.'

(Gamillscheg 1957: 462)

Later the infinitive gained ground at the expense of the gerund, and before the Old French period had replaced it altogether. In Late Latin *ad* was already being construed with the infinitive:

(35) Quomodo potest hic   nobis   carnem
      how   can   this-MASC/NOM us-DAT meat-ACC
      dare   ad manducare?
      give-INF to eat-INF
      'How can this man give us meat to eat?'

                         (*Vulgate*; cited in Gamillscheg 1957: 462)

The use of an allative-dative marker as a complementizer is common when
(as in English *want to V*, etc.) the tense of the complement is determined by
the nature of the main clause verb (Noonan 1985: 47–8), perhaps especially
when the infinitive suggests an action which is potential or future. It is
possible to see in this kind of phenomenon a common tendency toward a
mental association of "prospective" space with "prospective" time. The
pointing forward of the allative-dative to goal is inevitably linked to the
"forwardness in time" of the complement of *want*. Most verbs expressing
commands, requests, expectations, wishes, etc. have as part of their
semantics a goal, whether another person's action, or a desired object.

  Evidence from the history of English *to* does in fact illustrate the kind of
change involved, even though these origins are far from perspicuous. *To*
originally served as a preposition meaning 'toward' introducing a nominalized verb. It was, in other words, comparable with the Latin gerund. The
nominalized noun was in OE the infinitive, that is, the verb stem suffixed
with *-an/-ian*, as in *wyrcan* 'do, perform,' inflected with the dative case
marker *-e*, i.e., to *wyrcanne*:

(36) ne ðe   nan neodþearf ne lærde to wyrcanne ðæt
      nor you:DAT one need   not taught to perform   that
      ðæt þu   worhtest
      that you performed
      'nor did any necessity teach you to perform what you
      performed'

                                    (*c.* 880, Boethius 33.79.16)

In other words, the origins of the PDE *to*-infinitive lie in a verbal noun in a
prepositional phrase.

  The loss in the Middle English period of the case inflection, including case
inflection on the infinitive, allowed the *to* eventually to be reanalyzed as an
integral part of the verbal noun, which then could itself be prefixed with a
new preposition *for*,[4] e.g.:

(37) Þe hog louyth wel for to be in a foul place.
      'The hog well loves to be in a foul place.'

   (*c.* 1400, Lavynham; cited in Visser 1963–73: 1314)

7.4 Some counterexamples to unidirectionality in clause combining

There is substantial evidence that in most languages and most instances there is a continuum of development from more to less paratactic clause combining. However, there are some counterexamples. For instance, *although* is frequently used, especially by college students, as if it were *however*. This could be a hypercorrection resulting from literacy and learned punctuation, and therefore a temporary innovation. But a similar development that has withstood the test of a couple of centuries has been noted in Japanese.

In Modern Japanese, discourses of the following kind are possible:

(38) Taro-wa   wakai(-yo). Ga, yoku yar-u(-yo).
      Taro-TOP young(-*yo*). but well do-PRES(-*yo*)
      'Taro is young. But he does a good job.'

   (Matsumoto 1988: 340)

Here the two clauses may have the particle -*yo* on the predicate; the meaning of -*yo* is something like 'you know' in the colloquial sense of 'contrary to what you might be thinking'. *Ga* is a weakly adversative conjunction. An equivalent way of saying the same thing would be:

(39) Taro-wa   wakai-ga, yoku yar-u(-yo).
      Taro-TOP young-*ga*, well do-PRES(-*yo*)
      'Although Taro is young, he does a good job.'

   (*ibid.*)

In (39) *ga* is not a conjunction at the beginning of the second clause, as it is in (38), but a suffix on the predicate of the first clause. Moreover, *yo*, a sentence-final particle, may only appear on the second predicate in (39). Clearly (39) is a single sentence, whereas (38) consists of two sentences, an analysis supported by the intonation.

The hypothesis of unidirectionality would predict that the type of sentence illustrated by (39) is derived from a construction similar to that of (38). The single sentence would be thought to result from the collapsing of two separate sentences, and the reanalysis of *ga* from an independent conjunction in the second clause to a suffix in the first clause.

However, the historical data in fact suggests that the reverse occurred. Earlier Japanese texts point to sentences of the type in (39) as antecedents of those like (38), and indeed suggest that the type in (38) is relatively recent. The latter start to be recorded in the seventeenth century, especially in popular play scripts and similar texts suggesting a colloquial style.

The presence of counterexamples once more shows that the continua of grammaticalization are not exceptionless. Nevertheless, there is overwhelming evidence of the preponderance of changes from more to less paratactic modes of clause combining. Probably all languages have paratactic structures. At certain points, given certain traditions and discourse uses, dependent structures are innovated, and later renewed (M. Harris 1988).

7.5 Examples of the development of complex sentence constructions

We turn now to sketches of a few examples of the development of complex sentence structures, with the prime purpose of demonstrating the directionality of the change along various parts of the cline from juxtaposition to embedding. For a full-length diachronic study of one such process from the perspective of grammaticalization – the development of causal connectives in Old English – see Wiegand (1987).

7.5.1 *'That'-complementation in English*

Among standard examples of *that*-complementizers in English are:

(40) Bill thought that John had left.

(41) a. It was obvious that John had left.
  b. That John had left was obvious.

We sketch here some of the characteristics of the emergent *that*-complement structure in Old and Middle English.

Although the earliest records show that *OE þæt* behaved in some respects like its PDE equivalent, there are many examples of usage that suggest traces of a pronominal origin and a more hypotactic structure than is characteristic now (Mitchell 1986: Traugott 1992). Consider:

(42) Ða   on morgenne gehierdun þæt þæs   cyninges
  when/then in morning heard-PL DEM DEM:GEN king's
  þegnas þe him beæftan wærun þæt se cyning ofslægen wæs,
  thanes who him behind were COMP the king slain   was
  þa   ridon hie þider.
  then rode they thither

'When in the morning the king's thanes who had been left behind heard that he had been killed, then they rode up there.'

(ChronA (Plummer) 755.23)

The first *þæt* is a pronoun which anticipates the later complement clause, and the second *þæt* is the complementizer. There is a paratactic structure to complex sentences of this kind that may help us understand the functions of the two instances of *þæt*. As is usual in the older texts of OE, the relative clause is not embedded, but is located after the whole nucleus. What looks like a complement clause is still in part an appositional clause resuming the first *þæt*. The OE text is, then, not such a compressed rhetorical unit as our translation would suggest. It is more like the hypotaxis illustrated in (43):

(43)   Then in the morning the king's thanes heard this
       (these thanes had been left behind earlier)
       that the king had been slain.
       Then they rode up there.

The pattern of demonstrative pronoun + resumptive demonstrative represented by the *þæt* + *þæt* construction makes it possible to link the nuclear clause with its verb 'heard' to the margin headed by *þæt*, even though the relative clause 'who had been left behind earlier' intervenes. The stage represented by this example is already something more than merely paratactic, since the initial *þæt* of 'that the king had been slain' already marks the clause as a complement (a truly paratactic version would be: 'Then in the morning the king's thanes heard this: the king had been slain').

The pronominal status of the source of complementizer *þæt* is particularly striking in (44):

(44)   Þæt   gefremede Diulius hiora consul, þæt   þæt   angin
       DEM arranged   Diulius their consul, COMP DEM beginning
       wearð tidlice þurhtogen.
       was   in-time achieved
       'Their consul Diulius arranged (it) that it was started on time.'
                                                    (*c.* 880, Orosius 4 6.172.2)

The pre-verbal *þæt* in this example is a fronted (topicalized) object pronoun anticipating the complement introduced by the second *þæt*. (The third *þæt*, of course, is simply the quasi-definite article with the neuter noun *angin* 'beginning'.) Such correlative structures, especially correlatives which mark the beginning of both clauses, and their interdependency, are typical of hypotaxis in OE (and many earlier Indo-European texts). Such features are reminiscent of oral language and of strategies clarifying interdependencies in the flow of speech (for oral residue in early Old English prose syntax, see O'Neil 1977, Hopper 1992b).

The majority of instances of *þæt*-complements in OE are like (45), however, and do not reveal the pronominal origins of the construction overtly:

(45)   Dyslic biδ þæt   hwa   woruldlice speda forhogie for
       foolish is   COMP someone wordly   goods despise for
       manna herunge.
       men's praise
       'It is foolish to despise wordly goods in order to win the praise of
       men.'
                           (*c.* 1000, ÆCHom I, 4 60.32)

It appears that the complementizer *þæt* started out as a "copy" in the margin clause of the object pronoun in the nucleus. It was reanalyzed from a pronoun which was a constituent of the matrix clause to a complementizer that had a whole clause within its scope. Example (46) shows the use of *þæt* spreading to non-accusative object environments:

(46)   And þæs   us   ne scamaδ na,   ac þæs
       And DEM:GEN we:ACC not shames   never, but DEM:GEN
       us   scamaδ swyþe þæt   we bote   aginnan swa swa
       we:ACC shames much   COMP we atonement begin   so as
       bec   tæcan.
       books teach
       'And we are not at all ashamed of that, but we are ashamed of
       this: of beginning atonement in the way that the books teach.'
                        (*c.* 1010, WHom 20.3 160)

The impersonal verb *scamaδ* 'shames' in OE requires its experiencer argument (the person who is ashamed) to be in the accusative case, and the stimulus of the shame (the thing of which the experiencer is ashamed) to be in the genitive. Consequently, if *þæt* were still analyzed as an argument of the nucleus, it would have to be in the genitive case, since it is "stimulus" for *scamaδ*.

In the following example two features show that the *þæt* clause is in a hypotactic construction:

> (47) . . . þohte   gif he hi   ealle ofsloge,   þæt se   an
> . . . thought if he them all   slew-SUBJUNCT, that that one
> ne ætburste   þe   he sohte.
> not escape-SUBJUNCT that he sought
> '. . . thought that if he slew them all, the one he sought would
> not escape.'

> (*c.* 1000, ÆCHom I 5 82.10)

The reasons for thinking of the *þæt*-clause here as a complement include:

(a) The clause introduced by *þæt* is dependent and not appositive,
    since it is in the subjunctive, the "irrealis" mood required by the
    verb *þohte* 'thought.'

(b) The complementizer is clearly no longer a pronoun. If it were,
    one would expect it to precede the *if*-clause that depends on
    þohte.

However, the second point also shows that the complementizer is associated
directly with the proposition 'the one he sought would not escape,' and is
not yet a marker of the whole dependent structure. Another way of stating
this is to say that *þæt* does not govern "S-bar" (the set of branching
structures that includes all lower Ss), only S (i.e., its own immediate clause),
and is therefore not as fully syntacticized as it is in PDE. In PDE the
incorporation of the conditional clause into the complement would be
favored, as in the modern translation of (47).

There is no unequivocal evidence in OE for subject complements such as
are illustrated by (48a, b):

(48) a. It amazes me that they found the purse.
     b. That they found the purse amazes me.

It has been assumed that complements in impersonal constructions illustrated by predicate constructions such as (45) and impersonal constructions
such as (46) are subject complements (Lightfoot 1979). That is, it is assumed
that the subject of 'is foolish' is the entire clause 'that someone despise
wordly goods to win men's praise,' and that the subject of 'shames' is the
entire clause 'that we begin atonement in the way the books teach.' There is
no indisputable evidence, however, that subject complement clauses existed
in OE. For one thing there was in OE a "heavy constituent constraint" that
constituents that were long and full of content words should occur after
lighter and shorter constituents. There are no examples of complements
preceding the matrix verb.

Complements in constructions such as (45), with adjectival or nominal predicates, may simply have been complements of those constituents, just as the *þæt*-clause is the complement of *weddes* in (49):

(49)   . . . þonne beo ic gemyndig mines   weddes.[5]   þæt   ic
       . . . then   am I mindful   my-GEN pledge-GEN COMP I
       nelle   heonunforð   mancyn   mid wætere adrencan.
       not-will henceforward mankind with water   drown
       '. . . then I am mindful of my pledge that henceforward I will
       not drown mankind with water.'

                                              (*c* 1000, ÆChom I,1 22.11)

Similarly, complements in impersonals may have been complements of NPs in those constructions; in (46) the *þæt*-clause may be the complement of *þæs*.

An approach from grammaticalization which emphasizes continua of change and fixing of structure through plausible discourse strategies suggests that "movement" is relevant only at a later stage (Middle English) when the subject position came to be obligatorily filled. Even then, constructions such as (45) and (46) were not obligatorily (though frequently) introduced by 'it' or 'that.' The crucial evidence for the emergence of subject complements is the presence of complements in subject position. Warner (1982: 81) suggests that finite complements do not occur in subject position until the fourteenth century. An example is:

(50)   Þat þe þre kingis camen so fer bitokeneþ Cristis lordship.
       'That the three kings came so far signifies Christ's lordship.'
       (*c*. 1400, Wycliffe, WSerE i,341.28; cited in Warner 1985:23)

But even then, Warner shows, the complement has many more characteristics in common with what we are calling hypotactic clauses than with a truly subordinate clause. Koster (1978) suggests that evidence from constraints on the occurrence of subject complements in PDE (e.g., absence of inversion, as in *Did that John showed up please you?*) shows that full embedding in the sense that S can function as NP in subject position has in fact not occurred, and that these constructions are still hypotactic ("satellites" in Koster's terminology). All the same, the history of English finite complements shows a clear continuum from looser to tighter syntactic structuring, and spread from object to subject position.

7.5.2 *Relative clauses in English and Hittite*

We turn now to the development of relative clause structures, with particular attention to some of the discourse strategies that may contribute to increased dependency. Relative clauses correspond in many ways to adjectives, and indeed are sometimes called adjectival clauses. Languages exhibit different degrees of integration and interlacing of relative clauses, ranging from clauses which are placed outside the nucleus (see K. Hale 1976) to clauses which are closely attached to a head noun inside the nucleus.

Before we proceed, some terms will be necessary. Following Keenan (1985), we will use the notation Srel for the relative clause (whatever its degree of integration), and NPrel for the position in Srel of the relativized NP. Thus in *the woman whom you met*, Srel is *you met the woman*, and NPrel is the object of *you met*, i.e., *the woman* [you met [the woman]$_{NPrel}$]$_{Srel}$. The position of NPrel may be marked in a variety of ways which we will discuss further below: it may be marked by an inflected personal pronoun (e.g., *she*), an inflected demonstrative or interrogative pronoun (e.g., *who*), an uninflected subordinator (e.g., *that*), or nothing (the so-called "gap," as in *the woman you met*), or some combination of these. We will discuss some of the discourse strategies associated with different NPrel markings at the end of this section. But first we consider degree of integration as evidenced by position.

In his discussion of the early history of relative clauses in English, O'Neil (1977) shows that they started out essentially as adjuncts, that is, as paratactic clauses close to the end of the sentence. He hypothesizes that their path to integration within the matrix clause was via a stage of topicalization which moved certain relative clause structures to the left of the sentence; this is a stage of hypotaxis. Finally, clauses came to be embedded as dependent clauses immediately associated with their head nouns.

We introduce the paratactic stage of adjunction with example (51) (the uninflected relativizer *þe*, which is also widely used as a subordinator in OE, is glossed as SUB for "subordinator"):

(51) & þa men comon on East Engle þe   on þæm   anum scipe
      and the men came to East Anglia SUB on that one   ship
      wæron swiðe forwundode
      were very   wounded

'and the men who were on that sole (surviving) ship came to
East Anglia severely wounded'

(ChronA [Plummer] 897.51; cited in O'Neil 1977: 200)

Since the subordinator is uninflected (like PDE relative *that*), although it
marks the clause boundary, and the relevance of the clauses to each other, it
indicates nothing about the case of the relative. Particularly interesting
evidence of the paratactic nature of relative clause constructions in OE is
the existence (though rare) of relative constructions in which a relative
demonstrative pronoun followed by the subordinator *þe* has the case of the
head noun in the matrix clause, rather than the case it would carry as NPrel
in Srel:

(52)   Hi   adulfon gehwylcne dæl þæs   wyrtgeardes
       they dug   each   part that:GEN vegetable-garden:GEN
       þæs   þe þær ær   undolfen was.
       that:GEN SUB there before not-dug was
       'They dug every part of the vegetable garden that had been left
       undug before.'

(*c.* 1050, Gregory's Dialogues 202.3)

This reflects a discourse strategy in which the demonstrative is attributive to
the head noun, and anaphoric to it, as in 'of that vegetable garden: that one
had been left undug.' The function of the relative clause is simply to
characterize the NP in the matrix clause. Because the demonstrative simply
indexes the NP to be further characterized, it is misleading to call the
construction the "attracted relative," as the traditional terminology is. Such
terminology assumes that the relative pronoun will carry the case
appropriate to its function as NPrel in a dependent Srel clause. In other
words, the terminology assumes a syntactic structure that has somehow
become degenerate in use. From the perspective of grammaticalization,
however, the pronoun is well formed given the discourse strategy in which it
is being used.

More common in OE is a construction often known as "correlative" (the
term has to do with correlation between clauses, not with the relative!). In
this type of relative, both the relative clause and the matrix clause are full
clauses; only a distinctive marker on an NP marks dependency and linkage
to a following clause. This following clause contains an NP anaphoric to the
specially marked NP in the preceding clause (Keenan 1985: 164). This kind

of construction is illustrated by (53), in which the uninflected subordinator *þe* or *þæt* is followed by a personal pronoun in the case of NPrel:

(53) & þær is mid   Estum an mægð   þæt
      and there is among Ests   a   tribe:FEM:SG SUB
      hi   magon cyle gewyrcan
      they:NOM:PL[6] can   cold make
      'and there is among the Ests a tribe who are able to freeze (the dead)'

(c. 880, Orosius 1.21.13)

In (54) the adjoined clause is "impersonal," that is, there is no nominative subject associated with the verb:

(54) & ic gehwam   wille þærto tæcan þe   hiene
      and I whoever:DAT will   thereto direct SUB him:ACC
      his   lyst   ma   to witanne
      it:GEN would-please more to know
      '. . . and I shall direct anyone to it who would like to know more about it'

(c. 880, Orosius 3 3.102.22)

O'Neil (1977) suggests that dependency and integration (he calls it "intraposition") occur when relatives must be adjoined directly to the clause in which the head occurs, and, furthermore, subject relatives are topicalized to the left of that clause, as in (55):

(55) Ure ieldran þa   þe   þas   stowa ær   hioldon, hie
      our forbears those SUB these places previously held,   they
      lufodon wisdom.
      loved   wisdom.
      'Our forbears who previously possessed these places, they loved wisdom.'

(c. 880, CP LetWærf 31; cited in O'Neil 1977: 202)

This is clearly a more hypotactic structure than those discussed previously, since the relative occurs between the subject and the predicate, rather than after the predicate. But it is not fully embedded, since there is a cataphoric pronoun *hie* that points back to the subject, as the speaker keeps track of the flow of speech.

Fully embedded relatives, with no cataphoric or anaphoric elements, positioned immediately after their nominal heads, whatever the position of those heads in the clause, do not occur with any frequency until ME. An example is:

(56)   Thilke penance that is solempne is in two maneres.
       'The penance that is ceremonial is of two kinds.'
                         (*c.* 1390? Chaucer, *CT*, Parson's Tale, 106)

Just because relative clauses came to be embedded in English, we should not assume that embedding is a necessary endpoint of relativization. There is nothing intrinsically unstable about hypotactic relative clauses, which are very widespread and are known to have existed in the Indo-Aryan languages for several millennia (see Klaiman 1976).

We turn now to a partially different history of relative clauses, one that has been postulated for Hittite, a language that flourished from *c.* 1600 to 1200 BC. We will again be concerned with correlative relatives, but this time with their possible origins. Such relatives are found in languages as different from one another as Old English, Medieval Russian, and Warlpiri. A putative example from Hittite[7] is given in (57):

(57)   nu   Ú-NU-TUM ku-it   ku-e-da-ni   pé-eš-ki-it na-at
       and utensil   REL-INDEF to-someone he-gave   and-it
       Ú-UL ši-i-e(!)-eš-ki-it
       not   he-sealed
       'and the utensil which he gave to someone, he did not
       properly seal it'
                                              (Held 1957: 43)

This is translatable as 'He did not properly seal a utensil which he gave to someone,' or 'He gave someone a utensil without sealing it properly.' The elements *nu* and *na*, glossed 'and,' are sentence connectives which signal clause boundaries: they give the sense of the two clauses being adjoined rather than grammatically connected. The special marker *ku* is a pronoun with a stem *kw-*, which like its Latin cognate *qui-* (*quis* 'who?,' *qui* 'who (rel.),' *quidam* 'some, a certain') served as an inflectable relative-interrogative-indefinite pronoun stem.

The grammaticalization of correlatives in Hittite has been reconstructed by Justus (1976), with particular attention to the discourse strategies involved. She suggests that Hittite provides evidence of an initial stage in which a clause could be used to provide a thematic starting point, including a focal NP, for a segment of discourse which could be one or several following clauses. At this stage no marker was required. An example of such a construction is:

(58) ᵐTamnaššun-a hušwantan I$\underline{\text{ṢBATU}}$ š-an
Tamnašš-ACC alive-ACC they:seized PARTICLE-him
ᵘʳᵘHattuša   uwatet.
city:H.:DIRECTIONAL brought:3SG
'Tamnaššu (whom) they seized, he brought to Hattuša.'

(Justus 1976: 234)

Justus argues that the use of the relative-interrogative-indefinite pronoun *kw-* to mark the focal NP in thematic clauses of the type in (57) is a characteristic of somewhat later Hittite texts. But even at this later stage, she argues, the clause with the marked NP is only loosely connected to the "nucleus." An example such as (57), therefore, is to be construed as something like 'He gave a (some) utensil to someone and he didn't seal it,' with *ku-it* functioning as the indefinite marker of a noun phrase in an independent clause rather than a "relative pronoun." Justus suggests that what appears to be a correlative clause is in fact a topic clause that states a theme whose domain is not just the next clause but, potentially, several following clauses. Eventually the *kw-* came to be understood as grammatically linking the theme clause to the following clause, and could even be embedded:

(59) É   ᵈHalmašuittas É   ᵈIŠKURnaš BELI-JA Ù   É
house god-H:GEN house god-I.:GEN lord-my   and house
ᵈŠiunašummiš ABNI KASKALaz   kuit
god-S.:GEN I-built campaign:ABL PARTICLE:NOM/ACC
āššu   utahhun [?]   apēdanda
goods:NOM/ACC I-brought [them?] demonstr:INSTR
hališšijanun.
inlaid-1SG
'The temples of Halmašuitta, of the Stormgod my lord, and of Šiunašummi (which) I built I inlaid with the goods which I brought back from the campaign.'

(Justus 1976: 235)

The sentence contains a thematic clause, which translates as a relative clause in English, and a correlative clause; it can be translated literally as 'I built temples of the god Halmašuitta, the Stormgod, and the god Šiunašummi, and from the campaign which goods I brought back, with them I inlaid them.'

We have here, then, an example of a relative clause construction which was originally not a grammatical entity but simply part of the way in which discourses are organized in a particular language coming to be grammaticalized as an embedded clause.[8]

The preceding remarks about the emergence of relative clauses are valid only for the post-nominal and correlative types. Another type of relative clause, known as the pre-nominal type, is represented by the Tamil example in (60):

> (60) Anda paaDattai paDitta   paiyaNai kuuppiDu.
>   that lesson:ACC learn:PART boy:ACC call:IMP
>   'Call the boy that learned that lesson.'
>
> (Klaiman 1976: 160)

There is no relative pronoun, and the relative clause is embedded before the matrix noun and linked to it by a participial or special relative ending on the verb. According to Keenan (1985) only languages of the OV type have this kind of relative (though they typically also use post-nominal relatives as well).

The pre-nominal, participial type of relative clause represented in the Tamil example are probably not diachronically related to the other types we have discussed. It is in fact difficult to show any grammaticalization of pre-nominal relative clauses at all, since languages that have them appear always to have had them in virtually just that form. If change occurs, it does not result from any gradual extraposing or postposing of the participial relative but by starting anew, as it were, with the adjunct type. Not uncommonly both types exist together as possibilities, as in Estonian (see examples (26a, b) in Section 5.5.1. When this is the case, the pre-nominal participial clause is usually older and indigenous, the more clausal type newer and borrowed.[9] The development of pre-posed relatives is a topic for further study.

As indicated at the beginning of this section, NPrel (we should now specify post-nominal NPrel) can be marked by a number of different types of relativizer. One is personal pronouns, as in (54). These appear to be "place markers" in the discourse for NPrel, and are indexical of that position. Another type of marking is provided by "relative pronouns": inflectable pronouns that serve specific relativizing functions (e.g., they may move out of NPrel position to the beginning of Srel, as does the *wh*-pronoun in English). Such pronouns are demonstrative, interrogative, or indefinite pronouns in origin (*wh*-pronouns in English, *kw*-pronouns in Hittite). The sources of relative pronouns reflect the function of a relative clause in specifying or determining a noun from out of a domain of possible referents. Although there is rarely evidence that relative clauses derive directly from the grammaticalization of questions, this has sometimes been suggested, and it is easy to see the similarity between the two. A relative sentence such as (61) could with very little change be distributed over two parts of a discourse, as in (62):

(61)   The sheep which he stole was Squire Trelawney's prize ram.

(62)   Which sheep did he steal? – The sheep was Squire Trelawney's prize ram.

In Hittite texts it is sometimes impossible to tell whether the topic clause is to be interpreted as a question, to which the subsequent clause is the answer, or a correlative-nucleus construction: "The *kuis* and *kuit* may be relatives or interrogatives, depending on whether the two clauses are to be taken together or individually" (Held 1957: 40). An example is:

(63)   Ki-i-wa ku-it U-UL-wa SA   SAL ^{TUG}-NIG.LAM.MES.
       this   which not   garments of   woman
       'That which [is] this [here], are they not the garments of a woman?'/'What [is] this? Are they not the garments of a woman?'

(Held 1957: 40)

A third type of marking of the NPrel position is provided by uninflected relativizers. These may be derived by grammaticalization from demonstrative pronouns, as presumably was OE *ðe*, itself replaced by *that*. Such relativizers are often subordinators (or, more technically, complementizers). They are more grammatical than the pronouns from which they derive not only in their reduced form (they cannot carry inflections), but also in their more highly restricted privileges of occurrence. For example, in English neither the earlier *þe* nor the current *that* permits a preposition to precede, although the relative pronoun may:

(64)   a.   nyhst þæm tune   þe   se   deada man on lið
            next that   homestead SUB that dead man in lies
            'next to the homestead that the dead man lies in/next to the homestead in which the dead man lies/which the dead man lies in'

(*c.* 880, Orosius 1 1.22.2)

b.   *nyhst þæm tune on þe se deada man lið
'*next to the homestead in that the dead man lies'

On a scale of integration as evidenced by marking of NPrel (as opposed to position), the personal pronouns are least grammaticalized, the relative pronouns more so, the subordinators yet more so. The most grammaticalized way of marking NPrel along this continuum is zero or "gapping."

A topic much discussed in connection with relative clauses is the fact that not all potential NPrels can be relativized in a particular language, and that which NPrels may be relativized is predictable from the function in Srel and from the form of NPrel. Keenan and Comrie (1977) identified a functional "Accessibility Hierarchy" to account for these facts, now known as "the Keenan-Comrie Accessibility Hierarchy" (for further discussion, see Comrie 1981a, Keenan 1985). This hierarchy has the following form:

> subject > direct object > indirect object > object of pre- or post-position > possessor

where possessor (an oblique relation), is "low" on the hierarchy, and subject (a grammatical relation), is "high" on the hierarchy. If NPrel is expressed by a gap (and/or a subordinator) low on the hierarchy, then it can generally relativize all higher positions with the same form (Keenan 1985: 154). By contrast, if NPrel has the form of a personal pronoun, then only positions lower on the hierarchy can be predicted.

For instance, the fact that in English we can say *The woman I took the money from* (where NPrel is object of a preposition) allows us to predict that all positions to the left on the hierarchy may be relativized. Thus we can say *The woman I saw* (where NPrel is the object) and (with subordinator) *The woman that left*, or (in some varieties) *I know a woman will help you.*[10] The situation where NPrel is expressed by a personal pronoun is the opposite: here the fact that OE (and other languages such as Urhobo and Yiddish [Keenan 1985: 147]) allows subject NPrel pronoun forms predicts that other NPrels to the right on the hierarchy are allowed to be relativized. However, languages such as Hebrew do not allow subject NPrels to be expressed by personal pronouns, though Hebrew does allow NPrels that are objects or serve other functions on the right of the hierarchy to be so:

(65)   ha-sarim   she-ha-nasi   shalax otam la-mitsraim . . .
        the-ministers that-the-president sent   them to-Egypt . . .
        'the ministers that the president sent to Egypt'
                                      (Keenan 1985: 146)

Keenan and Comrie suggest that the accessibility hierarchy "directly reflects the psychological ease of comprehension" (1977: 88). We would rephrase this suggestion in somewhat different terms. We could hypothesize that the accessibility of highly grammaticalized forms of NPrel from left to right on the hierarchy (i.e., the motivation for relativizing first subjects, then direct objects, etc.) is a function of the tendency to integrate relationships that are frequently established, and that functions on the left of the hierarchy are frequently established because they are natural discourse collocations. On the other hand, what amounts to double marking (by a relativizer and a personal pronoun) in languages which allow or require the NPrel position to be marked by a personal pronoun inflected for number, case, and gender works from right to left on the hierarchy, affecting the oblique and object positions before the subject, because such extra, complex marking serves the purposes of identifying relationships that might not otherwise be fully clear to hearers.

This generalization may hold for other pronominal forms of NPrel as well. It is a well-known fact of the history of English that early ME had one relativizer, the subordinator *that*. When the new pronominal relativizer *wh-* came in, it did not start with subjects, but with indirect objects and possessives (for a detailed study of the development in Middle Scots, see Romaine 1982), in other words, on the right of the hierarchy. Presumably the more distinctive *wh-* forms served the purposes of identifying the less accessible, non-thematic, NPs precisely because the *wh-* forms were less generalized in their use, and therefore more expressive.

7.5.3 *From clause chaining to verb inflection in Lhasa*

The examples of the development of *that*-complements and of relative clause constructions have exemplified how paratactic structures may develop through hypotaxis to embedding. Throughout the process, the clauses serving as (pre)-complement or (pre)-relative have remained relatively identifiable as clauses in surface structure. Our next example illustrates the way in which a hypotactic clause chaining structure develops into an inflectional one with loss of clause boundary and hence of clausal identity in surface structure. Here we have a case of the development of maximal integration. The data is from Lhasa, a Tibeto-Burman language. The analysis and examples are from DeLancey (1991).

Like all Tibeto-Burman languages, Lhasa evidences clause chaining, which expresses sequence of events, as in (66). One or more verbs with non-final affixes are followed by a finite verb with tense-mood affixes.

(66) Khos   las=ka byas-byas zas -pa red.
      he:ERG work   did-NF   ate PERF
      'He worked and ate/having worked, he ate.'

(p. 9)

The "non-final" (NF) suffix -*byas* marks the verb as one of a series, and in this respect is comparable with the Japanese *te/de* suffix discussed above. The "final" verb, *zas* (glossed 'ate'), is inflected with a finite tense-aspect marker -*pa red* (historically derived from a nominalizer -*pa* and the copula *red*).

Constructions of the type in (66) express multiple events. However, according to DeLancey, three verbs, '*gro* 'go,' *yong* 'come,' and *sdad* 'sit, stay,' can occur as finite verbs preceded by verbs with or without the NF marker, and these constructions can express a single event, rather than a sequence of events. In such constructions '*gro* expresses not 'go' but distal directionality, *yong* 'come' expresses not motion but proximal directionality, and *sdad* 'sit, stay,' not stasis but aspectual continuation (as in *keep V-ing*):

(67) a. Kho 'dir   gom=pa brgyab (-byas) yongs- pa red.
          he here:LOC walked   (NF)   came   PERF
          'He walked here.' (not '*He walked here and came.')
      b. Khos   las=ka byas (-byas) sdad- pa red.
          he:ERG work   did (NF)   stay PERF
          'He was working/kept working.' (not '*He worked and
          stayed.')

(pp. 8–9)

DeLancey argues that because clause chaining is very frequent in Lhasa, some verbs, such as the three in question, may have come to be used frequently with non-final verbs where a sequenced event interpretation was pragmatically either redundant or implausible, and hence they came to be reanalyzed not as full verbs, but as markers of aspect. For example, '*gro* 'go' is informative as a motion verb in construction with a non-motion verb such as 'eat,' but it is redundant with respect to motion in construction with a verb of motion such as 'walk,' 'flee.' In the latter context, motion is demoted, directionality promoted.

The three verbs 'come,' 'go,' and 'stay' in their non-motion meaning may cooccur with a non-final markers, or they may not, which suggests that they are no longer full verbs in these uses. DeLancey calls them "serialized"

199

verbs. Other former full verbs, among them *tshar* 'finish,' and *myong* 'taste,' often occur as serialized verbs, and in such constructions express perfect. In volitional predicates with first person actors in statements and second person actors in questions (i.e., in highly local contexts based in speaker-hearer reference) they do not cooccur with non-final forms, and they do not have independent word tone. This suggests that they have gone further on the cline of grammaticalization than 'come,' 'go,' 'stay.' Example (68) illustrates *tshar* in its three coexistent uses: (a) main verb meaning 'finish' in an event separate from that expressed by the non-final verb, (b) serialized verb meaning 'finish' or 'perfect' in an event expressed by the non-final (or bare) verb, (c) grammaticalized suffix meaning 'perfect' functioning in the tense-aspect slot:

(68) a. Kho phyin-byas tshar -ba red.
    he   went-NF   finish PERF
    'He went and finished it.' (main verb)
  b. Kho phyin tshar -ba red.
    he   went finish PERF
    'He has gone.' (serialized form, without NF marker)
  c. Nga krom-la   phyin-tshar.
    I   market-LOC went-PERF
    'I've gone to the store.' (affix)

(pp. 10–11)

Yet other former verbs have been morphologized to the extent that they do not only fail to carry their own tone; they also lose nasalization. An example is *song* [sõ], [so], [s] 'evidential perfective' < *song* "which is an old suppletive perfective stem of 'go,' supplanted in this use in the modern languages by *phyin*" (p. 11).

The examples of the grammaticalization of the verbs show a cline of dependency from hypotaxis in clause chaining to the complete dependency of inflectional bonding. They also show the reduction of complex structure to simpler structure, and the accompanying total loss of boundary markers, in other words, integration, compression, and bonding. Like many other examples we have seen in this book they also illustrate the coexistence of different stages of grammaticalization (layering), and divergence in a highly local context. It should be noted further that although the particulars of the changes in Lhasa are very different from those of the development of auxiliaries in English (English does not have and never had clause chaining), and the full path from main verb to inflection has not yet occurred (and may perhaps never do so), nevertheless there are similarities: an erstwhile non-temporal main verb with a dependent verb has acquired temporal meaning, and the relationship between the erstwhile main and dependent verbs has changed such that the dependent verb has become the main verb or head of the construction.[11]

7.5.4 *From main clause construction to sentential adverb in contemporary English*

Our last example is from PDE, and illustrates both integration of structure via a shift from multiclause to single clause structure, and also how a discourse-oriented statistical analysis can suggest how to recognize possible ongoing grammaticalization processes.

As we have mentioned many times, grammaticalization can be thought of as a form of routinization of language (Haiman 1991). A form or a combination of forms occurs in discourse with increasing frequency, and from being an "unusual" way of making or reinforcing a discourse point comes to be the "usual" and unremarkable way to do so. The frequency with which such expressions occur will be one factor that determines whether or not they come to be regarded by the speech community as "grammatical." (Other factors are, of course, more obviously social: acceptance by broadcast and print media, endorsement by educational and other institutions, and so on.)

Our example is that of the emergence in PDE of "evidential parentheticals." Thompson and Mulac (1991) suggest that verbs of propositional attitude such as 'think' and 'guess' with first and second person subjects are coming to be parentheticals. Such verbs typically serve to introduce propositions, as in (69), where 'think' is the main verb and the sentence serves as an assertion that a certain belief is held by the speaker or a question concerning the belief state of the hearer:

(69)   a.   I think that the coup was planned by the CIA.
       b.   Do you think that the coup was planned by the CIA?

On the other hand, they may serve to qualify an assertion; they are then known as parentheticals:

(70)   a.   I think Commander Dalgleish writes poetry.
       b.   Commander Dalgleish writes poetry, I think.

Here the main verb is *writes*, and the sentence is a (qualified) assertion about an activity of Commander Dalgleish, not about the state of mind of the speaker. Alternatively, *think* and *guess* with second person subjects may serve to indicate interactive communication:

(71)   What's the point of that, do you think?

(Thompson and Mulac 1991: 322)

In such circumstances, there is no complementizer *that* and the parenthetical receives less stress than the main verb. Moreover, parenthetical *I/you think*, *I/you guess* have the same syntax as an adverb, in that they are not restricted to one position in the clause. A change of meaning is also noticeable. When it is parenthetical, *I think* is less certain than when it is non-parenthetical; the speaker is not staking out an epistemological position, but indicating the degree of validation of the statement by suggesting that he or she has no direct evidence for it. In other words, Thompson and Mulac suggest, the parenthetical is beginning to serve the kind of function often served by specialized clitics and particles expressing such modal distinctions as "witnessed," "deduced," "speculative," "hearsay," functions largely expressed in PDE by epistemic modals (e.g., *They must be students* 'I conclude they are students') and by adverbs such as *evidently, apparently,* etc.

From the perspective of the continuum of clause integration, we can see such parentheticals as instances of a complex sentence consisting of the nucleus with a verb of propositional attitude and a margin (e.g., *that Commander Dalgleish writes poetry*) has been reanalyzed as a single nucleus. The former margin is now the nucleus, and the former nucleus has been demoted to something that looks like a sentence adverb (comparable with *evidently, apparently,* etc.).

From a quantitative viewpoint, *think* and *guess* seem to be becoming distinct from other verbs of propositional attitude such as *suggest* and *believe* in that the former occur more frequently without *that*. Thompson and Mulac's data show the statistics reproduced in Table 7.1. They are also becoming distinct in that they account for 88% of all verb tokens with first or second person subjects. In other words, they appear to be becoming specialized (as *pas* was specialized into the negative in French, see Section

Table 7.1 *Occurrence of 'that' with 'think' and 'guess' versus all other verbs*

	− that	+ that	Total
think	622 (91%)	61 (9%)	683
guess	148 (99%)	2 (1%)	150
other	342 (75%)	112 (25%)	456

Source: based on Thompson and Mulac (1991: 320)

5.4.1). At the same time, they are coming to function as elements in the subjective domain of speaker attitude (as *be going to* did when it became a tense marker and *while* when it became a concessive, see Section 4.3.2). Only time will tell whether *guess* and *think* will continue along this path of development, and whether they will serve as the model to other verbs of propositional attitude such as *believe* or *suppose* at some time in the future.

8
Some further issues

8.1 Introduction

In this chapter we outline some of the topics concerning transmission of grammaticalization processes that deserve further attention as the study of grammaticalization continues. In particular we will touch briefly on some of the claims that have been developed in much linguistic work during the present century, and the challenges posed to them by the study of grammaticalization. These assumptions have to do with distinctions that, while based in some empirical realities, have too often become idealized into absolute binary opposites, for example, claims regarding the role in change of child versus adult language acquisition, of parametric changes versus grammaticalization, and of evolutive versus contact-induced change. Finally, we pay particular attention to changes associated with pidginization and creolization, since they have much to contribute to the future study of grammaticalization.

There are many other topics we could have covered pertaining to transmission of changes involved in grammaticalization, such as spread across styles, registers, and communities, including the influence of literacy. These are all important topics, and are central to any complete understanding of grammaticalization. However, given the limitations of space, we have chosen not to elaborate on them in this book. For a few examples of work in these areas the reader is referred to Labov (1972), Milroy (1980), Heath (1983), Schiffrin (1987).

8.2 Grammaticalization versus parametric change

Language acquisition has long been regarded as a major factor in language change. In the early part of this century, Hermann Paul (1920) was particularly concerned with developing a theory of the relationship between child language acquisition and "evolutive" change, that is, change that is regarded as only minimally affected by outside factors, such as conquest, demographic changes, or migrations. More recently, child language acquisition has been accorded a central theoretical place in generative theory, whether synchronic or diachronic, because it is seen as the potential locus for insights into learnability, that is, into the human-specific cognitive factors that make language possible.

One of the pioneers of work on phonological change in the generative framework was Halle (1964). A hypothesis current at that time (and still prevalent in various forms) was that it is at least theoretically possible to conceive of an "optimal grammar," one which characterizes what a speaker knows, with only a few rules, and furthermore that shorter descriptions (containing shorter and fewer rules) are more highly valued than longer ones. Working with this assumption, Halle explored the questions whether and how a distinction could be made between changes that affect the overall simplicity of a grammar and those that do not. His conclusion was that data from different dialects of the same language showed that the differences could be characterized in terms of degree of simplicity. For our purposes, what is especially important about the article is that Halle formulated a hypothesis about the role of language acquisition in language change that underlies almost all subsequent work within the generative framework:

> The ability to master a language like a native, which children possess to an extraordinary degree, is almost completely lacking in the adult. I propose to explain this as being due to deterioration or loss in the adult of the ability to construct optimal (simplest) grammars on the basis of a restricted corpus of examples. The language of the adult . . . need not, however, remain static . . . I conjecture that changes in later life are restricted to the addition of a few rules in the grammar and that the elimination of rules and hence a wholesale restructuring of his [sic] grammar is beyond the capabilities of the average adult.
>
> (p. 344)

According to this view, the discontinuity between adults and children enables major changes, but the discontinuities within a person's life do not. As we will see below, the distinction is not nearly as sharp as Halle proposed.

This kind of view, which made a sharp binary distinction between child and adult acquisition, was elaborated and refined by Andersen (1973) and Lightfoot (1979). The issue has recently been taken up with much vigor in Lightfoot (1989, 1991), within the theory of "Principles and Parameters" (see Section 3.2). As we have seen, Lightfoot hypothesizes that children bring to language learning and hence to change a "disposition to learn" which is neurologically inbuilt and therefore constrains what can be learned and in what ways grammars can be different from generation to generation. The inbuilt constraints are hypothesized to be rather abstract parameters which can be set differently by different generations, resulting in "structural reanalysis."

According to Lightfoot, new parameter settings are characterized by the following six properties (Lightfoot 1991: 167–9; examples are ours, based on material referred to in this book).

(a)   They are manifested by a cluster of changes that occur simultaneously, e.g., loss in English of both "inversion and negative sentences" such as *Left he?, He left not*, and introduction of *do*-support into interrogative and negative sentences (see Section 3.4.3).

(b)   They can set off chain reactions, e.g., word order changes, such as shifts from OV to VO (see Section 3.5.1).

(c)   They tend to take place more rapidly than other changes and to show S-curve phenomena, that is, gradual beginnings, rapid spread, and gradual tapering off (Kroch 1989a, 1989b). Lightfoot contrasts changes evidenced by S-curves with "grammaticalization and morphological change, involving the loss of gender markers (Jones 1988), the reduction of verbal desinences ["inflections"], or the loss of the subjunctive mood, [which] generally take place over long periods . . . This kind of gradual cumulativeness is generally not a hallmark of new parameter setting."

(d)   Obsolescence of earlier rules and forms, e.g., nominative and accusative marking on subject of non-finite clauses in Finnish (Section 5.2.2). Lightfoot suggests that "a form can hardly drop out of the language for expressive reasons . . . Obsolescence must be due to a structural 'knock-on' effect, a by-product of something else which was itself triggered by the kind of positive data that are generally available to children."

(e)   Significant change in meaning "is generally a by-product of a new parameter setting." Lightfoot exemplifies this with shifts in the meaning of *like* from 'please' to 'enjoy.' However, in the case of this example, it is clear that the 'please' meaning existed in OE (Fischer and van der Leek 1987). Significant changes in meanings that we have discussed include meaning changes in the development of main verbs into auxiliaries and affixes (see especially Chapters 3–5).

(f)   Parameter setting occurs in response to shifts in unembedded clauses only. For example, Lightfoot claims that the OV > VO shift in English occurred in response to input from main clauses only (for some discussion see 3.5.1, where it is pointed out that OV is not used exclusively in subordinate clauses).

The perspective of grammaticalization challenges virtually all of these claims. Fundamentally, the approach from grammaticalization argues that the grammaticalization of lexical items or constructions is enabled by pragmatic factors; indeed, much of grammaticalization in its early stages is the conventionalizing in certain local contexts of conversational inferences as morphosyntactic reanalysis occurs (Chapter 4). In general it can be shown that meaning change accompanies rather than follows syntactic change. Lightfoot identifies lack of total arbitrariness in change with chain reactions set off by new parameters. By contrast, the perspective from grammaticalization suggests that very few changes are arbitrary, precisely because of the pragmatic inferencing that constrains them. Many researchers in the field would also argue that arbitrariness is the exception rather than the rule because of the pervasiveness of iconicity in the organization of linguistic material (see Sections 2.3, 4.3.1 and 7.2).

Equally fundamental to the perspective of grammaticalization is the fact that changes are shown to be gradual. They are gradual along various dimensions. There is the dimension of clines, which do not exhibit rigid category differences. For example, the cline of clause combining shows that embedding is a rather special case of complex sentence formation (Chapter 7), a fact which calls into question the usefulness of the claim that children respond only to unembedded structures. There is the dimension of functional hierarchies such as animacy, definiteness, or thematic relations (the accessibility hierarchy discussed in connection with relative clauses in 7.5.2). Changes occur at different rates and different times along clines, and very rarely go to completion. Furthermore, obsolescence is gradual, often leaving what can be called detritus in the system (see Chapter 6) and usually does not show characteristics otherwise posited for parameter changes.

We have presented a unidirectional hypothesis of grammaticalization (Chapter 5). As we have seen (Section 4.1), Bybee (1985) argues that this unidirectionality results from cognitive processes alone. We have argued, with others such as Heine, Claudi, and Hünnemeyer (1991a), that unidirectionality results not from cognitive strategies alone but also from discourse production strategies in which speakers and hearers negotiate communication. A production model which refers to communicative purpose can account for the fact that over time certain linguistic properties may simply not be felt to serve communicative purposes any more and can therefore be consciously or unconsciously eliminated. Obsolescence therefore does not have to be a product of "a structural knock-on effect".

There is certainly evidence that changes may cluster, that they may occur in S-curves, and that they may have what appear to be chain reactions.

From the perspective of grammaticalization developed here, these are not evidence for parameter settings, but rather of a tendency of speakers and hearers to organize information in accessible ways. Such ways of organizing information include head–modifier (Section 3.5.1), and given–new (Sections 6.4.2, 7.5.2).

Another way of addressing the question of whether to distinguish parametric from minor changes is to distinguish those kinds of changes that cross-linguistically have a kind of "typological ripple" or "cascading effect" (Buckingham in discussion of Lightfoot, see Lightfoot 1989: 335) from those that are more language-specific. For example, word order shifts are of the former kind. But the phenomenon of the English modals is a far more language-specific change (e.g., despite somewhat similar word order changes from pre-French times on, French shows only partial development of a modal category, and, at least in standard French, there is no equivalent of empty *do*). Furthermore, as we have seen in Section 3.4.3, what has been considered the "phenomenon of the modals" in English is actually very much a function of which ones were selected for research (other modals such as *have to, be to, try to*, etc. have not undergone the same kinds of structural changes as *have, may, can, shall, will*) etc.

Once this kind of distinction is made between cross-linguistic "cascade effects" and more language-specific changes, the question becomes one of whether there is a fundamental distinction to be made between those changes that show rapid spread and those that do not. Absent extensive studies of different changes to demonstrate this, the answer can only be speculative. It will of course take several generations, indeed centuries of studies of child language acquisition, only recently made possible by the advent of tape and video recordings, to provide experimental evidence for the hypothesis about children's role in language change. Even then the data will be only partially comparable, because acquisition data is by definition non-written, whereas historical data prior to the advent of recording technologies is by definition written, and therefore subject to different constraints.

Valuable as parameter setting is as a concept, not least as a strong hypothesis against which to test analyses, evidence from grammaticalization is only one challenge to the hypothesis. Another, not unrelated one is from language change in general – parametric change is defined in Lightfoot's work by its end result, but if it is fundamentally different in nature from other kinds of changes, one would expect it to be different in its beginnings (Disterheft, forthcoming). A further challenge is provided by the evidence from studies of acquisition. It is becoming less and less clear that children do indeed innovate in ways that are fundamentally different from those of adults. As early as 1982, Bybee and Slobin, studying children's acquisition of verb forms such as *send–sent, sing–sang–sung*, and their innovations, such as *think–thunk*, concluded that: "there is nothing particularly special about the relation between small children's innovative forms and morphophonemic change. The innovations of older children and adults, although perhaps rare, where they can be elicited, may also serve as predictors of change" (Bybee and Slobin 1982: 36–7). As we will see in the next section, the study of creoles confirms the conclusion that children and adults do not contribute to change in fundamentally different ways.

8.3 Contact

The model of change discussed in Section 3.2. is conceived as monogenetic and concerned with evolutive change. It models transmission of whole systems, or interrelated sets, of lexical, phonological, morphological, syntactic, and semantic rules. This approach has arisen out of a tradition that started with comparative linguistics and that has persisted in the very largely different context of generative grammar. However different they have been, nevertheless both of these traditions have idealized homogeneity of language and of transmission, whereas in fact most actual situations involve contact, at the minimum with speakers of other dialects, whether social, regional, or stylistic (see Weinreich, Labov, and Herzog 1968, and Thomason and Kaufman 1988 for especially clear studies of the consequences of heterogeneity for an understanding of how language changes).

However skeptical most researchers in grammaticalization may be about the usefulness of the model of change discussed in Chapter 3, Figure 3.1, for the most part they too have privileged transmission in relatively homogeneous contexts. We have been no exception. However, we turn here briefly to the question whether studies of contact situations raise any special issues regarding grammaticalization. A full study of this question would deserve a book in itself. Of greatest interest to us here is the development of pidgins and creoles because they illustrate in rather extreme form a number of theoretical issues, and provide a large number of insights into processes of grammaticalization (for overviews see Bickerton 1988, Foley 1988, Muysken 1988, Romaine 1988; for fuller discussion see Hymes 1971, Valdman and Highfield 1980, Mühlhäusler 1986, Rickford 1987).

We ignore situations of contact that entail only partial external influence on subparts of a linguistic system. One situation in contact that we ignore is that of "borrowing," which often involves extensive incorporation of foreign elements in only one area of the language, typically the lexicon, with minimal influence elsewhere. Ordinarily the kinds of items borrowed are independent words and morphemes (Weinreich 1953), although very occasionally morphological paradigms may be borrowed (Thomason and Kaufman 1988: 20 cite the unusual case of Mednyi Aleut, with Russian finite verb morphology but with other largely Aleut grammar and vocabulary). English is an example of a language which has borrowed lexical items extensively, from Scandinavian (e.g., *give*), French (e.g., *table*), Latin (e.g., *tubular*), and many other languages. As a result of the influx of French vocabulary, it has developed a system of stress alternation such as is found in *real–reality–realistic*, but nevertheless it has undergone little radical syntactic or morphological change. For the most part changes in English can be said to be system-internal and evolutive. A second situation that we ignore is one of language admixture across a wide area, such as is evidenced by the Balkan and the Dravidian languages (see Sandberg 1968 [1930] and Masica 1976, respectively). Instead, we take a brief look at pidgins and creoles, languages that not only evidence extensive influence of two or more languages on each other but also have long been shown to provide special insight into language development and transmission.

The study of pidgin and creole languages is especially important for historical linguistics because contemporary varieties are relatively recent in origin (three or four centuries at the most), and exemplify rapid change in non-literate situations, unlike most of the more traditional subjects of historical and comparative linguistics, which may have millennia of history, much of it written. Furthermore, pidgins and creoles challenge many basic assumptions about homogeneity and the role of adults and children in language change.

A pidgin is a non-native contact language which develops typically in a social situation characterized by major class distinctions and by numerical disparities between these classes (e.g., a slave economy in which the number of slaves is far greater than that of the landowners). Often several mutually unintelligible languages are involved, with one language being used as the socially and politically prestigious standard. Examples where the prestige language was English include West African Pidgin English, Hawaiian Pidgin English, and Tok Pisin, spoken in Papua New Guinea. Studies of adult Tok Pisin speakers in the 1960s and 70s revealed that this group was developing a nativized (creole) version of the language, with some extensive grammaticalization, for example, the development of relative clauses, cliticization, and phonological reduction (cf. *baimbai* 'bye-and-bye' > *bai* 'later, future'). Although the rate of development was considerably faster among children, the changes themselves did not originate with them but with adults (Sankoff 1980). Studies of pidgin development and especially of adults nativizing a pidgin, at least in situations like those of Papua New Guinea, therefore call into question the hypothesis that change occurs primarily in the transmission between generations, and is attributable primarily to children.

Pidgins are no one's native languge. Although their lexicon is mixed, it is usually predominantly derived from the language of the socially dominant group, known as the "lexifier language," with some features of the languages of the socially subordinate group. (The language of the socially dominant group, e.g., colonialists or slave traders, is often called the "superstrate language," that of the socially subordinate group is often called the "substrate language.") Pidgin studies have shown that there are several kinds of pidgins, ranging from minimal communication devices which are highly unstable, e.g., jargons used in limited domains such as trade or labor recruitment, to more complex pidgins arising from relatively stable situations and used in a wide variety of linguistic contexts, e.g., West African Pidgin English, to extended pidgins used as general lingua francas, e.g., Melanesian Pidgin English (Foley 1988).

One of the topics that has been particularly challenging in the development of thinking about the role of children versus adults in language change has been the question of whether creoles provide some privileged evidence for the biologically determined program that enables language acquisition. One strong hypothesis that has been put forward is Bickerton's that certain creole situations exhibit evidence for a "bioprogram" or innate language-specific neurological disposition that permits children who have no extensive consistent language input to create a new language out of the bits and pieces of degenerate input they encounter. One such situation, it has been hypothesized, was exemplified in Surinam in the eighteenth century, where after a revolution the slaves dispersed into the bush and developed Saramaccan Creole (Byrne 1987). However, McWhorter (1992) challenges the claim that Saramaccan Creole exhibits bioprogram characteristics, on the grounds that many features of the language attributed to the bioprogram, such as verb serialization, have similarities in African languages that are likely to have contributed to the Creole. Another putative situation providing evidence for the bioprogram was, according to Bickerton, to be found in Hawaii in the late nineteenth century, where many mutually unintelligible languages were spoken, and where there was "no preexisting language in common" (Bickerton 1984: 174). Evidence for the development of the bioprogram was alleged to be provided by Hawaiian Creole speakers in their seventies, eighties and nineties. However, the interpretation of their speech was made on the assumption "that the speech of individuals does not change appreciably after adulthood is reached" (*ibid.*), an assumption that appears to have seriously skewed the interpretation of the data.

In an early characterization of the bioprogram, Bickerton (1981: 212) hypothesized that it had the following semantic-syntactic features:

(a)   specific/non-specific
(b)   state/process
(c)   punctual/non-punctual
(d)   causative/non-causative

A later version hypothesized that it had the syntactic characteristics of a limited simple clause, one which assigns only subject and object, but no other case markers, and therefore no prepositions (Bickerton 1984: 179). More recently still, Bickerton has put forward the radical hypothesis that "there is a single set of universal syntactic principles. These principles are absolute and do not undergo any form of variation, parametric or other"; all variation is, according to this theory, a function of acquisition of lexical items and of processes acting on them (Bickerton 1988: 272). In other words, in all its versions the bioprogram is hypothesized to be neurologically far more restricted than Universal Grammar; nevertheless, it has much in common with that hypothesis. Attractive though the concept of a bioprogram may seem, there does not appear to be any empirical evidence that the distinctions proposed uniquely pre-date any extant creole (see discussion of Bickerton's 1984 target article and later work such as Rickford 1987, Sankoff 1990, Baker 1991). Furthermore, as we have seen, evidence from other pidgins and creoles suggests that adults may play a significant role in language development. It is therefore unlikely that creoles provide unique insights into human genetic coding that is available to all first language acquisition users whatever their input, and only to them (as is Bickerton's position). Rather, they appear to be among the broader characteristics of language available in the process of language development, either in adult life or in child language situations.

What the study of pidgins and creoles can provide, however, is a window on grammaticalization in situations of extreme contact that support generalizations that have been developed with regard to grammaticalization in relatively homogeneous contexts, as well as suggesting further directions for work. It is to these that we now turn, beginning with some brief morphosyntactic characterizations of the languages in question.

Minimal pidgins probably cannot be said to "have a grammar." However, they typically share certain characteristics. Among them the following characteristics relevant to grammaticalization (or absence of it) are often cited:

(a) a lexicon comprised largely the two major categories N and V
     (e.g., Tok Pisin *sik* used for 'be sick, disease')
(b) lack of word formation rules in the lexicon
(c) periphrasis (e.g., Tok Pisin *haus sik* 'hospital,' *gras bilong pisin* 'father,' literally 'grass of bird')
(d) temporal expressions expressed by adverbs or particles (e.g., Tok Pisin *baimbai* 'later, future,' *pinis* 'finished, completed, past'); no consistent means of expressing tense, aspect, or modality
(e) absence of inflection and allomorphy
(f) absence of clefting, topicalization, etc., largely resulting from absence of fixed word order
(g) absence of embedding
(h) absence of stylistic variants

Such pidgins are characterized by slow speech and exhibit only minimal morphology. Both may be associated with speakers' unfamiliarity with the language, and with speakers' tendency to use minimal effort, especially in situations where discourse is limited to basic practical affairs.

Bickerton illustrates minimal pidgins of this type by an example of Hawaiian Pidgin spoken by a person of Japanese descent and recorded in 1913:

(1) Bilding–hai pleis–wal pat–taim–nautain–aen den–nau tempicha
     eri taim sho yu.
     'There was an electric sign high up on the wall of the building
     which showed you what time and temperature it was.'

                                                      (Bickerton 1984: 175)

If pidgins stabilize they may acquire more extensive morphology, most especially predicate markers (PM), object markers, aspectual particles, and some embedding structures. This suggests attention to expressivity and to hearers' need for clarity. An example from West African Pidgin English will illustrate some of these characteristics of a stable pidgin. The passage is excerpted from a narrative about the outwitting of a king by a clever boy called Sense-pass-king or 'Wiser-than-king':

(2) Sens-pas-king i   bin   gow, i   mas-fut   fo rowt,
     Sense-pass-king PM PAST go,   PM makes-foot for road,
     waka trong   fo   hil, sowtey i   rish   fo king
     walks vigorously   fo   up-and-down hills, so-that PM reaches at king
     i   tong. King i   tok sey, yu don   kom. Meyk yu
     his palace king PM talk say, you COMPL come. make you
     klin ma het. Biabia i   don   plenti tumos   fo ma
     clean my head. hair   PM COMPL grow too-much for my
     het. Sens-pas-king i   bin   don   gri sey,   i
     head. Sense-pass-king he PAST COMPL agree say/COMP, PM
     go bap   king i   het.
     go barber king his head
     'Wiser-than-king began his journey. Up and down hill he went, and so finally he arrived at the king's palace. The king said, "You have come. Shave my head (because) my hair has grown too long." Wiser-than-king agreed to cut the king's hair.'

                    (Traugott 1976a: 71, based on Schneider 1966: 177)

Note in particular the constructions *tok sey* and *gri sey* which are the kinds of construction we noted in Section 1.3.2. in connection with the development in Ewe of the complementizer *bé*. The West African construction has been translated literally (i.e., "calqued") into the lexifier language, English. Another notable feature is the periphrastic possessive, as in *king i tong* in the inflectional possessive, not the periphrastic, order of PDE. The predicate marker construction will be discussed further below.

Minimal pidgins are important for the study of grammaticalization, since they can be regarded as illustrating a stage prior to grammaticalization itself, that is, a stage in which semantic properties predominate, and structural properties are highly limited. The stabilization of pidgins, and the acquisition by these pidgins of grammatical characteristics, has the potential to give us first-hand insight into early stages of grammaticalization. Stable pidgins demonstrate that "essential communication" such as is often associated with pidgins does not follow a principle of "one meaning – one form" such as one might associate with attention to clarity for hearers. Rather, speakers economize by using the same lexical item for several syntactic functions and also by using periphrasis (Mühlhäusler 1986). Morphosyntactic organization is typically periphrastic (occasionally agglutinative in more elaborate pidgins), and supports the view that grammaticalization originates in lexical items and phrases.

By contrast to pidgins, creoles are typically thought of as native languages, although extensive use of a stable pidgin may in some instances lead to the development of some characteristics in the pidgins that are normally associated with creoles. Among often-cited characteristics of creoles are (a)–(c) below.

(a) Articles: a distinction is made between definite referential (3a), indefinite referential (3b), and indefinite non-referential (3c) (for the differences, see Section 6.4.1):

(3)   a.   Mi bai di buk.
           'I bought the book (that you already know about).'
      b.   Mi bai wan buk.
           'I bought a (particular) book.'
      c.   Mi bai buk.
           'I bought a book (or books).' (even the speaker does not know which book[s])

                              Guyanese Creole; Bickerton 1977: 58)

(b) Tense-modality-aspect systems: periphrastic expressions are widely found. Bickerton (especially 1984) argues that they are typically sequences of the following type: ± anterior[1] tense, ± irrealis modality and ± non-punctual aspect markers, in that order, e.g.: Hawaiian Creole *bin* [+anterior] – *go* [+irrealis] – *stei* [+non-punctual] V 'would have been V-ing').

(c) A distinction is made between realized (+realis) complementation as in (4a) and unrealized (−realis) complementation as in (4b):

(4)   a.   Il   desid   al met posoh ladah.
           'she decided go put fish   in-it' [inference: she did what she decided to do]
      b.   Li ti   pe ale aswar   pu al bril lakaz sa   garsoh-la
           he TNS M go one-evening for go burn house that boy-the
           me lor sime ban dayin fin   atke   li.
           but on path PL witch COMPL attack him
           'He would have gone that evening to burn the boy's house, but on the way he was attacked by witches.'

                  (Mauritian Creole; Bickerton 1981: 60–1, citing Baker 1972)

In (4a) *al* expresses realized events, in (4b) *pu al* expresses unrealized events.

(d) Multiple negation: in negative sentences, typically non-definite subjects, non-definite verb phrase constituents and the verb must all be negated:

> (5) mi neva sii notn in dat bilin.
>   'I never saw anything in that building.'
>
> (Guyanese Creole; Rickford 1987: 148)

(e) Clause dependency, especially relativization:

> (6) mi witnis da wid mi ai   wo gaad gi   mi . . . dii kozn
>   I   witness that with my eyes that God give me . . . the cousin
>   wo swiit   na waan fu gu.
>   that intoxicated not want to go
>   'I witnessed that with my own eyes which God gave me . . . the
>   cousin who was intoxicated did not want to go.'
>
> (Guyanese Creole; Rickford 1987: 153)

(f) Focusing by leftward movement:

> (7) Enikain laengwij ai no kaen spik   gud.
>   any-kind language I not can   speak well
>   'There's no kind of language that I can speak well.'
>
> (Hawaiian Creole, 1896; cited in Bickerton 1984: 176)

Like pidgins, creoles show a considerable range of elaboration, specifically from varieties furthest from the standard (known as "basilects") to varieties close to the standard (known as "acrolects"). This kind of range has been variously described. One model is that of a continuum, with individual speakers having mastery over part of this continuum (see Bickerton 1975, and, from a somewhat different viewpoint, Rickford 1987). Such a model provides strong evidence for the non-discreteness of categories.

Theories of pidgin and creole development often refer to "pidgin simplification" and "creole elaboration." There is no question that the lexicon and coding of pidgins is relatively simple. However, to characterize the process of pidginization as one of simplification can be misleading, depending on which language(s) one starts from. Clearly an early stage pidgin is simpler than any native language. However, when linguists speak of "pidgin simplification," they usually mean simplification of the lexifier language. Since most speakers of a pidgin are not speakers of that lexifier language, and therefore have not internalized its grammar, there can be no evolutive development of that grammar, and the notion of simplification in this sense is misplaced (Traugott 1976b). It is also misplaced in so far as it suggests that speakers of the lexifier language developed the pidgin or creole to communicate with speakers of the subordinate languages; however, the evidence suggests that the languages were developed by speakers of the subordinate languages to facilitate communication among themselves because their native languages were mutually unintelligible (e.g., Whinnom 1971). What we can most plausibly say regarding the emergence of a pidgin is that a restricted system is innovated based on the lexicon of the lexifier language, and some principles, probably universal, of minimal grammatical organization. This is basically an abductive process. The process of pidgin stabilization is a process of complexification of morphosyntactic organization as well as of the lexicon. The process of creolization is a significantly more extensive process of complexification. To the extent that creoles are the result of child language acquisition, they call into question the assumption of much historical linguistics mentioned in the preceding section that rule simplification is the result of child language acquisition, because the creole is always more complex than the pidgin.

Another important theoretical point in connection with pidgins and creoles has to do with the extent to which the grammars are thought to be "mixed." Even though pidgins are always regarded as mixed languages, nevertheless, they are typically described in terms of the lexifier language (e.g., English, French, Portuguese, German). This is in part a practical matter, owing to uncertainty about which socially subordinate languages were originally involved. One problem that has arisen from this approach has already been mentioned: researchers tend to think of simplification of the lexifier language. Another problem is that those who think in terms of "simplification" of the lexifier language tend to think of that language in terms of the standard, rather than the vernacular, which is inevitably the input to a pidgin. Wrong comparisons may therefore be made because vernacular language is often less morphologically complex than the standard, and the lexicon also is often less complex. In some cases there may even be substantial differences in syntax. For example, as mentioned in 1.3.3, Lambrecht (1981) discusses features of non-standard French, including the facts that topic/anti-topic structures abound, and that clitic pronouns have become bound to verbs as agreement markers. In (8) we find topic *ma femme* and the bound agreement marker *il*, which shows only agreement, not gender (contrast the anaphoric feminine pronoun *elle*). In (9) we find the agreement marking bound pronoun *il*, and anti-topic (i.e., post-posed topic) *garçon*:

(8) Ma femme il   est venu.
     my wife   AGR has come

(Lambrecht 1981: 40)

(9) Il-attend   devant la   porte, le   garçon.
     AGR-wait before the door, the boy

(Lambrecht 1981: 74)

Because anti-topic rightward NP shift is frequent in non-standard French, verb–subject order abounds, in contrast to standard French which has subject–verb order, as in (10):

(10) Le garçon attend devant la porte.
      the boy waits before the door

The so-called predicate markers of West African Pidgin (*i* in (2)) and many other pidgin and creole languages bear a resemblance to the bound pronouns in non-standard French (and also vernacular English, cf. *Jane, she called me up this morning*). This suggests that where mismatches between pidgins or creoles and the lexifier language occur, they may originate in vernacular varieties of the lexifier language, or possibly in the subordinate language, or both, and considerable care needs to be taken in assessing possible origins of any construction.

Where creoles are concerned, because they are thought of as native languages, and tend to be treated as examples of child language acquisition, the approach again tends to be one-dimensional. The focus is on innovations with the lexifier language as the target. However, evidence has recently emerged in some communities of recreolization, that is, movement, often sociopolitically motivated, away from the standard and refocusing on the norms of an older creole system (Le Page and Tabouret-Keller 1985). Such changes have some resemblance to the adaptive changes mentioned in Section 5.6. Whether they will lead to structural reanalysis and further differentiation of grammars remains to be seen.

It used to be said, as a simplification, that stable pidgins and creoles had the grammar of the subordinate languages and the lexicon of the lexifier language. This claim has been studied in some detail in the context of Melanesia, where various pidgins including Tok Pisin have stabilized over the last hundred and fifty years. For example, Keesing (1991) has argued that Vanuatu (Bislama) and Solomons Pijin provide exceptionally good insight into the relationship between a pidgin and the languages that contribute to it (he calls them the "donor" languages), because the pidgins are and have over a long time been in direct contact not only with English but with Melanesian languages. This is in contrast to the pidgins arising in the Caribbean during colonial times, which have had far less stable contact with the African languages. Keesing shows that many features of the pidgins can be attributed to the Eastern Oceanic Austronesian languages of the area calqued into morphology that looks like English. In other words, an Eastern Oceanic Austronesian form is translated into a semantically roughly equivalent form in English, but may serve the grammatical purposes of the Eastern Oceanic Austronesian form. He suggests that there are, therefore, "formulas of equivalence" that show that the pidgins are less innovative than is often thought, and more dependent on the extant structure of surrounding languages. One example is the use of serial constructions and object markers, as in (11), which is approximately equivalent to the Kwaio example in (12):

(11) Tek-em   kam.
      take-OBJ come
      'Bring it.'

(12) Ori-si-a   mai.
      ask-TRANSITIVE-it hither
      'Ask about it.'

                                        (Keesing 1991: 322–3)

Another is the use of *des*/*tes* < English 'just' in precisely the position in which the local languages use an aspect marker. Keesing cites (14) as the Bislama equivalent of Vetmbao (South Malekula) (13):

(13) Naji nga-mandrxa mun.
      him he-ASP   drink
      'He has just drunk.'
                (Charpentier 1979: 353; cited in Keesing 1991: 326)

(14) Em i   tes trink.
      him he ASP drink
      'He just drank.'

These examples alone do not, of course, make the case for the development of "formulas of equivalence," but, together with many others, they suggest that at least where there is the opportunity for long-term stability of both the pidgin and the native languages, there is evidence that formulae of expression from the subordinate language may be as important as or more important than formulae from lexifier languages in the process of grammaticalization. The examples also reveal once again that highly localized constructions and recurrent constructions or formulae are the key loci of grammaticalization.

Further evidence for the importance of recognizing multiple as well as single sources of input to grammaticalization can be seen from the development of creoles such as Sri Lanka Portuguese Creole. Portuguese, the lexifier language, is VO. Tamil, the substratum language, is OV. The Sri Lanka Portuguese Creole has taken the resources of the Portuguese preposition *para* 'for' and used it as a postposition, with phonological reduction to *pə*, in an OV structure. Compare:

(15) a. **Portuguese**
      Eu tinha dado o   dinheiro a/para João.
      I   have given the money to/for John

    b. **Tamil**
      Nān calli-yay   jon-ukku kuṭu-tt   iru-nt-an.
      I   money-ACC John-DAT give-PAST be-1-SG

    c. **Sri Lankan Portuguese**
      Êw diñeru jon-pə   jā-dā   tiña.
      I   money John-DAT give-COMPLETIVE give-PAST
      'I had given John the money.'
                  (I. Smith 1987: 83; cited in Romaine 1988: 40)

The study of the development of mixed languages demands that more attention be paid to multiple origins of grammatical structures. Contact has been an important factor for most languages, and a strictly monogenetic view of grammaticalization is ultimately inappropriate. A fuller understanding of similarities and differences in transmission through language acquisition by adults as well as children in homogeneous and heterogeneous communities needs to be integrated with the study of grammaticalization. Until such work is done, it is methodologically sound to attempt to account for internal evolutive changes within a community before looking outside for possible and often not plausible borrowings. As Thomason and Kaufman caution:

> an external explanation for a particular structural change is
> appropriate . . . [only, PH and ET] when a source language and a
> source structure in that language can be identified. The identification
> of a source language requires the establishment of present or past
> contact of sufficient intensity between the proposed source language
> and the recipient language . . . The proposed source-language
> structures need not be, and frequently are not, identical to the

innovated structures in the recipient langugae, but a successful claim
of influence must of course provide a reasonable account of any
reinterpretation or generalization that has occurred as a result of the
interference.

(Thomason and Kaufman 1988: 63–4)

Reasonable interpretations will be based in principled understandings of the
mechanisms and motivations for change including grammaticalization.

NOTES

Chapter 1

1   We follow Quirk *et al.* (1973: 88) in analyzing *be going to* as a future rather than as a "prospective aspect" (Comrie 1976: 64–5). This is because it has distinct deictic properties based in the speaker's point of view (see Section 4.3.2).

2   Punctuation in examples from other authors and texts has been standardized. Dates of periods, authors and works are often not known with certainty; dates given in the book are approximate only.

3   We owe this example to Tony Hurren.

4   At least the first person is probably maintained inferentially in all examples of *lets*.

5   This and all other examples from Old English in this book are cited in the form given in Healey and Venezky (1980).

Chapter 2

1   This and other translations in this chapter are by Paul Hopper.

2   A third kind of iconicity mentioned is metaphorical iconicity, in which a representative characteristic of a referent is represented by something else. We may think here of examples like *My love is a rose*, in which certain characteristics of love (beauty, difficulty, etc.) are represented by the parallel of a specific flower plant that has special beauty but also thorns.

Chapter 3

1   Heine, Claudi, and Hünnemeyer (1991a) and especially Heine (forthcoming) regard the coexistence of older and newer meanings and forms and small differences between stages as peculiar to grammaticalization. They are certainly particularly characteristic of grammaticalization, but not definitional.

2   See, however, Heine, Claudi, and Hünnemeyer (1991a: 231), who, in arguing for continuous as well as discrete shifts in the process of grammaticalization, imply that some changes may not be abrupt.

3   Lord (1976: 182) specifies only minimal reanalysis, consisting of relabeling the syntactic category; we assume a more significant reanalysis along the lines of Heine and Reh (1984: 38).

4   Fleischman's translation is 'public matters.'

5   Lightfoot uses superscript bars where we use prime marks to signify hierarchies of levels: double prime signifies "larger phrase," single prime signifies "smaller phrase." The last V rule has been added. The rules have been simplified somewhat for the purposes of presentation here.

6 A very similar path of development is reported for the history of English *have*-perfects by Carey (1990).

7 In Chapter 7 we will argue that in fact few clauses were strictly speaking subordinate in OE; rather they were loosely dependent in a way associated with "hypotaxis."

8 "Loss" is actually too strong a term; V2 became recessive, but generalized later to some contexts in which it had not been available earlier, see Stockwell (1984).

9 He also uses the term "simplification," but since it is extremely difficult to define, this term is avoided here.

10 It is of course possible to regard analogy in the sense of rule generalization as itself a type of reanalysis, since under rule generalization the linguistic contexts in which a rule may operate are extended or reanalyzed. The basic distinction still holds, however, between reanalysis that introduces new rules and reanalysis whereby the new rule spreads.

Chapter 4

1 Weinreich, Labov, and Herzog (1968) have called this the "actuation problem."

2 The process by which inferences become polysemies is often called "lexicalization." However, the term "lexicalization" also refers to a different process whereby meaning distinctions that were formerly expressed by independent morphemes come through phonological and other changes to be monomorphemic (e.g., the forms *lay* versus *lie*, or *set* versus *sit*, are said to be "lexicalized" as a result of the loss of the former causative morpheme -*i*- that followed the verb stem). It has also been used for "the systematic relations between meaning and surface expression" in a language (Talmy 1985). To avoid confusion, we prefer to distinguish by a different term the processes by which pragmatic inferences become polysemies.

3 However, for some (Indo-)Guyanese speakers, *corner* has been grammaticalized as a preposition, e.g., *He live corner one rumshop* 'He lives diagonally across the street from a rumshop' (John Rickford, p.c.).

4 A related use is found in Halliday (1985), who regards expansions of constituents, for example expansion of NP to S (e.g., complementation), as metaphors or abstractions.

5 Speaker's viewpoint is minimal, except when directional *go* is contrasted with *come* (*He was going to see his aunt and then coming to see his sister*).

6 And in a paper entitled 'The origin of *do*-support," presented at a Stanford Linguistics Colloquium, 1991.

7 The date of composition is a matter of continued debate; the traditional view is that *Beowulf* dates back to *c.* 750; more recently it has been dated *c.* 1000.

Chapter 5

1 We do not include the nominal genitive because this is more appropriately defined as a clitic, cf. *The man across the street's fence.*

2 Timberlake translates as 'Does one think this to be a sin?'

3 "The genitive subject of the participial clause in a system without subject-to-object raising" (Timberlake 1977: 147).

4 Because the proclitic numeral *sa*- otherwise appears only before classifiers, such examples may wrongly suggest that it is the head noun which has been elided rather than the classifier.

5 As mentioned in note 1 to Chapter 4, "lexicalization" is used in the linguistic literature to mean a number of different things. We have here differentiated between "lexicaliza-

tion," the process by which material develops into or is recruited to form lexical items, and "semanticization," the process whereby formerly inferred meanings become part of the polysemous structure of a grammatical item.

6 We owe this observation to Dan Slobin.

Chapter 6

1 The term "morphologization" is sometimes also used for the development of phonological alternations that occur as the result of phonological changes in specific morphological contexts, in other words, of morphophonemic alternations, as found in the English past tense form *-ed* ([t ~ d ~ əd]).

2 Andersen's figures are based on work in Polish by Theodora Rittel (1975). For the full reference to Rittel, see Andersen 1987: 50.

3 The distinction between derivational and inflectional morphology is not clear-cut. For discussion, see Bybee (1985: Chapter 4).

4 The history of *kill* is interesting in this connection, since it originates in a causal form of the verb *cwel-* 'die,' *cwel-j-* 'die + causative.'

5 Includes derivational as well as inflectional forms.

6 The forms identified as pre-Pali are reconstructed, hence the asterisks.

7 According to Hock, the second person form is irregular and has no morpheme boundaries.

8 The strong declension was used in the absence of a demonstrative.

9 We owe these examples to Michael Noonan.

Chapter 7

1 We use the same features as Foley and Van Valin (1984: 242), but for a different analysis. Foley and Van Valin consider some constructions to be "co-subordinate," that is, +dependent/−embedded. These clause combinations, which are typically instances of switch reference or verb serialization (clause combinations which are under the scope of one operator, e.g., declarative), are more rather than less syntactically bonded than those which are +dependent/+embedded. This is a theoretically problematic analysis, since it treats the two "plus" features as less dependent than one of the possible +/− combinations. We agree with C. Lehmann (1988) that dependency and bondedness are best treated as two separate criteria within the cluster of clause combining properties.

2 A slightly different "constellation" of four properties is suggested in Langacker (1991). Others have suggested a larger number of properties. For example, Haiman and Thompson (1984) suggest seven, C. Lehmann (1988) suggests six.

3 Some education psychologists have mistakenly thought that even with the intonation rise the construction is incoherent. Labov (1969) exploded then-current pedagogical assumptions that because certain Black speakers used the intonation pattern and not the segmental *if*, they did not understand conditional constructions and were "verbally deprived." Clearly, rising intonation has a grammatical function.

4 See Warner 1982, Chapter 5, for discussion of the Middle English rules.

5 Punctuation in OE did not serve the same purposes as it does in PDE; it probably signaled intonation patterns for purposes of reading sermons aloud. It is possible that the first period might have indicated sentence-final pause, but the second evidently does not.

6 As a collective, 'tribe,' though grammatically singular, can have plural agreement (cf.

in PDE dialect variants between 'the committee is . . .' and 'the committee are . . .').

7 In citing Hittite examples, we follow the transliteration given in the source from which the citation is taken.

8 However, M. Hale would presumably argue that examples with definite relative clauses, such as (59), had a different history from indefinite relatives such as (57) because, according to his analysis, indefinite relative *kui-* is topicalized, whereas definite relative *kui-* cannot be topicalized (1987: 48).

9 Literary German, which has pre-posed, participial relatives, may be an exception to this.

10 Such constructions were used in writing in earlier English; they have largely disappeared in writing, but are still found in spoken English (Bailey 1973: 165).

11 Zwicky (forthcoming) provides evidence that in English the auxiliary–main verb construction is actually not adequately described as dependent–head; rather, the auxiliary has properties intermediate between dependent and head; this is exactly what one would expect on the assumption that change occurs along a continuum in small rather than giant steps.

Chapter 8

1 "Anterior" tense is also known as "relative" past tense – an event is marked as occurring prior to another, without respect to speaker time.

REFERENCES

Adams, Karen L., and Nancy Frances Conklin. 1973. Toward a theory of natural classification. In Claudia Corum, T. Cedric Smith-Stark, Ann Weiser, eds., *Chicago Linguistic Society* 9: 1–10.

Ahlqvist, Anders, ed. 1982. *Papers from the 5th International Conference on Historical Linguistics*. Amsterdam: Benjamins.

Akatsuka, Noriko. 1986. Conditionals are discourse-bound. In Traugott *et al.*, 333–51.

Allan, Keith, and Kate Burridge. 1991. *Euphemism and Dysphemism: Language Used as Shield and Weapon*. New York: Oxford University Press.

Andersen, Henning. 1973. Abductive and deductive change. *Language* 49: 765–93.

1980. Morphological change: towards a typology. In Fisiak, ed., 1–50.

1987. From auxiliary to desinence. In Martin B. Harris and Paolo Ramat, eds., *Historical Development of Auxiliaries*, 21–51. Berlin: Mouton de Gruyter.

1989. Understanding linguistic innovations. In Leiv Egil Breivik and Ernst Håkon Jahr, eds., *Language Change: Contributions to the Study of its Causes*, 5–27. Berlin: Mouton de Gruyter.

Anderson, Lloyd. 1986. Evidentials, paths of change, and mental maps: typologically regular asymmetries. In Wallace Chafe and Johanna Nichols, eds., *Evidentiality: The Linguistic Coding of Epistemology*, 273–312. Norwood, NJ: Ablex.

Anderson, Stephen. 1977. On mechanisms by which languages become ergative. In Li, ed., 317–63.

1988. Morphological change. In Newmeyer, ed., Vol. 1, 324–62.

Anttila, Raimo. 1977. *Analogy*. The Hague: Mouton.

1988. Causality in linguistic theory and in historical linguistics. Review article. *Diachronica* 5: 159–80.

1989 [1972]. *Historical and Comparative Linguistics*. Amsterdam: Benjamins, 2nd edn [1st edn 1972, New York: Macmillan].

Atlas, Jay D., and Stephen C. Levinson. 1981. *It*-clefts, informativeness, and logical form. In Peter Cole, ed., *Radical Pragmatics*, 1–61. New York: Academic Press.

Austin, Peter, ed. 1988. *Complex Sentence Constructions in Australian Languages.* Amsterdam: Benjamins.

Axmaker, Shelley, Annie Jaisser, and Helen Singmaster, eds. 1988. *Berkeley Linguistics Society: General Session and Parasession on Grammaticalization* (*Berkeley Linguistics Society* 14). University of California, Berkeley.

Bailey, Charles-James N. 1973. The patterning of language variation. In Richard W. Bailey and Jay L. Robinson, eds., *Varieties of Present-Day English*, 156–89. New York: Macmillan.

Baker, Philip. 1972. *Kreol: A Description of Mauritian Creole.* London: Hurst.
1991. Causes and effects. *Journal of Pidgin and Creole Languages* 6: 267–78.

Baldi, Philip. 1976. The Latin imperfect in *bā. Language* 52: 839–50.

Bean, Marian C. 1983. *The Development of Word Order Patterns in Old English.* London: Croom Helm.

Benveniste, Émile. 1968. Mutations of linguistic categories. In Lehmann and Malkiel, eds., 85–94.

Berlin, Brent, and Paul Kay. 1969. *Basic Color Terms: Their Universality and Evolution.* Berkeley and Los Angeles: University of California Press.

Berndt, C. H., and R. M. Berndt. 1951. An Oenpelli monologue: culture-contact. *Oceania* 22: 24–49.

Bever, T. G., and T. Langendoen. 1972. The interaction of speech perception and grammatical structure in the evolution of language. In Robert P. Stockwell and Ronald K.S. Macaulay, eds., *Linguistic Change and Generative Theory*, 32–95. Bloomington: Indiana University Press.

Bickerton, Derek. 1975. *Dynamics of a Creole System.* Cambridge: Cambridge University Press.
1977. Pidginization and creolization: language acquisition and language universals. In Albert Valdman, ed., *Pidgin and Creole Linguistics*, 49–69. Bloomington: Indiana University Press.
1981. *Roots of Language.* Ann Arbor: Karoma.
1984. The language bioprogram hypothesis. *The Behavioral and Brain Sciences* 7: 173–221 (target article and responses).
1988. Creole languages and the bioprogram. In Newmeyer, ed., Vol. 2, 268–84.

Binnick, Robert I. 1991. *Time and the Verb: A Guide to Tense and Aspect.* New York: Oxford University Pres.

Blakemore, Diane. 1987. *Semantic Constraints on Relevance.* Oxford: Blackwell.
1990. Constraints in interpretation. In Hall *et al.*, eds. 363–70.

Bolinger, Dwight. 1975. *Aspects of Language.* New York: Harcourt Brace Jovanovich, 2nd edn.
1977. *Meaning and Form.* London: Longman.
1984. Intonational signals of subordination. In Brugman, Macaulay, *et al.*, 401–13.

Bossong, Georg. 1985. *Empirische Universalienforschung: differentielle Objekt-markierung in den neuiranischen Sprachen.* Tübingen: Gunter Narr.

References

Bréal, Michel. 1991 [1882]. George Wolf, ed. and translator, *The Beginnings of Semantics; Essays, Lectures and Reviews*. Stanford: Stanford University Press.

Brinton, Laurel. 1988. *The Development of English Aspectual Systems*. Cambridge: Cambridge University Press.

Forthcoming. The origin and development of quasimodal *have to* in English. *Papers from the 10th International Conference on Historical Linguistics, Amsterdam, 1991*.

Brown, Cecil. H. 1976. General principles of human anatomical partonomy and speculations on the growth of partonomic nomenclature. *American Anthropologist* 3: 400–24.

Brown, Cecil H., and Stanley R. Witkowski. 1983. Polysemy, lexical change and cultural importance. *Man* (NS) 18: 72:89.

Brugman, Claudia, Monica Macaulay, *et al.* 1984. *Proceedings of the Tenth Annual Meeting of the Berkeley Linguistics Society*. University of California, Berkeley (*Berkeley Linguistics Society* 10).

Burrow, T., and S. Bhattacharya. 1970. *The Pengo Language*. Oxford: Clarendon Press.

Bybee, Joan L. 1985. *Morphology: A Study of the Relation between Meaning and Form*. Amsterdam: Benjamins.

1990. The semantic development of past tense modals in English. In Wolfgang Wölck, Betty L. Brown, and Dan Devitt, eds., *Buffalo Working Papers in Linguistics 90–91*, 13–30. Special Issue for Paul Garvin.

Bybee, Joan L., and Östen Dahl. 1989. The creation of tense and aspect systems in the languages of the world. *Studies in Language* 13: 51–103.

Bybee, Joan L., and William Pagliuca. 1985. Cross-linguistic comparison and the development of grammatical meaning. In Jacek Fisiak, ed., *Historical Semantics and Historical Word Formation*, 59–83. Berlin: de Gruyter.

1987. The evolution of future meaning. In Ramat *et al.*, eds., 108–22.

Bybee, Joan L., William Pagliuca, and Revere D. Perkins. 1991. Back to the future. In Traugott and Heine, eds., Vol. 2, 17–58.

Bybee, Joan L., and Dan I. Slobin. 1982. Why small children cannot change language on their own. In Ahlqvist, ed., 29–38.

Byrne, Francis. 1987. *Grammatical Relations in a Radical Creole*. Amsterdam: Benjamins.

Campbell, Lyle. 1991. Some grammaticalization changes in Estonian and their implications. In Traugott and Heine, eds., Vol. 1, 285–99.

Canale, Michael. 1976. Implicational hierarchies of word order relationships. In William Christie, ed., *Current Progress in Historical Linguistics*, 36–69. Amsterdam: North-Holland.

Carey, Kathleen. 1990. The role of conversational implicature in the early grammaticalization of the English perfect. In Hall *et al.*, eds., 371–80.

Chafe, Wallace. 1970. *Meaning and the Structure of Language*. Chicago: University of Chicago Press.

1988. Linking intonation units in spoken English. In Haiman and Thompson, eds., 1–27.

Charpentier, J.-M. 1979. *Le Bislama(n): pidgin des Nouvelles-Hébrides*. Paris: SELAF.

Chomsky, Noam. 1981. *Lectures on Government and Binding: The Pisa Lectures*. Dordrecht: Foris Publications.

Chung, Sandra. 1977. On the gradual nature of syntactic change. In Li, ed., 3–55.

Clarke, Eve V. 1978. Locationals: existential, locative, and possessive constructions. In Greenberg *et al.*, eds., Vol. 4, 85–126.

Claudi, Ulrike, and Bernd Heine. 1986. On the metaphorical base of grammar. *Studies in Language* 10: 297–335.

Cole, Peter. 1975. The synchronic and diachronic status of conversational implicature. In Cole and Morgan, eds., 257–88.

Cole, Peter, and Jerry L. Morgan, eds. 1975. *Speech Acts* (Syntax and Semantics Vol. 3). New York: Academic Press.

Comrie, Bernard. 1976. *Aspect*. Cambridge: Cambridge University Press.

1978. Ergativity. In W. P. Lehmann, ed. 1978b, 329–94.

1980. Morphology and word order reconstruction: problems and prospects. In Fisiak, ed., 83–96.

1981a. *Language Universals and Linguistic Typology*. Oxford: Blackwell.

1981b. *The Languages of the Soviet Union*. Cambridge: Cambridge University Press.

Corbett, Greville G., Scott McGlashen, and Norman Fraser, eds. Forthcoming. *Heads in Grammatical Theory*. Cambridge: Cambridge University Press.

Craig, Colette. 1991. Ways to go in Rama: a case study in polygrammaticalization. In Traugott and Heine, eds., Vol. 2, 455–92.

Croft, William. 1990. *Typology and Universals*. Cambridge: Cambridge University Press.

1991. *Syntactic Categories and Grammatical Relations*. Chicago: University of Chicago Press.

Cruse, D. A. 1986. *Lexical Semantics*. Cambridge: Cambridge University Press.

Dahl, Östen. 1985. *Tense and Aspect Systems*. Oxford: Blackwell.

DeLancey, Scott. 1981. An interpretation of split ergativity and related patterns. *Language* 57: 626–57.

1991. The origins of verb serialization in Modern Tibetan. *Studies in Language* 15: 1–23.

Denison, David. 1985. The origins of periphrastic DO: Ellegård and Visser reconsidered. In Roger Eaton, Olga Fischer, Willem Koopman, and Frederike van der Leek, eds., *Papers from the 4th International Conference on English Historical Linguistics*, 44–60. Amsterdam: Benjamins.

1990. Auxiliary and impersonal in Old English. *Folia Linguistica Historica* 9: 139–66.

Dietrich, W. 1973. *Der periphrastische Verbalaspekt in den romanischen Sprachen*.

References

Tübingen: Niemeyer.

Dirven, René. 1985. Metaphor as a basic means for extending the lexicon. In Paprotté and Dirven, eds., 85–119.

Disterheft, Dorothy. 1990. The role of adaptive rules in language change. *Diachronica* 7: 181–98.

Forthcoming. Parameter resetting. *Papers from the 10th International Conference on Historical Linguistics, Amsterdam, 1991.*

Dixon, R. M. W. 1979. Ergativity. *Language* 55: 59–138.

1982 [1969]. Olgolo syllable structure and what they are doing about it. In *Where Have all the Adjectives Gone?*, 207–10. Berlin: Mouton [first published in *Linguistic Inquiry* 1: 273–76, 1969].

Dressler, Wolfgang U. 1985. *Morphonology: The Dynamics of Derivation.* Ann Arbor: Karoma.

1988. Language death. In Newmeyer, ed., Vol 4, 184–5.

Dryer, Matthew S. 1991. SVO languages and the OV:VO typology. *Journal of Linguistics* 27: 443–82.

Du Bois, John W. 1985. Competing motivations. In Haiman, ed., 1985b, 343–65.

1987. The discourse basis of ergativity. *Language* 63: 805–55.

Ebert, Robert. 1976. Introduction. In Steever *et al.*, eds., vii–xviii.

Ellegård, Alvar. 1953. *The Auxiliary Do.* Stockholm: Almquist and Wiksell.

Faltz, Leonard. 1988. *Reflexivization: A Study in Universal Syntax.* New York: Garland.

Fillmore, Charles J., Paul Kay, and Mary Catherine O'Connor. 1988. Regularity and idiomaticity in grammatical constructions: the case of *let alone*. *Language* 64: 501–38.

Finegan, Edward, and Niko Besnier, 1989. *Language: Its Structure and Use.* San Diego: Harcourt Brace Jovanovich.

Fischer, Olga, and Frederike van der Leek. 1987. A 'case' for the Old English impersonal. In Willem Koopman, Frederike van der Leek, Olga Fischer, and Roger Eaton, eds., *Explanation and Linguistic Change*, 79–120. Amsterdam: Benjamins.

Fisiak, Jacek, ed. 1980. *Historical Morphology.* The Hague: Mouton.

Fleischman, Suzanne. 1982. *The Future in Thought and Language: Diachronic Evidence from Romance.* Cambridge: Cambridge University Press.

Fodor, Janet Dean. 1977. *Semantics: Theories of Meaning in Generative Grammar.* New York: Thomas Crowell.

Foley, William A. 1988. Language birth: the processes of pidginization and creolization. In Newmeyer, ed., Vol. 4, 162–83.

Foley, William A., and Robert D. Van Valin. 1984. *Functional Syntax and Universal Grammar.* Cambridge: Cambridge University Press.

Fries, Charles C. 1940. On the development of the structural use of word-order in Modern English. *Language* 16: 199–208.

Gabelentz, George von der. 1891. *Die Sprachwissenschaft. Ihre Aufgaben,*

Methoden, und bisherigen Ergebnisse. Leipzig: Weigel.

Gamillscheg, Ernst. 1957. *Historische französiche Syntax.* Tübingen: Niemeyer.

Geeraerts, Dirk. 1986. Functional explanations in diachronic semantics. In Alain Bossuyt, ed., *Functional Explanations in Linguistics* (= *Belgian Journal of Linguistics* 1), 67–93. Brussels: Editions de l'Université de Bruxelles.

Geis, Michael L., and Arnold M. Zwicky. 1971. On invited inferences. *Linguistic Inquiry* 11: 561–6.

Genetti, Carol. 1991. From postposition to subordinator in Newari. In Traugott and Heine, eds., Vol 1, 227–55.

Gilliéron, Jules Louis. 1902–10. *Atlas linguistique de la France.* Paris: Champion.

Givón, T. 1971. Historical syntax and synchronic morphology: an archaeologist's field trip. *Chicago Linguistic Society* 7: 394–415.

   1973. The time-axis phenomenon. *Language* 49: 890–925.

   1979. *On Understanding Grammar.* New York: Academic Press.

   1982. Tense-aspect-modality: the creole prototype and beyond. In Paul J. Hopper, ed. *Tense-aspect: Between Semantics and Pragmatics*, 115–63. Amsterdam: Benjamins.

   1985. Iconicity, isomorphism, and non-arbitrary coding. In Haiman, ed., 1985b, 187–219.

   1989. *Mind, Code and Context: Essays in Pragmatics.* Hillsdale, NJ: Erlbaum Associates.

   1990. *Syntax: A Functional–Typological Introduction*, Vol. 2. Amsterdam: Benjamins.

   1991a. The evolution of dependent clause morpho-syntax in Biblical Hebrew. In Traugott and Heine, eds., Vol. 2, 257–310.

   1991b. Serial verbs and the mental reality of 'event': grammatical vs. cognitive packaging. In Traugott and Heine, eds., Vol. 1, 81–127.

Green, Georgia M. 1989. *Pragmatics and Natural Language Understanding.* Hillsdale, NJ: Erlbaum Associates.

Greenberg, Joseph H. 1960. A quantitative approach to the morphological typology of language. *International Journal of American Linguistics* 26: 178–94.

   1966a. Some universals of language with particular reference to the order of meaningful elements. In Greenberg, ed., 1966b, 73–113.

   ed. 1966b. *Language Universals, with Special Reference to Feature Hierarchies.* The Hague: Mouton, 2nd edn.

   1974. The relation of frequency to semantic feature in a case language (Russian). *Working Papers on Language Universals, Stanford University*, 16: 21–89. Reprinted in Keith Denning and Suzanne Kemmer, eds., *On Language: Selected Writings of Joseph H. Greenberg*, 207–26. Stanford: Stanford University Press, 1990.

   1978a. How does a language acquire gender markers? In Greenberg *et al.*, eds., 1978. Vol. 3, 47–82.

1978b. Generalizations about numeral systems. In Greenberg *et al.*, eds., 1978, Vol. 3, 249–95.

1985. Some iconic relationships among place, time, and discourse deixis. In Haiman, ed., 1985b, 271–81.

1991. The last stages of grammatical elements: contractive and expansive desemanticization. In Traugott and Heine, eds., Vol. 1, 301–14.

Greenberg, Joseph H., Charles A. Ferguson, and Edith Moravcsik, eds. 1978. *Universals of Human Language*. Stanford: Stanford University Press, 4 vols.

Grice, H. Paul. 1975. Logic and conversation. In Cole and Morgan, eds., 41–58.

Haiman, John. 1972. Phonological targets and unmarked structures. *Language* 48: 365–77.

1978. Conditionals are topics. *Language* 54: 564–89.

1980. The iconicity of grammar. *Language* 56: 515–40.

1983. Iconic and economic motivation. *Language* 59: 781–819.

1984. Hua: a Papuan language of New Guinea. In Timothy Shopen, ed., *Languages and their Status*, 35–90. Cambridge: Winthrop.

1985a. *Natural Syntax: Iconicity and Erosion*. Cambridge: Cambridge University Press.

ed. 1985b. *Iconicity in Syntax*. Amsterdam: Benjamins.

1991. Motivation, repetition and emancipation: the bureaucratization of language. In H. C. Wolfart, ed., *Linguistic Studies Presented to John L. Finley*. Memoire 8, Algonquian and Iroquoian Linguistics (Winnipeg, Manitoba), 45–70.

Haiman, John and Sandra A. Thompson. 1984. "Subordination" in universal grammar. In Brugman, Macaulay *et al.*, *Berkeley Linguistics Society* 10: 510–23.

eds. 1988. *Clause Combining in Grammar and Discourse*. Amsterdam: Benjamins.

Hale, Kenneth. 1973. Deep–surface canonical disparities in relation to analogy and change: an Australian example. In Thomas Sebeok, ed., *Current Trends in Linguistics, 11: Areal and Typological Linguistics*, 401–58. the Hague: Mouton.

1976. The adjoined relative clause in Australia. In R. M. W. Dixon, ed., *Grammatical Categories in Australian Languages*, 78–105. Canberra: Australian Institute of Aboriginal Studies.

Hale, Mark. 1987. Notes on Wackernagel's Law in the language of the Rigveda. In Calvert Watkins, ed., *Studies in Memory of Warren Cowgill (1929–1985)*, 38–50. Berlin: de Gruyter.

Hall, Kira, Jean-Pierre Koenig, Michael Meacham, Sondra Reinman, and Laurel A. Sutton, eds. 1990. *Berkeley Linguistics Society: General Session and Parasession on the Legacy of Grice (Berkeley Linguistics Society* 16). University of California, Berkeley.

Halle, Morris. 1964. Phonology in generative grammar. In Jerry A. Fodor and

Jerrold J. Katz, eds., *The Structure of Language: Readings in the Philosophy of Language*, 334–52. Englewood Cliffs, NJ: Prentice-Hall.

Halliday, M. A. K. 1961. Categories of the theory of grammar. *Word* 17: 241–92.

1985. *An Introduction to Functional Grammar*. London: Arnold.

Halliday, M. A. K. and Ruqaia Hasan. 1976. *Cohesion in English*. London: Longman.

Hammond, M., and M. Noonan, eds. 1988. *Theoretical Morphology*. New York: Academic Press.

Harris, Martin. 1978. *The Evolution of French Syntax: A Comparative Approach*. London: Longman.

1982. On explaining language change. In Ahlqvist, ed., 1–14.

1988. Concessive clauses in English and Romance. In Haiman and Thompson, eds., 71–99.

Harris, Roy, and Talbot Taylor. 1989. *Landmarks in Linguistic Thought*. London: Routledge.

Hawkins, John A. 1983. *Word Order Universals*. New York: Academic Press.

Healey, Antonette diPaolo, and Richard L. Venezky. 1980. *A Microfiche Concordance to Old English*. University of Toronto: The Dictionary of Old English Project, Centre for Medieval Studies. [Also available in electronic form: Angus Cameron, Ashley Crandell Amos, Sharon Butler, and Antonette diPaolo Healey, *The Dictionary of Old English Corpus in Electronic Form*. University of Toronto: Dictionary of Old English Project.]

Heath, Shirley. 1983. *Ways with Words: Language, Life and Work in Communities and Classrooms*. Cambridge: Cambridge University Press.

Heine, Bernd. Forthcoming. Grammaticalization chains. *Studies in Language*.

Heine, Bernd, and Mechthild Reh. 1984. *Grammaticalization and Reanalysis in African Languages*. Hamburg: Helmut Buske.

Heine, Bernd, Ulrike Claudi, and Friederike Hünnemeyer. 1991a. *Grammaticalization: A Conceptual Framework*. Chicago: University of Chicago Press.

1991b. From cognition to grammar – evidence from African languages. In Traugott and Heine, eds., Vol. 1, 149–87.

Held, Warren H., Jr. 1957. *The Hittite Relative Sentence*. Baltimore: Linguistic Society of America (Language Dissertation no. 55).

Heusler, Andreas. 1921. *Altisländisches Elementarbuch*. Heidelberg: Winter, 2nd edn.

Hock, Hans Henrich. 1991 [1986]. *Principles of Historical Linguistics*. Berlin. Mouton de Gruyter, 2nd edn.

Hockett, Charles F. 1947. Problems of morphemic analysis. *Language* 23: 321–43. Reprinted in Martin Joos, ed., *Readings in Linguistics, I. The Development of Descriptive Linguistics in America 1925–1926*, 229–42. Chicago: University of Chicago Press, 1966.

Hodge, Carlton T. 1970. The linguistic cycle. *Language Sciences* 13: 1–7.

References

Hoenigswald, Henry. 1966. Are there universals of linguistic change? In Greenberg, ed., 1966b, 23–41.

Hook, Peter E. 1974. *The Compound Verb in Hindi*. Ann Arbor: Center for South Asian Studies.

    1991. The emergence of perfective aspect in Indo-Aryan languages. In Traugott and Heine, eds., Vol. 2, 59–89.

Hopper, Paul J. 1986a. Discourse function and typological shift: a typological study of the VS/SV alternation. In W. P. Lehmann, ed., *Language Typology 1985. Papers from the Linguistic Typology Symposium, Moscow, 9–13 December 1985*, 123–41. Amsterdam: Benjamins.

    1986b. Some discourse functions of classifiers in Malay. In Collette Craig, ed., *Noun Classes and Categorization*, 309–25. Amsterdam: Benjamins.

    1987. Emergent grammar. In Jon Aske, Natasha Beery, Laura Michaelis, and Hana Filip, eds., *Berkeley Linguistics Society* 13: 139–57.

    1990. Where do words come from? In William Croft, Keith Denning, and Suzanne Kemmer, eds., *Studies in Typology and Diachrony (for Joseph Greenberg)*, 151–60. Amsterdam: Benjamins.

    1991. On some principles of grammaticization. In Traugott and Heine, eds., Vol. 1, 17–35.

    1992a. Phonogenesis. In William Pagliuca, ed., *Proceedings of the 23rd Annual Milwaukee Conference on Linguistic Change*. Amsterdam: Benjamins (to appear).

    1992b. A discourse perspective on syntactic change: Text-building strategies in Early Germanic. In Edgar Polomé and Werner Winter, eds., *Reconstructing*. Berlin: Mouton de Gruyter.

Hopper, Paul J., and Janice Martin. 1987. Structuralism and diachrony: the development of the indefinite article in English. In Ramat *et al.*, eds., 295–304.

Hopper, Paul J., and Sandra Thompson. 1984. The discourse basis for lexical categories in universal grammar. *Language* 60: 703–83.

    1985. The iconicity of the universal categories "noun" and "verb." In Haiman, ed., 1985b, 151–83.

Horn, Laurence R. 1972. '*On the Semantic Properties of Logical Operators in English.*' Ph.D. dissertation, University of California at Los Angeles.

    1984. Toward a new taxonomy for pragmatic inference: Q-based and R-based implicature. In Deborah Schiffrin, ed., *Meaning, Form and Use in Context: Linguistic Applications*, GURT 84, 11–42. Washington DC: Georgetown University Press.

    1989. *A Natural History of Negation*. Chicago: University of Chicago Press.

Humboldt, Wilhelm von. 1825. Über das Entstehen der grammatikalischen Formen und ihren Einfluß auf die Ideenentwicklung. *Abhandlungen der Königlichen Akademie der Wissenschaften zu Berlin*, 401–30.

1988 [1836]. *On Language*. (On the Variety of Human Language Structure and its Implications for the Intellectual Development of Humanity.) Translation by Peter Heath of *Über die Verschiedenheit des menschlichen Sprachbaus und ihren Einfluß auf die geistige Entwicklung des Menschengeschlechts*, 1836. Cambridge: Cambridge University Press.

Hyman, Larry M. 1975. *Phonology: Theory and Analysis*. New York: Holt, Rinehart and Winston.

Hymes, Dell. 1971. *Pidginization and Creolization of Languages*. Cambridge: Cambridge University Press.

Ihalainen, Ossi. 1976. Periphrastic *do* in affirmative sentences in the dialect of East Somerset. *Neophilologische Mitteilungen* 77: 608–22.

Jackendoff, Ray. 1983. *Semantics and Cognition*. Cambridge, MA: The MIT Press.

1990. *Semantic Structures*. Cambridge, MA: The MIT Press.

Jakobson, Roman. 1965. Quest for the essence of language. *Diogenes* 51: 21–37.

1966. Implications of language universals for linguistics. In Greenberg, ed., 1966b, 263–78.

1971. Closing statement: linguistics and poetics. In Thomas A. Sebeok, ed., *Style in Language*, 350–77. Cambridge, MA: The MIT Press.

Jakobson, Roman, and Morris Halle. 1956. *Fundamentals of Language*. The Hague: Mouton.

Jeffers, Robert J., and Ilse Lehiste. 1979. *Principles and Methods for Historical Linguistics*. Cambridge, MA: The MIT Press.

Jeffers, Robert J., and Arnold M. Zwicky. 1980. The evolution of clitics. In Elizabeth Closs Traugott, Rebecca La Brum, and Susan Shepherd, eds., *Papers from the 4th International Conference on Historical Linguistics*, 221–31. Amsterdam: Benjamins.

Jones, Charles. 1988. *Grammatical Gender in English: 950–1250*. London: Croom Helm.

Joseph, Brian D., and Richard D. Janda. 1988. The how and why of diachronic morphologization and de-morphologization. In Hammond and Noonan, eds., 193–210.

Justus, Carol. 1976. Relativation and topicalization in Hittite. In Li, ed., 213–46.

Kaisse, Ellen M. 1982. Sentential clitics and Wackernagel's Law. In Daniel P. Flickinger, Marlys Macken, and Nancy Wiegand, eds., *West Coast Conference on Formal Linguistics*, 1–14. Stanford University: Linguistics Department.

Katz, Jerrold J., and Jerry A. Fodor. 1963. The structure of a semantic theory. *Language* 39: 170–210.

Keenan, Edward L. 1985. Relative clauses. In Shopen, ed., Vol. 2, 141–70. Cambridge: Cambridge University Press.

Keenan, Edward L., and Bernard Comrie. 1977. Noun phrase accessibility and universal grammar. *Linguistic Inquiry* 8: 63–99.

References

Keesing, Roger M. 1991. Substrates, calquing and grammaticalization in Melanesian Pidgin. In Traugott and Heine, eds., Vol. 1, 315–42.

Kemenade, Ans van. 1987. *Syntactic Case and Morphological Case in the History of English*. Dordrecht: Foris.

Kemmer, Suzanne. Grammatical prototypes and competing motivations in a theory of linguistic change. In Garry Davis and Gregory Iverson, eds., *Explanation in Historical Linguistics*, 145–66. Amsterdam: Benjamins.

Forthcoming a. Middle voice, transitivity, and the elaboration of events. In Barbara Fox and Paul Hopper, eds., *Voice: Form and Function*. Amsterdam: Benjamins.

Forthcoming b. *The Middle Voice*. Amsterdam: Benjamins.

Kiparsky, Paul. 1968. Linguistic universals and linguistic change. In Emmon Bach and Robert T. Harms, eds., *Universals in Linguistic Theory*, 171–202. New York: Holt, Rinehart and Winston.

1988. Phonological change. In Newmeyer, ed., Vol 1, 362–415.

1992. Analogy. *International Encyclopedia of Linguistics* 1: 56–61. Oxford: Oxford University Press.

Klaiman, M. H. 1976. Correlative clauses and IE syntactic reconstruction. In Steever *et al.*, eds., 159–68.

Klavans, Judith L. 1985. The independence of syntax and phonology in cliticization. *Language* 61: 95–120.

König, Ekkehard. 1986. Conditionals, concessive conditionals, and concessives. In Traugott *et al.*, 229–46.

Koster Jan. 1978. Why subject sentences don't exist. In S. Jay Keyser, ed., *Recent Transformational Studies in European Languages*. Cambridge: Cambridge University Press.

Kroch, Anthony S. 1989a. Function and grammar in the history of English: periphrastic DO. In Ralph W. Fasold and Deborah Schiffrin, eds., *Language Change and Variation*, 133–72. Amsterdam: Benjamins.

1989b. Reflexes of grammar in patterns of language change. *Language Variation and Change* 1: 199–244.

Krupa, Viktor. 1966. *Morpheme and Word in Maori*. The Hague: Mouton.

1968. *The Maori Language*. Moscow: Nauka Publishing House.

Kuno, Susumu, and Etseko Kaburaki. 1977. Empathy and syntax. *Linguistic Inquiry* 8: 627–72.

Kuryłowicz, Jerzy. 1945–9. La nature des procès dits analogiques. *Acta Linguistica* 5: 121–38. Reprinted in Eric P. Hamp, Fred W. Householder, and Robert Austerlitz, eds., *Readings in Linguistics 2*, 158–74. Chicago: University of Chicago Press, 1966.

1964. *The Inflectional Categories of Indo-European*. Heidelberg: Winter.

1965. The evolution of grammatical categories. Reprinted in J. Kuryłowicz, 1976, *Esquisses linguistiques*, Vol. 2, 38–54. München: Fink.

Kytö, Merja. 1991. *Variation and Diachrony, with Early American English in*

Focus. Frankfurt-am-Main: Peter Lang.

Labov, William. 1969. The logic of non-standard English. *Georgetown Monographs in Languages and Linguistics* 22: 1–43. Reprinted in William Labov, *Language in the Inner City: Studies in Black Vernacular English*, 210–40. Philadelphia: University of Pennsylvania Press, 1972.

1972. *Sociolinguistic Patterns*. Philadelphia: University of Pensylvania Press.

1974. On the use of the present to explain the past. In Luigi Heilman, ed., *Proceedings of the 11th International Congress of Linguists*, 825–52. Bologna: Mulino.

Lakoff, George. 1984. Performative subordinate clauses. In Brugman, Macaulay, *et al.*, 472–80.

1987. *Women, Fire, and Dangerous Things: What Categories Reveal about the Mind*. Chicago: University of Chicago Press.

Lakoff, George, and Mark Johnson. 1980. *Metaphors we Live by*. Chicago: University of Chicago Press.

Lakoff, Robin. 1972. Another look at drift. In Robert P. Stockwell and Ronald S. Macaulay, eds., *Linguistic Change and Generative Theory*. Bloomington: Indiana University Press.

Lambrecht, Knud. 1981. *Topic, Antitopic and Verb Agreement in Non-Standard French*. Amsterdam: Benjamins.

Langacker, Ronald W. 1977. Syntactic reanalysis. In Li, ed., 57–139.

1985. Observations and speculations on subjectivity. In Haiman, ed., 1985b, 109–50.

1990. Subjectification. *Cognitive Linguistics* 1: 5–38.

1991. *Foundations of Cognitive Grammar*, Vol. 2. Stanford: Stanford University Press.

Lass, Roger. 1980. *On Explaining Language Change*. Cambridge: Cambridge University Press.

Lausberg, Heinrich. 1962. *Romanische Sprachwissenschaft*. Berlin: de Gruyter, 3 vols.

Lehmann, Christian. 1982. *Thoughts on Grammaticalization: A Programmatic Sketch*. Vol. I (Arbeiten des Kölner Universalien-Projekts 48). Köln: Universität zu Köln. Institut für Sprachwissenschaft.

1985. Grammaticalization: synchronic variation and diachronic change. *Lingua e Stile* 20: 303–18.

1988. Towards a typology of clause linkage. In Haiman and Thompson, eds., 181–225.

1989. Latin subordination in typological perspective. In Gualtiero Calboli, ed., *Subordination and other Topics in Latin: Proceedings of the Third Colloquium on Latin Linguistics*, 153–79. Amsterdam: Benjamins.

Lehmann, Winfred P. 1978a. The great underlying ground-plans. In Lehmann 1978b, ed., 1–55.

ed. 1978b. *Syntactic Typology: Studies in the Phenomenology of Language*.

References

Austin: University of Texas Press.

Lehmann, W. P., and Y. Malkiel, eds., 1968. *Directions for Historical Linguistics: A Symposium*. Austin: University of Texas Press.

Lehrer, Adrienne. 1974. *Semantic Fields and Lexical Structure*. Amsterdam: North-Holland.

Le Page, Robert B., and A. Tabouret-Keller. 1985. *Acts of Identity*. Cambridge: Cambridge University Press.

Levinson, Stephen C. 1983. *Pragmatics*. Cambridge: Cambridge University Press.

Li, Charles N., ed. 1975. *Word Order and Word Order Change*. Austin: University of Texas Press.

ed. 1976. *Subject and Topic*. New York: Academic Press.

ed. 1977. *Mechanisms of Syntactic Change*. Austin: University of Texas Press.

Li, Charles N., and Sandra A. Thompson. 1974. Historical change of word order: a case study of Chinese and its implications. In John M. Anderson and Charles Jones, eds., *Historical Linguistics 1: Syntax, Morphology, Internal, and Comparative Reconstruction*, 200–17. Amsterdam: Benjamins.

1976a. Development of the causative in Mandarin Chinese: interaction of diachronic processes in syntax. In Masayoshi Shibatani, ed., *The Grammar of Causative Constructions* (Syntax and Semantics, Vol. 6), 477–92. New York: Academic Press.

1976b. Subject and topic: a new typology of language. In Li, ed., 457–90.

Lichtenberk, Frantisek. 1991a. On the gradualness of grammaticalization. In Traugott and Heine, eds., Vol. 1, 37–80.

1991b. Semantic change and heterosemy in grammaticalization. *Language* 67: 475–509.

Lightfoot, David. 1979. *Principles of Diachronic Syntax*. Cambridge: Cambridge University Press.

1982. *The Language Lottery: Toward a Biology of Grammars*, Cambridge, MA: The MIT Press.

1988. Syntactic change. In Newmeyer, ed., Vol. 1, 303–23.

1989. The child's trigger experience. *Brain and Behavioral Sciences* 12: 321–75 (target article on pp. 321–4 and responses on pp. 334–75).

1991. *How to Set Parameters: Arguments from Language Change*. Cambridge, MA: The MIT Press.

Longacre, Robert. 1985. Sentences as combinations of clauses. In Shopen, ed., Vol. 2, 235–86.

Lord, Carol. 1976. Evidence for syntactic reanalysis: from verb to complementizer in Kwa. In Steever *et al.*, eds., 179–91.

1982. The development of object markers in serial verb languages. In Paul J. Hopper and Sandra A. Thompson, eds., *Studies in Transitivity* (Syntax and Semantics, Vol. 15), 277–300. New York: Academic Press.

Lüdtke, Helmut. 1980. Auf dem Wege zu einer Theorie des Sprachwandels. In Helmut Lüdtke, ed., *Kommunikationstheoretische Grundlagen des*

238

Sprachwandels, 182–252. Berlin: de Gruyter.

Lyons, John. 1968. *Introduction to Theoretical Linguistics*. Cambridge: Cambridge University Press.

1977. *Semantics*. Cambridge: Cambridge University Press, 2 vols.

Malkiel, Yakov. 1979. Problems in the diachronic differentiation of near-homonyms. *Language* 55: 1–36.

1981. Drift, slope, slant. *Language* 57: 535–70.

Masica, Colin P. 1976. *Defining a Linguistic Area: South Asia*. Chicago: University of Chicago Press.

Matthiessen, Christian, and Sandra A. Thompson, 1988. The structure of discourse and 'subordination.' In Haiman and Thompson, eds., 275–333.

Matisoff, James A. 1982 [1973]. *The Grammar of Lahu*. Berkeley: University of California Press, 2nd printing.

1991. Areal and universal dimensions of grammatization in Lahu. In Traugott and Heine, eds., Vol. 2, 383–53.

Matsumoto, Yo. 1988. From bound grammatical markers to free discourse markers: history of some Japanese connectives. In Axmaker *et al.*, eds., 340–51.

McCawley, James D. 1968. The role of semantics in a grammar. In Emmon Bach and Robert T. Harms, eds., *Universals in Linguistic Theory*, 125–69. New York: Holt, Rinehart and Winston.

McWhorter, John H. 1992. Substratal influences on Saramaccan serial verb constructions, *Journal of Pidgin and Creole Languages* 7: 1–53.

MED: The Middle English Dictionary. 1956–. Ann Arbor: University of Michigan Press.

Meillet, Antoine. 1912. L'évolution des formes grammaticales. *Scientia* (Rivista di Scienza) 12, No. 26, 6. Reprinted in Meillet 1958, 130–48.

1915–16 [1958]. Le renouvellement des conjonctions. *Annuaire de l'École pratique des Hautes Études*, Reprinted in Meillet 1958, 159–74.

1958. *Linguistique historique et linguistique générale*. Paris. Champion.

Mikola, Tibor. 1975. *Die alten Postpositionen des Nenzischen (Juraksamojedischen)*. The Hague: Mouton.

Milroy, Lesley. 1980. *Language and Social Networks*. Baltimore: University Park Press.

Mitchell, Bruce. 1986. *Old English Syntax*. Oxford: Clarendon Press, 2 vols.

Mithun, Marianne. 1984. How to avoid subordination. In Brugman, Macaulay, *et al.*, eds., 493–509.

1988. The grammaticization of coordination. In Haiman and Thompson, eds., 331–59.

1991. The role of motivation in the emergence of grammatical categories: the grammaticization of subjects. In Traugott and Heine, eds., Vol. 2, 159–84.

Mühlhäusler, Peter. 1986. *Pidgin and Creole Linguistics*. Oxford: Blackwell.

Muysken, Peter. 1988. Are pidgins a special type of language? In Newmeyer, ed.,

Vol. 2, 285–301.

Newmeyer, Frederick J., ed. 1988. *Linguistics: The Cambridge Survey.* Cambridge: Cambridge University Press, 4 vols.

Nichols, Johanna. 1986. Head-marking and dependent-marking grammar. *Language* 62: 56–117.

Nichols, Johanna, and Alan Timberlake. 1991. Grammaticalization as retextualization. In Traugott and Heine, eds., Vol. 1, 129–46.

Noonan, Michael. 1985. 'Complementation.' In Shopen, ed., Vol. 2, 42–140.

OED: The Oxford English Dictionary. 1989. Oxford: Clarendon Press, 2nd edn. [Available in electronic form on CD-ROM.]

O'Neil, Wayne. 1977. Clause adjunction in Old English. *General Linguistics* 17: 199–211.

Ortony, Andrew, ed. 1979. *Metaphor and Thought.* Cambridge: Cambridge University Press.

Paprotté, Wolf, and René Dirven, eds. 1985. *The Ubiquity of Metaphor.* Amsterdam: Benjamins.

Paul, Hermann, 1920. *Prinzipien der Sprachgeschichte.* Halle: Niemeyer, 5th edn.

Peirce, Charles Sanders. 1931. *Collected Papers,* ed. by Charles Hartshorne and Paul Weiss. Cambridge, MA: Harvard University Press.

Pérez, Aveline. 1990. Time in motion: grammaticalisation of the *be going to* construction in English. *La Trobe University Working Papers in Linguistics* 3: 49–64.

Pinkster, Harm. 1987. The strategy and chronology of the development of future and perfect tense auxiliaries in Latin. In Martin B. Harris and Paolo Ramat, eds., *The Historical Development of Auxiliaries,* 193–223. Berlin: Mouton de Gruyter.

Plank, Frans. 1984. The modals story retold. *Studies in Language* 8: 305–64.

Pullum, Geoffrey K., and Arnold M. Zwicky. 1983. Cliticization vs. inflection: the case of English *n't. Language* 59: 502–13.

Quirk, Randolph, Sidney Greenbaum, Geoffrey Leech, and Jan Svartvik. 1973. *A Concise Grammar of Contemporary English.* New York: Harcourt Brace Jovanovich.

Ramat, Anna Giacalone, Onofrio Carruba, and Giuliano Bernini, eds. 1987. *Papers from the 7th International Conference on Historical Linguistics.* Amsterdam: Benjamins.

Reddy, Michael J. 1979. The conduit metaphor – a case of frame conflict in language about language. In Ortony, ed., 284–324.

Rickford, John R. 1987. *Dimensions of a Creole Continuum: History, Texts, and Linguistic Analysis of Guyanese Creole.* Stanford: Stanford University Press.

Romaine, Suzanne. 1982. *Socio-Historical Linguistics: Its Status and Methodology.* Cambridge: Cambridge University Press.

1988. *Pidgin and Creole Languages.* London and New York: Longman.

Rude, Noel. 1991. Verbs to promotional suffixes in Sahaptian and Klamath. In

Traugott and Heine, eds., Vol. 2, 185–99.

Sadock, Jerrold. 1991. *Autolexical Syntax: A Theory of Parallel Grammatical Representations*. Chicago: University of Chicago Press.

Samuels, M.L. 1972. *Linguistic Evolution: With Special Reference to English*. London: Cambridge University Press.

Sandberg, Kristian. 1968 [1930]. *La Linguistique balkanique: problèmes et résultats*. Paris: Klinksiek.

Sankoff, Gillian. 1980. *The Social Life of Language*. Philadelphia: University of Pennsylvania Press.

    1990. The grammaticalization of tense and aspect in Tok Pisin and Sranan. *Language Variation and Change* 2: 295–312.

Sapir, Edward. 1921. *Language: An Introduction to the Study of Speech*. New York: Harcourt Brace Jovanovich.

Sapir, J. David. 1977. The anatomy of metaphor. In J. David Sapir and J. Christopher Crocker, eds., *The Social Use of Metaphor: Essays on the Anthropology of Rhetoric*. Philadelphia: University of Pennsylvania Press.

Saussure, Ferdinand de. 1986 [1922]. *Course in General Linguistics*. Translated and annotated by Roy Harris. La Salle: IL: Open Court Press. [The source text is *Cours de linguistique générale*, 2nd edn, 1922.]

Schachter, Paul. 1985. Parts-of-speech systems. In Shopen, ed., Vol 1, 3–61.

Schiffrin, Deborah. 1987. *Discourse Markers*. Cambridge: Cambridge University Press.

Schneider, G.D. 1966. *West African Pidgin-English: A Descriptive Linguistic Analysis with Texts and Glossary from the Cameroon Area*. Athens, Ohio.

Schwegler, Armin. 1988. Word-order changes in predicate negation strategies in Romance languages. *Diachronica* 5: 21–58.

    1990. *Analyticity and Syntheticity: A Diachronic Perspective with Special Reference to Romance Languages*. Berlin: de Gruyter.

Searle, John R. 1979. Metaphor. In Ortony, ed., 92–123.

Shapiro, Michael. 1991. *The Sense of Change: Language as History*. Bloomington: Indiana University Press.

Shibatani, Masayoshi. 1991. Grammaticization of topic into subject. In Traugott and Heine, Vol. 2, 93–133.

Shopen, Timothy, ed. 1985. *Language Typology and Syntactic Description*. Cambridge: Cambridge University Press, 3 vols.

Silverstein, Michael. 1976. Hierarchy of features and ergativity. In R. M. W. Dixon, ed., *Grammatical Categories in Australian Languages*, 112–71. Canberra: Australian Institute of Aboriginal Studies.

Slobin, Dan I. 1977. Language change in childhood and in history. In John MacNamara, ed., *Language Learning and Thought*, 185–214. New York: Academic Press.

    1985. Cross-linguistic evidence for the language-making capacity. In Dan I. Slobin, ed., *The Cross-Linguistic Study of Language Acquisition. Vol 2:*

Theoretical Issues, 1157–1256. Hillsdale, NJ: Erlbaum Associates.

Smith, Henry. 1992. *Restrictiveness in Case Theory*. Ph.D. dissertation, Stanford University.

Smith, I. R. 1978. Realignment and other convergence phenomena. *University of Melbourne Working Papers in Linguistics* 4: 67–76.

Sperber, Dan, and Deirdre Wilson. 1986. *Relevance, Communication and Cognition*. Cambridge, MA: Harvard University Press.

Steever, Sanford B., Carol A. Walker, and Salikoko S. Mufwene, eds. 1976. *Papers from the Parasession on Diachronic Syntax*. Chicago: Chicago Linguistic Society.

Stein, Dieter. 1990a. *The Semantics of Syntactic Change: Aspects of the Evolution of* do *in English*. Berlin: Mouton de Gruyter.

1990b. Functional differentiation in the emerging standard language: the evolution of a morphological discourse and style marker. In Henning Andersen and Konrad Koerner, eds., *Historical Linguistics 1987: Papers from the 8th International Conference on Historical Linguistics*, 489–98. Amsterdam: Benjamins.

Stern, Gustav. 1931. *Meaning and Change of Meaning: With Special Reference to the English Language*. Bloomington: Indiana University Press.

Stockwell, Robert P. 1984. On the history of the verb-second rule in English. In Jacek Fisiak, ed., *Historical Syntax*, 575–92. Berlin: Mouton.

Stoffel, C. 1901. *Intensives and Down-toners*. Heidelberg: Winter.

Sweetser, Eve E. 1988. Grammaticalization and semantic bleaching. In Axmaker *et al.*, 389–405.

1990. *From Etymology to Pragmatics: Metaphorical and Cultural Aspects of Semantic Structure*. Cambridge: Cambridge University Press.

Talmy, Leonard. 1976. Semantic causative types. In Masayoshi Shibatani, ed., *The Grammar of Causative Constructions* (Syntax and Semantics Vol 6), 43–116. New York: Academic Press.

1983. How language structures space. In Herbert Pick and Linda Acredolo, eds., *Spatial Orientation: Theory, Research and Application*, 225–82. New York: Plenum Press.

1985. Lexicalization patterns: semantic structure in lexical forms. In Shopen, ed. Vol. 3, 57–149.

1988. Force dynamics in language and cognition. *Cognitive Science* 2: 49–100.

Thomason, Sarah Grey, and Terrence Kaufman. 1988. *Language Contact, Creolization, and Genetic Linguistics*. Berkeley: University of California Press.

Thompson, Sandra A., and Robert Longacre. 1985. Adverbial clauses. In Shopen, ed., Vol. 2, 171–234.

Thompson, Sandra A., and Anthony Mulac. 1991. A quantitative perspective on the grammaticization of epistemic parentheticals in English. In Traugott and Heine, eds., Vol. 2, 313–29.

Timberlake, Alan. 1977. Reanalysis and actualization in syntactic change. In Li, ed., 141–80.

Traugott, Elizabeth [Closs]. 1965. Diachronic syntax and generative grammar. *Language* 41: 402–15.

Traugott, Elizabeth Closs. 1976a. Pidgins, Creoles, and the Origins of Vernacular Black English. In Deborah Sears Harrison and Tom Trabasso, eds., *Black English: A Seminar*, 57–93. New York: Wiley.

1976b. Natural semantax: its role in the study of second language acquisition. In S.P. Corder and E. Roulet, eds., *Actes du 5ème Colloque de linguistique appliqué de Neuchâtel. The Notions Simplification, Interlanguages and Pidgins and their Relation to Second Language Pedagogy*, 132–62. Geneva: Droz.

1978. On the expression of spatio-temporal relations. In Greenberg *et al.*, eds., Vol. 3, 369–400.

1982. From propositional to textual and expressive meanings: some semantic–pragmatic aspects of grammaticalization. In Winfred P. Lehmann and Yakov Malkiel, eds., *Perspectives on Historical Linguistics*, 245–71. Amsterdam: Benjamins.

1985a. 'Conventional' and 'dead' metaphors revisited. In Paprotté and Dirven, eds., 1985, 17–56.

1985b. Conditional markers. In Haiman, ed., 1985b, 289–307.

1989. On the rise of epistemic meanings in English: an example of subjectification in semantic change. *Language* 65: 31–55.

1992. Old English syntax. In Richard Hogg, ed., *The Cambridge History of English, Vol. 1: Old English*, 168–289. Cambridge: Cambridge University Press.

Traugott, Elizabeth Closs, and Bernd Heine, eds. 1991. *Approaches to Grammaticalization*. Amsterdam: Benjamins, 2 vols.

Traugott, Elizabeth Closs, and Ekkehard König. 1991. The semantics–pragmatics of grammaticalization revisited. In Traugott and Heine, eds., Vol. 1, 189–218.

Traugott, Elizabeth Closs, Alice ter Meulen, Judy Snitzer Reilly, Charles A. Ferguson, eds. 1986. *On Conditionals*. Cambridge: Cambridge University Press.

Trubetzkoy, N. 1929. Zur allgemeinen Theorie der phonologischen Vokalsysteme. *Travaux du Cercle Linguistique de Prague* 1: 39–67.

Ullmann, Stephen. 1964. *Semantics: An Introduction to the Science of Meaning*. Oxford: Blackwell.

Valdman, A., and A. Highfield eds. 1980. *Theoretical Orientations in Creole Studies*. New York: Academic Press.

Vennemann, Theo. 1975. An explanation of drift. In Li, ed., 269–305.

Vincent, Nigel. 1978. Is sound change teleological? In Jacek Fisiak, ed., *Recent Developments in Historical Phonology*, 409–30. The Hague: Mouton.

1979. Word order and grammatical theory. In Jürgen M. Meisel and Martin D.

Pam, eds., *Linear Order and Generative Theory*. Amsterdam: Benjamins.

1982. The development of the auxiliaries HABERE and ESSE in Romance. In Nigel Vincent and Martin Harris, eds., *Studies in the Romance Verb*, 71–96. London: Croom Helm.

Forthcoming a. Head versus dependent marking: the case of the clause. In Corbett *et al.*, eds.

Forthcoming b. The role of periphrasis in theory and description. *Papers from the 10th International Conference on Historical Linguistics, Amsterdam, 1991*.

Visser, F. Th. 1963–73. *An Historical Syntax of the English Language, Parts I–III*. Leiden: E. J. Brill.

Wackernagel, Jacob. 1892. Über ein Gesetz der indogermanischen Wortstellung. *Indogermanische Forschungen* 1: 333–436.

Warner, Anthony. 1982. *Complementation in Middle English and the Methodology of Historical Syntax*. University Park: The Pennsylvania State University Press.

1983. Review article on David Lightfoot, *Principles of Diachronic Syntax*. *Journal of Linguistics* 19: 187–209.

1990. Reworking the history of the English auxiliaries. In Sylvia Adamson, Vivien Law, Nigel Vincent, and Susan Wright, eds., *Papers from the 5th International Conference on English Historical Linguistics*, 537–58. Amsterdam: Benjamins.

Watkins, Calvert. 1964. Preliminaries to the reconstruction of Indo-European sentence structure. In H. Lunt, ed., *Proceedings of the 9th International Congress of Linguists (Cambridge, Mass.)*, 1035–45. The Hague: Mouton.

Weinreich, Uriel. 1953. *Languages in Contact*. The Hague: Mouton.

Weinreich, Uriel, William Labov, and Marvin I. Herzog, 1968. Empirical foundations for a theory of language change. In Lehmann and Malkiel, eds., 95–189.

Werner, Heinz, and Bernard Kaplan. 1963. *Symbol-Formation: An Organismic-Developmental Approach to Language and the Expression of Thought*. New York: Wiley.

Whinnom, Keith. 1971. Linguistic hybridization and the 'special case' of pidgins and creoles. In Dell Hymes, ed., *Pidginization and Creolization of Languages*, 91–115. Cambridge: Cambridge University Press.

Wiegand, Nancy. 1987. *Causal Connectives in the Early History of English: A Study in Diachronic Syntax*. Ph.D. dissertation, Stanford University.

Wierzbicka, Anna. 1980. *Lingua Mentalis: The Semantics of Natural Language*. New York: Academic Press.

1988. *The Semantics of Grammar*. Amsterdam: Benjamins.

1989. *The Alphabet of Human Thoughts*. Linguistic Agency, University of Duisburg, Ser. A, Vol. 245. Duisburg: Universität Duisburg Gesamthochschule.

Wilkins, David. Forthcoming. Natural tendencies of semantic change and the
    search for cognates. In Mark Durie, ed., *The Comparative Method Reviewed*.
    London: Oxford University Press.
Zwicky, Arnold. 1985. Clitics and particles. *Language* 61: 283–305.
    Forthcoming. Heads, bases, and functors. In Corbett *et al.*, eds.

INDEX OF NAMES

INDEX OF LANGUAGES

GENERAL INDEX